# SUNKEN TREASURE

Robert F. Burgess

# SUNKEN TREASURE: SIX WHO FOUND FORTUNES

DODD, MEAD & COMPANY
NEW YORK

1   2   3   4   5   6   7   8   9   10

**Library of Congress Cataloging-in-Publication Data**

Burgess, Robert Forrest.
Sunken treasure.

1. Treasure-trove.   I. Title.
G525.B8682   1987          910.4'53          87-24444
ISBN 0-396-08848-1

*This book is dedicated to my mother and father—
to my father for giving me his love of the outdoors,
and an early appreciation for adventure,
and to my mother, for her steady encouragement to
always follow my dream
no matter where it went, so long as it led to happiness.*

Happy are those who can dream dreams
and are willing to pay the price to live them.

# Contents

# Part VI
# Melvin Fisher:
# Today's the Day     **257**

# Preface

"Some may be tall, some may be short, some may be quiet, some may be voluble, but the first characteristic that all treasure hunters have is an obsession," said Treasure Salvors Company Vice-President, Bleth McHaley.

"There is no way of getting away from a treasure . . . once it fastens itself upon our mind," wrote Joseph Conrad.

Who among us does not thrill to the thought of being able to dive down into the sea to find a long lost treasure of gold and silver coins; of ornate rings and gem-studded jewelry; of big and little bars and ingots of precious metal worth millions of dollars; of centuries-old riches lying there on the ocean bottom just for the taking?

That part we can certainly all identify with, but most of us know nothing about what it takes to be a successful treasure salvor. In this book I have tried to go beyond the story of the cliché treasure diver—the diver of daring feats, near escapes from death, and the seemingly easy finding of a fortune just waiting to be taken. Instead, I have focused first on the actual historical events that created the attractive treasure targets. Then looked closely at the key individuals who were destined to work the puzzle that had baffled their kind for centuries. In the end I have sought to learn why they alone found the treasure when all others had failed.

What were their secrets for success? What factors were there in the lives of these six treasure hunters that made them different? What drove them to excel in this highly competitive field in which most fail? Why were they so obsessed in their search? Why had they risked their lives, their fortunes, against overwhelming odds? How did they begin, and how did they end up?

These are some of the questions I asked in writing this book. The answers are all here, often in the treasure salvors' own words and deeds. It may surprise readers to learn that, for many of these individuals, the actual "getting" of a treasure is not nearly as important as the challenge of "going" for it, or that, from an early, impressionable age, what really fastens on some men's minds is not "treasure," as Joseph Conrad thought, but another obsession—an insatiable thirst for adventure.

What they did, how they did it, and for whatever reasons, here are the secrets of the world's most successful treasure salvors.

# Acknowledgments

How difficult it is to acknowledge all of the significant contributors to this work, when their contributions actually began over forty years ago. At that time, none of my boyhood friends nor I realized that our adventures would eventually be responsible for a book. But in part, this is true. They helped me build my first diving rig out of a World War II gas mask, 50 feet of air hose, and a primitive gasoline-powered air pump. Without their help I would never have dared make that first dive to 30 feet underwater in a cold, dark Michigan lake, seeking "sunken treasures" on a long-forgotten shipwreck. That boyhood quest was the springboard that launched me on many similar underwater adventures in the years to come—all of which contributed directly to this book. So, I gratefully express my appreciation to my stalwart companions, Bob and Fletcher Failing, Jerry Bricker, Jim Korecki, and Jim Post, whose help made those prescuba diving adventures of 1943 and 1944 possible.

Up to that time, we were all largely under the spell of several adventure writers. Of all the books we read, their common denominator was adventure—adventure under water or adventure in connection with long lost treasure. Naturally, Robert Louis Stevenson's *Treasure Island* and Jules Verne's *Twenty Thousand Leagues Under the Sea* were our bibles, not to mention the adventures of Tom Swift and the Hardy Boys. They were all our heroes. Two particular books that fired our imaginations were Colonel John D. Craig's *Danger is My Business*, and Lieutenant Harry E. Rieseberg's *I Dive for Treasure*. As research for this book revealed, Rieseberg's highly imaginative adventure writing is probably largely responsible for my generation of treasure salvors. For their contribution to our lives and to this book, I owe them a special debt of gratitude.

I wish to express my appreciation to the treasure hunters and underwater archaeologists of the past few years who made a special effort to help me with my research, either through interviews or through the sharing of their knowledge and expertise. They are: former Florida state underwater archaeologist Carl J. Clausen; archaeologist R. Duncan Mathewson III; photographer Don Kincaid; historical researcher Dr. Eugene Lyon; lawyer David Horan; and treasure divers Arthur McKee, Jr., Mel Fisher, and Robert F. Marx.

For help in documenting their most recent achievements, I am indebted to Barry Clifford, Burt D. Webber, Jr., anthropologist Edwin Dethlefsen, and authors John Grissim and Arthur T. Vanderbilt II.

Whenever my research takes me to Florida's Department of Archives, History, and Records Management, I can always expect full cooperation from this group of historians, archaeologists, preservationists, and technicians, who work with the complex problems of Florida's period shipwreck management and contract programs. Those who were especially helpful in furnishing me with information and valuable background data for the 1715 Spanish treasure fleet recoveries and ongoing work in this area are Jim Miller, Jim Dunbar, Herb Bump, Jamie Levy, Frank Gilson, and Roy Lett. Thank you for always being there when I needed you.

Other no less important contributors include Mrs. Arthur McKee, Jr; sport diver Alex Kuze; treasure hunter Raymond Braun; my expert clipping artist Marjorie Parker; publisher and friend Val Martin, for the loan of the vast and unlimited resources of his clipping services; Ernie Richards and Bob Weller for their knowledgeable input regarding Florida East Coast beach finds and the ongoing salvage of treasure from the 1715 fleet; and my underwater photographic assistants and models, Terry Zimmerman, Robert Sofge, John Harvey, and Mark Yelvington. To all of you, thank you for your help.

# PART I

## Arthur McKee, Jr.: The Treasure Hunter's Treasure Hunter

# Chapter 1

## Please God: Two Silvers, One Gold, and a Platinum

Staring through the faceplate of his 72-pound Miller-Dunn diving helmet, Art McKee saw the Bahamian seascape around him suddenly dissolve in a white haze. But the loss of visibility never even slowed his shuffling gait across the soft sand bottom. He would have been where he was, doing what he was doing, if he had to do it all by feel alone. Instinctively, Art knew how to solve his poor visibility instantly. Since the water came up chin high in his hardhat, all he did was take a mouthful and spit it on his misted faceplate. Instant vision again!

Sunlight shafted through the azure water around him like celestial spotlights. The eroded terrain framed by his faceplate should have resembled an underwater Garden of Eden, with lush outcroppings of amber pineapple coral, large pillow-shaped grooved beds of white brain coral, giant purple sea fans, all held together and fenced in by wavy stands of rust-colored fire coral. But now there was none of this.

What had once been, maybe a half-century earlier, was now a coral graveyard. What remained was dead or dying—sad, wilted, gray, fuzzy shapes that barely resembled the vibrantly colored living reef. This was all due, Art realized, to a few men's selfish greed.

He was diving near Gorda Cay in the Bahamas. Gorda was well inhabited with a population that lived off the sea. More impatient than most, some of the inhabitants had found a quick and easy way to get lobsters out of holes in the reef. They poured bleach into the holes. The lobsters ran out and the native divers scooped them up, dumped more bleach into other holes, and caught more lobsters.

The only trouble with this method was that the bleach killed everything else—the tiny marine polyps that built the reef, the tiny fish and sponges that hid there. Ultimately, it wiped out the entire area.

This is why Art stared disgusted at the coral graveyard that men had made for themselves. It seemed that they never learned.

But Art and his friends were looking for another kind of grave and, from the way his heart was pumping (almost as fast as the compressor jetting cool air into his helmet), there was evidence now that they were close.

The story that Art McKee and his friends had kept secret for so long had to do with sunken ships and treasure. About three hundred years earlier, a ship loaded with silver bars sank in a hurricane off the Pacific coast near Panama. The Spanish quickly responded by salvaging most of the silver. Brought ashore, the silver was loaded onto the backs of a mule train and made its way northward through the steaming jungles to Portobelo first, then Cartegena on the fever-ridden coast of the Gulf of Mexico. There, Indians loaded it aboard a Spanish galleon, the *Maravilla*, a ship bound for Spain by way of Havana.

Many weeks later, joined by other treasure-laden vessels, the fleet left Havana, worked its way up the Florida Straits, and, in the vicinity of Little Bahama Bank, encountered another severe storm. At night, in the ensuing chaos, the *Maravilla* struck another vessel and sank.

Once again the Spanish sent salvagers to the site. Some of the treasure was recovered, but two small salvage vessels, with the *Maravilla* silver aboard, wrecked near Gorda Cay. Again, what could not be salvaged was left to the whims of the sea.

Years later, Gorda Cay fishermen puzzled over the odd-shaped black pieces of metal that washed up on their beach near one end of the island. Charlie Brookfield, a man with a penchant for preserving wildlife and an itch to find buried treasure, contacted McKee in the Florida Keys. Brimming with the kind of repressed enthusiasm of a treasure hunter positive that he has the one and only copy of an authentic treasure map tucked under his belt, Brookfield didn't beat around the bush.

"Hey Art," he said. "I know of a wreck near Gorda Cay, where some silver coins washed up on the beach dated 1651, 1652, and 1653! Get your dive helmet and let's go!"

Art wasn't all that fired up by the story. He had heard of coins found on a beach before. Usually, that was all there was. Hardly worth a trip to the islands.

When Brookfield sensed McKee's reticence, the jovial past president of Miami's Audubon Society let out a little bit more of the exciting information.

"Friend of mine there, a native named Kyle, thinks he's found the wreck. Big pile of ballast rocks with cannon sticking out it. Says he struck a cannon with a rod and saw no rust. Must be brass."

That statement was all that was needed to light McKee's fire. As a salvage diver, McKee knew brass meant money. During the war, he had dived up plenty of it from old shipwrecks in the Keys. Maybe the cannon were not brass but bronze, which meant even bigger bucks. And then there was the silver. . . .

"How soon can we get it together?" asked McKee.

Brookfield fanned his hands. "Soon as you like."

Within days fired-up treasure hunters led by Brookfield and McKee had rounded up a similar group of enthusiastic investor treasure hunters, charted a 36-foot twin-screw Mathews cruiser, and headed for the Bahamas with McKee's Miller-Dunn helmet and compressor ready for action.

Things clicked right along. Off Gorda Cay, McKee donned

his rig and dropped down to the bottom near shore. Prowling around in the surge from the surf, he found several cannonballs.

Then they searched the beach. No coins appeared. Brookfield found his source, Kyle Lightburn, and pressed him for information about the location of the shipwreck.

The black man waved his hand toward the shimmering sea. "Mon, she's right out there. Ya can poke her wit de grain." He was speaking of the 18-foot-long crawfish pole armed with multiple spear tips natives used for skewering lobsters from a boat.

The group boated out to where Kyle directed and there indeed found ancient cannon protruding from a pile of scattered ballast rocks. McKee was now moving around this ancient ship's grave in the graveyard of dead coral. He wondered what was underneath all those cantalope-size river rocks, once used to keep the ship upright when the winds and the seas tried to roll it over. For the record, McKee filmed the site just as they found it, intending later to add the footage to what were to be the first authentic films ever made of actual Spanish treasure wrecks.

He had just finished shooting a sequence showing the old cannon sticking out of the rock pile like lengths of sewer pipe, and was cradling the heavy Bolex housing in the crook of his arm, when an urgent tug on his lifeline told him he was wanted topside.

Surfacing, McKee stared at his tender through a quickly misting faceplate. Spitting a gulp of seawater at the blurry image, he saw the man beckon him to the dive ladder. Charlie Brookfield hung over the side like a boat fender, apparently itching to tell him something.

Shrugging off the hissing Miller-Dunn with the tender's help, McKee heard Brookfield's voice booming down the ladder at him.

"Hey Art, Kyle's found a pile that looks a lot more promising over there," pointed Brookfield. "I saw something through the glass-bottom bucket you need to check out. We'll head over in the dinghy. You guys follow with the big boat."

From the pitch of his voice, McKee knew his friend had spotted something intriguing.

Brookfield and the Bahamian took off in the small pot-bellied dinghy. Lanky Kyle stood perfectly balanced like a stork in the bow, poling the boat along with his grains, while Brookfield draped himself over the stern, face down in the glass-bottom bucket skidding in the rippled wake. He didn't intend to miss seeing an inch of that bottom.

McKee and the others cranked up the Mathews and gentled it over to the pair in the dinghy. Kyle had his pole jammed in the bottom. As they drew alongside and dropped anchor, Brookfield jabbed his thumb toward the bottom, beaming back at them. McKee hurried into his dive gear.

Down the ladder he went, clearing the faceplate as he descended the dozen or so feet through the lukewarm water to the hard-packed white sand bottom. The air hissed in rapid pulses into his helmet. No heavy camera housing to worry with this time, McKee carried nothing more cumbersome than a small army surplus pick and shovel combination, the kind infantrymen used for digging foxholes in World War II.

McKee slogged along the bottom in his black tennis shoes, leaving a curious trail of footprints in the sand. With the water warm as it was, he perspired in his helmet. Even his eyeballs seemed to steam. And always, just when he needed to see something, his faceplate misted, as it did at the very moment he reached the long pile of ballast rocks and Kyle's long pole marking the general area of interest.

Clearing the plate, McKee saw the pole resting beside something long and gray shaped like a large loaf of bread. "Probably pig iron," he thought.

Lurching over beside the rock pile, he whacked it with his pick.

The object never budged. "Whew," thought McKee. "Must be grown to the bottom." Pushing harder, he finally saw the thing turn over and roll down into the ballast. Then he glimpsed white metal.

Carefully, because he could not bend over without losing his helmet, McKee squatted and hoisted up on it. "Holy Christmas," he wheezed. "Feels like a chunk of lead."

He struck it again with his pick. There was no mistaking the silvery gleam. "Lead, hell!" he thought. His heart was once again outdistancing the seemingly slowpoke throbs of the compressor, as he signaled for a rope.

Throwing fast hitches around the bar, McKee followed it up. At the surface, to keep it from banging into the hull, he grabbed it like a mother clutching a baby to her breast and started up the ladder with it.

McKee weighed 185 pounds, his helmet weighed 72 pounds, the bar he clutched would tip the scales at 60 pounds. With all of it on a ladder built to support little more than the weight of a swimmer, something had to give.

One of the rungs went.

So did McKee and the bar. As it shot past, he somehow managed to grab the bottom unbroken ladder rung and hang on, still cradling the bar in his arms, as his companions hauled it up and dragged him in behind it.

Even as his tender lifted his helmet, McKee heard the others hammering at the bar and exclaiming, "It's got to be silver! Look at that big cross of Spain on it!" Someone else said, "The color where he hit it. Sure as hell, that's silver!" And one of the other fellows chimed in, "Good God, it *is* silver! We're all rich!"

Everyone seemed to be jumping up and down and slapping each other on the back, before McKee could get a close look at the bar. Then he was doing it, too. They joyously beat each other on the back like a bunch of guys who had just won their first football game in high school.

Then, one of them yelled, "Art, are there any more of 'em down there?"

McKee nodded. "Yeah, I think I saw the end of another one right beside it!"

"Then what the devil you doing standing around up here?"

So McKee ducked into the Miller-Dunn and jumped over the side again, dropping down to the bottom so fast, the pressure made his ears snap and pop.

Back to the ballast pile he went. There he found the half-remembered gray shape. Half-buried in the ballast, it was wedged under a cannonball with a big purple sea fan growing atop it. McKee pushed it aside and there it was, the big gray loaf-sized bar.

Deciding to take a few frames of it just the way it was, McKee climbed back up the vessel's dangling descent line and had them hand him the Bolex-16 movie camera.

Back on the bottom, he filmed the first pictures ever made of a silver bar being recovered from a Spanish shipwreck.

Naturally, the filming had to be a two-man operation. One of Art's shipmates thrashed down, clothes and all, wearing black and white leather shoes, to do the honors with the Bolex.

"Lucky he got it on the first take," McKee murmured seconds later, as the bug-eyed, purple-faced fellow dropped the camera and rocketed back to the surface.

Again McKee hitched the bar to the rope and they hauled it up. As he helped lift it, the bar seemed heavier. "Maybe its just my imagination," he thought.

He started prowling through the ballast pile. Again there was Charlie Brookfield's prodding crawfish pole pointing out yet another bar. This one had such a big piece of ballast rock attached to it that McKee could hardly move it. But he managed to topple it over.

On the underside of the bar, a small area had been eaten away by electrolytic action. In the slanting rays of the late afternoon sun, McKee stared at the spot, hardly believing his eyes.

*It was yellow!* He rubbed it with his thumb. It stayed yellow. "My God!" he thought. "It's a bar of gold!"

Excited to the extent that he could hardly tie the rope around the bar, McKee waved gleefully for them to haul away. Helping it, he was certain this bar was much heavier than the other two. As it pendulumed through the mirrored surface, Art huffed and puffed from a combination of physical exhaustion and the excitement of the finds.

Moments later, sounds filtered down from the boat above . . . wild deck thumping . . . muffled shouts. McKee imagined everyone going wild. He caught himself chuckling almost hysterically in his helmet. "Jeeze, I can't believe it. We're really all gonna be rich!"

Adrenaline surged into his system. Back on the rock pile, he almost leaped at it in his eagerness to find more. Looking up, he saw Charlie Brookfield's face framed by the round glass-bottom bucket. Lipreading him, McKee saw him say, "It's gold!"

"Boy-o-boy-o-boy!" was all McKee could sputter. He *knew* that last bar was a helluva lot heavier than the others.

McKee had been underwater practically all day. By now, he was cold and shivering, but he was unaware of it. All he could think was, "Gee whiz, Charlie said it's gold. The first two were silver. Now if I can just find one made of platinum, we'll all retire!"

McKee now attacked the rock pile with a vengeance bordering on sheer need. Adrenaline gushed into his system like a runaway bilge pump. He *had* to find that platinum bar before he ran out of daylight. He had to make their day. It was there . . . somewhere . . . maybe under that next layer of rocks.

He labored furiously, pushing, shoving, kicking aside the ballast. Nothing mattered any more. It was getting later and later. The compressor seemed to be lagging behind his gasps for air. He swore at its laziness. Sweat trickled into his smarting eyes. His helmet steamed like a Turkish bath. McKee cursed, spit at it, and kept chopping at the rocks with his pick. By now, too, he had a severe case of the shakes, of which he was totally unaware.

Suddenly, as he brought up his pick in a vigorous upswing, he stumbled forward. The pick's blade smashed through his helmet's faceplate.

Water gushed in. Swirling sharp shards of glass sliced his ear. He was being smothered. He struggled to get out of his flooded helmet.

They had to chase him down current to catch him. As they dragged his limp body over the side of the small boat, he was throughly whipped.

"We got the two silvers . . . and the gold . . . but I sure wanted to find a platinum," he gasped to Charlie Brookfield, as they returned to the cruiser.

"Gold? What gold?" asked Brookfield.

McKee sat up. "When you saw me looking at you in the bucket you said, 'It's gold.' "

"Naw, it's just as silver as the rest," said Brookfield. "When I saw you shivering, I asked *'Are you cold?'* "

McKee reacted like a punctured inner tube.

The three silver bars weighed 60, 70, and 75 pounds individually. The 70-pound bar was purchased by the Smithsonian Institution in Washington, which announced that it was their most outstanding acquisition of the year.

Art McKee never forgot the incident. Every time he saw a piece of gold after that, he remembered it. Years later, he told me: "The thing is, when you find the stuff you have no thought about time. It means nothing to you. No feeling. You can cut yourself and you don't even notice it. You find silver, then you want gold. You get gold, then you want platinum. You never get enough. You've got the fever. Once you get it, you can't stop. Nothing will stop you until the day you drop dead."

# Chapter 2

# On the Trail to Treasure

*"Bridgetown, New Jersey. November 2, 1910.* That's where and when I was born," said the fellow who was to be known ever after as Arthur McKee, Jr. "I attended high school up there and that was the extent of my schooling. After that I went to school with the fish—schools of fish."

He was a tough, wiry youngster, not particularly tall for his generation, but lean, well proportioned, and considered good-looking by a number of Bridgetown young ladies.

He never did care much for school, probably because most of the subjects seemed dull and uninteresting. But dull or not, he treated them all with his youthful brand of lighthearted humor. Nothing escaped his sharp eye; nor were details ever forgotten.

He was an outdoors boy. Often he went by himself to the woods or into the swamps, just to wander around. He got a canoe and would take it to a stream's headwaters and follow that waterway as far as it went. He took the 17-foot canoe to a river and followed it to Delaware Bay. Then he crossed the bay in the canoe.

A kind of youthful wanderlust kept nipping at his heels.

The first book he had ever read on his own—not because he was told to, but because he wanted to—was directly responsible for shaping the rest of Art McKee's life. At least in part. Another book took care of the rest of it.

The first was *On the Bottom* by Commander Edward Ellsberg. It was precisely the kind of book to appeal to a boy like McKee. It was about submarines and the adventures of navy deep-sea divers. It was the tensely told tale of the S-51 submarine: how they raised it and lost it, then raised it again. McKee was with them on every breathless page.

His next voluntary reading was a book by Lieutenant Harry E. Rieseberg titled *I Dive for Treasure*. Like many youngsters his age—an entire generation of them—McKee was instantly caught up in the grand sense of adventure that Rieseberg wrote about with such an elegant, if not exactly accurate, flourish of his fanciful imagination. What red-blooded American boy could help but be stirred right down to the jackknife in his brass-eyeleted high-top boots to read about Rieseberg in brass helmet and full deep-sea diver regalia, stomping down the streets of old sunken Port Royal, looking up at the ancient pirate port's old earthquake-wrecked buildings, while hearing the ghostly peal of the town's tower bell tolling mournfully in the currents—tolling, one knew, for the dead souls of drowned pirates, who had left their booty behind for Rieseberg to find.

Rieseberg always got the booty, but you can bet that most of it was literary. You can bet, too, that McKee read his words for gospel. If Rieseberg wrote that he found shipwrecks with full sails flying manned by skeleton crews guarding chests of gold and silver, who dared doubt? Of his valiant hand-to-tentacle fights to the death with giant octopuses, a generation of ocean-divers-to-be got sweaty-palmed every time they read the passage. It was the stuff of adventure, all about the deep, dark ocean's depths with enough shipwrecks, sunken treasures, and dangers to last a man a lifetime. Best of all, it was all there, just waiting to be found!

As a kind of garnish for these books, McKee consumed everything he found at the local library about King Tut's treasure, the Aztecs, and the Incas. He was especially impressed by the story of Cortez and Montezuma. Though he detested history as such, it all fed the fire.

In the summers he was a lifeguard at a big lake in south Jersey. He went to an aquatic school and, armed with Red Cross safety instructor's training, he taught youngsters to swim and dive. Like other similarly inclined teenagers inspired by certain kinds of literary works, McKee built himself a diving helmet.

"I took an old 5-gallon can with a bicycle pump for air," he later remembered with a chuckle. "We nearly drowned ourselves."

He found he did a lot better without the gear. He had no trouble swimming and free diving. Every spare moment he had was spent on or in the water.

The world is made up of two kinds of people. There is nothing much in between. People are either water people with a strong affinity to the water, or they are landsmen with deep roots and a generally subconscious dislike of water. McKee was a water person. His whole life was to point in that direction—always toward water. For fun he free-dived for big freshwater turtles, letting them pull him around the bottom, before steering them to the surface. Such water ventures as these were his baptism.

A key turning point in Art's life occurred the day a big storm struck Bridgetown. It was the aftermath of a hurricane. The results of it blew him onto the course he was to follow from then on.

It all started as a disaster. When the storm struck Bridgetown it washed out the dam. As a result, two big oyster schooners had struck the bridge that connected east Bridgetown to west Bridgetown and destroyed the link.

Considering conditions ripe for adventure, down the rain-swollen rampaging river came McKee and a buddy in their canoe. Reaching the bridge, they struck a piling. The cedar canoe wrapped around it, snapping itself in two, while the boys rode the flood the rest of the way down the river.

A hard-hat professional diver was summoned by the city to

survey damage to the bridge. With the lake practically gone down the drain, so to speak, lifeguard McKee's job was less than enviable. The city still paid him to sit up in his wooden tower overlooking all that stinking mud and rotting mussels. So there he sat, day in and day out. His job was to keep people from wading out across the lake and getting stuck in the mud. The local newspaper even wrote an article about him. They said Arthur McKee was no longer a lifeguard; he was a "mudguard."

Not long after that, McKee started looking around for a more challenging job. He met the helmet and hose diver evaluating damage to the bridge and told him he was looking for work.

"You can't dive in my gear," said the man, "but if you get permission from your folks, I'll hire you to tend my lines."

That's the way he started, as a line-tender for the diver, doing all the topside work, all the time itching more and more to try out that marvelous diving gear for himself.

One Sunday morning the opportunity presented itself. By now McKee knew that his boss drank a lot every weekend. By Monday he never was much good. So McKee always washed down his canvas rubberized dive suit Saturday afternoons and hung it up to dry. It seldom got used before Monday afternoon. One Sunday, while the suit's owner was sleeping off his Saturday night binge, McKee persuaded a friend to help him into the dive suit and see what the big adventure was all about.

In no time McKee was dressed in the bulky canvas suit with its overweighted lead shoes. As his buddy lowered the heavy brass helmet onto the suit's metal collar and dogged it in place, McKee made a final request through the open faceplate. "No matter what happens," he said, "keep the air coming."

"Sure. Don't worry about a thing," his buddy said, starting up the air pump and clamping shut McKee's faceplate.

Inside the helmet the cool air gushed down on the boy's head. He stood up in the canvas bag of a suit that could have held two people his size and clumped over to the ladder leading down into the river.

Despite the oversized, overweighted lead boots, he somehow got down it. On the last rung he instinctively held his breath and stepped off.

Down he went like an anchor, with hose, line, and bubbles trailing his rapid descent into the blackest black McKee had ever seen in his life.

His ears hurt something fierce from the unequalized pressure, but by working his jaw and jamming his nose against the cold, moist faceplate, as he had heard one should do, he managed to equalize things, easing the pain in his brow.

He had encountered the bottom almost gently, mostly because it was the ooziest kind of mud and he had gone well into it. As he tried to move, he almost toppled backward into the stygian mire that had him by the legs.

His breathing was a mile a minute, mostly from the excitement. But the air was plentiful and it blew cool on his sweat-dripping head.

McKee tried bending forward at the waist, the way he knew divers did when they walked on the sea floor. But the abrupt changing of his center of balance almost toppled him forward, helmet down, into the muck.

Quickly he learned to compensate for the enormous weight attached to both ends of his body, not to mention the ungainly lead belt about his waist, which was now so loose, it hung a lot closer to the vicinity of his knees. In fact, if it went much farther, it would have tripped him up.

So, first things, first, McKee managed an upright squat that somehow allowed him to grip the lead belt and inch it higher. Then by twisting it over and over, he took up some of the slack.

Visibility below never improved. He guessed his boss must have always worked like that in the dark. Leaning into the current, McKee got first one leg, then the other out of the muck. Eventually, he reached a harder-packed bottom that enabled him to move more freely. He was also now aware that the water was squeezing him so hard, the suit was pressing painful folds deep into his thighs and abdomen. It was like being clutched by an enormous hand.

McKee knew what the problem was, but he didn't know

how to correct it. It had something to do with the valves on his helmet, which could let the air pressure in the suit counteract the squeeze. But his boss had never explained that part. McKee hoped he wouldn't stumble off a drop-off into deeper water, because he had read about the consequences of doing so. The increased pressure might be bad enough to squeeze a diver right up into his helmet. He never forgot reading about one deep sea diver who went deep too fast and, when they pulled him up, he was nothing but jelly in his helmet. They spooned him out.

McKee shivered and decided that, since he couldn't see, he'd better not walk much farther or the same thing might happen to him. He decided he had better come up.

Suddenly, the thought pushed him to the brink of panic. *He didn't know how to come up!* It was the valves again. There was something you did that allowed the escaping air to partially inflate the suit and actually airlift the diver to the surface.

Again, McKee was afraid to touch anything having to do with the valve adjustment. Vaguely he knew the danger of a diver ascending too quickly. McKee surely didn't want to die with the bends. He wasn't informed about the exact reason for the bends, but he knew it was named that because whatever happened bent you double and you died in agony. Lieutenant Rieseberg made sure all his readers understood the details of that.

So there he stood, wondering what to do next.

He couldn't go up. He didn't dare go down. And he couldn't get out of the suit by himself. It flashed through his thoughts that this was sure one helluva way to start a career as a deep-sea diver.

Finally, McKee decided the only thing left to do was to walk out of the river—helmet, hoses, boots, and all.

For a moment he had to run things over in his mind and be absolutely certain which way was back—which way went toward shore and which went out into the deep black mud of the river bottom.

Believing he had it straight, he pivoted clumsily and started clumping off in the direction he prayed was toward shore. Gradually, the pressure seemed less of a squeeze on his body. He hoped his friend on the air pump would understand his intentions and somehow help.

Gradually, McKee's small, round faceplate window turned from black to brown. He was indeed moving toward shore, but experiencing more difficulty lifting his weighted boots up and over the steepening terrain.

Finally, it was more level. He had negotiated the drop-off. Only now he was really into soupy mud.

He slogged through it as best he could, but it finally got him. Thanks to a combination of sheer overweight, awkwardness, and exhaustion, he finally slurped forward, helmet first, into the gunk.

"*Jeezo-peezo*," he swore to himself, "what have I done now?"

He thrashed his arms and legs weakly, but all that seemed to do was make him sink deeper in the ooze. There was no use trying to see anything out the faceplate now. It was once again black. In fact, after struggling for several moments, he no longer knew whether he was on the bottom or deep under it. The thought of being buried there in the mud and having his air finally stop brought on a spasm of renewed effort to free himself from the sticky mess.

How much time passed he wasn't able to tell. Things were getting pretty desperate, when suddenly he felt his lifeline tighten.

Lying face down, he knew the line was no longer going upward toward the surface. It was stretching taut toward shore. Someone was hauling on it!

McKee fought to get to his knees. The tightening line helped. Once up that far, he crawled, or rather swam, through the mud, his progress due mostly to the strong pull on the line.

In moments he was out of the mud and into the weeds, then he glimpsed daylight through his tiny helmet window.

Through the streaming weeds and mud that encased him, he saw his buddy wildly waving his arms, while he directed a half-dozen men dressed in their Sunday black coats and vests, all lined up and hauling on his heavy lifeline like a tug-of-war team. Together they skittered McKee in his weed-shrouded deep-sea diving suit all the way to the beach.

It took the boys the rest of the day and well into the evening to clean all the filth from the dive suit, but finally they got it looking clean and properly hung up to dry. Next morning, when McKee's boss came down to the barge, the first thing he did was to feel his diving suit.

"Good gosh!" he exclaimed. "Still wet. Musta rained last night."

"Uh-huh. Sure musta," murmured McKee.

It was 1934. His diving adventure was to be the first of many to follow.

# Chapter 3

# Finding the Capitana

McKee worked for the diver on other projects on the Delaware River, learning all he could about the business of helmet and hose diving. Eventually, a football injury he had sustained in high school brought on the next major turning point in his life.

It was his left knee. Doctors operated and removed some of the cartilage. After that, it bothered him more. The muscle in his thigh and calf got smaller. McKee went to an osteopath. He worked on it three times a week, finally improving the condition, so that the muscles once again would support the joint. He advised the young man to do lots of swimming to help strengthen the leg. There was only one place in the country where McKee knew he could swim in warm tropical seas all year around—Florida.

He packed his gear and headed south to the Sunshine State.

Once in Florida he never stopped until he reached the Keys. There he applied for and got a job as chief diver on the navy underwater pipeline. It carried drinking water from the mainland at Homestead through the hundreds of tiny islands comprising the long, curving archipelago that ends in Key West. Whenever that 15-inch pipe broke down, McKee was called out to repair it. For two years of doing this he learned a lot about diving helmet and hose rigs in heavy tides. For those times when the sea's surge threatened to sweep him away in his Miller-Dunn 72-pound helmet, McKee built a 115-pound helmet to hold him down against the tides.

Whenever he had free time he swam, exercising his bad knee as much as possible. Soon it got so much better, he no longer limped. He became city recreational director at Homestead and reveled in the outdoor life he had made for himself. On his days off, he dived the inshore reefs, supplying local gift shops with coral and marine specimens. Eventually, in this pursuit, he realized there were a lot of old shipwrecks scattered along this coast.

At first, he began going offshore with his hard-hat diving rig and a tug, salvaging old brass and iron off the wrecks. There was always a good market for these things, along with the old curios McKee sometimes scavenged off the old hulks to sell to the tourist shops.

The more he saw on the bottom, the more it fascinated him. He was in the right place at the right time. Few others were doing what he was doing. Naturally, the sponge divers were operating off the Gulf Coast, and other hard hats were stashing coral in their boats for easy sales ashore. But in those days the coral went on forever; the sea had relatively few fellows diving with this comparatively expensive kind of diving gear. The invention of equipment as uncomplicated as scuba gear, which would virtually open the ocean bottom to everyone, was not due for another twenty years. McKee and his hard hatters had it all right in the palm of their hands. And he for one was taking advantage of it.

One day in 1938, a commercial fisherman he had befriended dropped by Homestead to see him. His name was Reggie Roberts.

"Hey, McKee," he said. "You interested in old cannon?"

"Sure. Why not?" asked McKee. "Their iron sells as good as any other. Where are they?"

"Spotted some sticking out of an old pile of ballast rock down by Plantation Key," said the fisherman. "Why don't you bring your diving rig and come on down. I'll take you out fishing and show you the wreck."

"It's a deal," grinned McKee.

That weekend he met Roberts down the coast and loaded his Miller-Dunn helmet, hoses, and compressor aboard his tug. Then they headed out for the wreck site.

Three and a half miles off Plantation Key, Roberts eased his old weather-beaten tugboat alongside a shadow on the bottom and dropped anchor.

Leaning over the rail, peering down into the translucent blue water, McKee whistled aloud. "Looks like a beauty. Anybody been on it yet?"

"I doubt it," called Roberts from the wheelhouse. "It looks untouched."

McKee quickly geared up, cranked up his compressor, and went down to look it over.

In 27 feet of water he saw what remained of the wreck—a hill of ballast rock 15 feet high, 40 feet wide, and 100 feet long. Scattered at odd angles and protruding from the pile of stones were more old iron cannon than McKee had ever seen before— at least twenty of them of varying lengths.

McKee picked around the base of the rock pile, fanning away the sand and pulling out coral-encrusted chunks with odd-shaped pieces of metal and wood fragments sticking out of them. Eagerly, he gathered a bucketful of these pieces along with several encrusted cannonballs. Then he surfaced to examine his finds.

Twenty minutes later, the deck around him was littered with his finds. But after examining them, he was disappointed.

"Only thing I can identify is the cannonball," he told Roberts. "Rest of it looks like junk."

His heavily tanned companion in the tattered baseball cap shrugged. "That's what I figured, but you never know."

McKee picked through the rocklike chunks, breaking off

some of the odd-shaped pieces of blackened metal. He thought he would see if anyone ashore knew what they were.

Some days later, he drove to the University of Miami and located a professor reputed to be knowledgeable about such subjects.

The man put on his glasses and studied the pieces of metal carefully.

"Shaped like that, they're not coins," he said. "I think they're pieces of lead. Perfectly worthless."

"Thanks," said McKee.

Not too satisfied with the professor's snap judgment, McKee stopped by a jewelry store and showed the owner his finds.

The man promptly identified them as heavily sulphided silver coins.

"Boy-o-boy!" McKee left the store walking on air, grinning from ear to ear. People he passed on the street stopped and stared after him.

On his next trip on the wreck he found a gold coin. It was a Spanish gold escudo. Cupping it in the palm of his hand, he stared at the small heavy pool of yellow gleaming as brightly as the day it was minted. Turning it over, he saw stamped on the coin the date 1721. It indicated that the ship had sunk sometime after that date. But what ship?

McKee began searching libraries for whatever information he could find about shipwrecks of that period. Exhausting all the sources he could think of, he wrote a letter to various institutions in Spain.

Months passed. Then one day McKee received a large package from the director of the Archives of the Indies in Seville. In it were copies of old Spanish documents and a photograph of a chart showing not only the wreck that McKee had found, but the locations of eighteen other shipwrecks in the Florida Keys that had occurred when the Spanish treasure fleet of 1733 was struck by a hurricane in the Florida Straits.

From translations of these documents, McKee learned that

the pile of ballast stone Reggie Roberts had showed him off Plantation Key was once the *Capitana el Rui*, flagship of the fleet.

"Whew!" McKee exclaimed as he read a translation of the ship's manifest list, which told what that one vessel had carried as cargo—over 5 million pesos worth of treasure!

His heart was still racing over that fact when he read another document. It revealed that Spanish salvagers had recovered all of the *Capitana*'s treasure after the ship sank.

That was not the happiest of news for this budding treasure hunter, but it didn't slow McKee down. He shifted his dive barge to the site over the wreck and, in his Miller-Dunn helmet, he attacked the hill of ballast rocks with a vengeance, spending as much as ten hours a day by himself on the bottom. The one-man task was a prodigious one. It involved moving all of those cantalope-and-larger-sized smooth river rocks from one side of the shipwreck to the other, then hand-fanning the sand pockets beside the ship's rotten timbers in search of treasure and artifacts.

Gradually, he began to find things. His collection of treasure grew. That year, 1938, with friends helping, McKee and his crew shifted some 250 tons of ballast rock to get at the artifacts they believed lay beneath the sand.

Wholesale digging in the bottom was out of the question, because of the danger of overlooking things as small as coins. Up until then, they fanned the bottom with their hands, moving the sand by degrees. But this proved so slow, that McKee tried to think of a more practical underwater excavation device.

Recalling that the navy used something called an airlift to deepen harbors, McKee borrowed the idea and applied it to his shipwreck excavation. An airlift operated on the principle of a vacuum cleaner, one that worked underwater. To create the suction, compressed air was injected into a length of pipe near its nozzle. As the air rushed toward the surface, it drew water with it, creating a strong enough suction at the nozzle to dig holes in the bottom far faster than divers could by hand. This was the first time such a device was used to excavate a shipwreck. From then on, every treasure hunter and underwater archaeologist were to use the device for excavating.

In the years that followed his work on the *Capitana*, McKee and his partners recovered an astonishing amount of artifacts and treasure, astonishing in the fact that the wreck had already been salvaged previously by the Spaniards. For this reason, probably, most of McKee's finds proved to be artifactual in nature. They recovered over twenty different sizes of iron cannon, more than a thousand silver coins dated before 1733, silver statues, religious medals, candlesticks, pewter mugs and plates, jewelry, buttons and buckles, navigational instruments, daggers, swords, pistols, tons of cannonballs and grapeshot, broken crockery, ship's blocks and bits of ropes, and wreckage, a 3-ton anchor, and many more tons of coral-encrusted clusters, some of which contained everything from a court sword to a gold coin.

"At one time, I had so many pieces of my shipwreck packed, sacked, and stacked around my house, that I was running out of living space," said McKee.

It was not news to him that tourists were very interested in both shipwrecks and sunken treasure. But, despite all the things he had collected, he still didn't have enough to outfit a museum. The real museum of sunken treasure—that enormous pile of round river rocks and rotting timbers—lay on the bottom of the ocean 3½ miles offshore.

McKee, always the innovator, began wondering how feasible it would be to ferry tourists out to the wreck and get them to pay to watch divers working on the bottom salvaging the treasure of an authentic Spanish galleon.

McKee set his idea in motion, painting signs that offered the public a chance of a lifetime—a visit to a treasure wreck being salvaged by deep-sea divers.

The idea was as successful as his airlift. The signs literally sucked the tourists off the Key's overseas Highway 1 and funneled them into his treasure-hunting operation. The public willingly paid to ride out on the glass-bottom barge and stare down at the divers. McKee reaped no great profit from this operation, but the tourists ended up paying his crew's gasoline and food expenses from the tour.

Not content to merely look, however, people began to say, "Gee whiz, I'd sure like to go down there and do some of that."

Though these were prescuba days, McKee saw the possibilities quite clearly.

"Okay," he said. "I'll put you down on the wreck, where you can see it at close range. The price will be ten bucks."

As an added inducement, McKee printed up a number of official-looking documents to attest to the fact that so-and-so had dived to the bottom of the ocean as a deep-sea diver on the wreck of a Spanish treasure galleon. Untold numbers of tourists paid their ten dollars not just to get the trip, but to own that prestigious-looking document. Surely, many ended up framed proudly on walls.

Gradually, McKee came to realize that what they were doing was tearing the shipwreck to pieces, literally destroying the very thing the tourists were paying to see. From that came another great idea.

"Let's take all the ballast and cannon, pick them up, and put them back atop the pile to make it more photogenic," he told his crew. "Then we will make movies of it. If they pay for it, we'll let people come down and photograph our authentic Spanish galleon."

And that's what happened. A film was made for CBS, an hour-long presentation for the "Odyssey" show. Another was made for the Hiram Walker people; then came "Secret Cargo," for Canadian Club. John Craig for "Of Lands and Seas," filmed a feature about McKee's wreck. McKee became so popular, he was invited to appear on television's "We the People" and other such shows. The whole thing began to snowball, so much so, that McKee began to fear interference from others who might wish to profit similarly with his shipwreck.

In the early 1940s McKee applied to the state of Florida for a lease to protect the wrecks in his area, so that he could continue his operations unmolested by modern-day pirates.

For the next eight years, McKee had a perfect arrangement—a popular concession unlike anything in the world. From
the *Capitana*, as well as other old shipwrecks along the coast,
McKee recovered enough interesting items to eventually fill a
museum he built in 1949 like a concrete fortress on the beach.

He selected the site in a novel way. One day he was filming
aerial scenes of the *Capitana* on a dead, flat calm. He was
shooting movies with a 16-millimeter Bolex out the open door of
a Piper Cub, when the engine suddenly sputtered.

"Sounds like trouble!" shouted the pilot. "We'd better
head in."

Instead of flying back to Marathon where he came from,
the pilot flew straight in toward the beach highway. As they
crossed the coast, McKee looked down and saw an enormous
rock pit. It later proved to measure 970 feet long, 200 feet wide,
and 18 feet deep. There was no outlet to the sea, but McKee
thought to himself, "Wow, what a place to operate from, if that
pit could be opened to the sea!"

Once on the ground, McKee learned that the pit was in
solid coral rock. He bought 25 acres of land, with the big hole
right in the middle of it and the whole spread reaching from the
highway to the ocean.

He got a group of friends together. They pooled their
money, then dug the channel, giving the pit its opening to the
sea. After that, they decided they needed more money to
operate. They formed a corporation, called McKee's Museum of
Sunken Treasure, a Florida corporation authorized to sell twenty
thousand shares of stock at ten dollars a share.

It was a two hundred thousand dollar corporation. McKee
kept 51 percent of the stock and, over the years, he gradually
acquired 81 percent of it. The museum was to help McKee pay
for some of his future treasure-hunting adventures. He had
learned the first most important rule of becoming a professional
treasure hunter: *find a way to eat your cake and have it at the same
time.*

# Chapter 4

# Treasure Troubles

Despite the corporation and the museum, before he could adequately salvage the shipwreck he had leased from the state, McKee began having his first major problems with treasure.

In the beginning, it started with other treasure hunters who believed that all old abandoned shipwrecks were largely in the ocean's public domain; they belonged to anyone who had the wherewithall to work them. They firmly believed that no one had the right to legislate these long-forgotten sites, and moreover, they refused to go along with any "so-called" laws that allowed one salvager the rights to a lot of abandoned shipwrecks to the exclusion of everyone else.

Naturally, when word got out that McKee held an exclusive salvage lease from the state of Florida to work not only the *Capitana*, but a number of other old shipwrecks scattered between Cape Canaveral and the upper Florida Keys, rival treasure hunters bristled.

Eventually, it led to outright confrontations.

McKee had had the situation largely to himself for so many years, he was used to the idea that a few rival treasure hunters would be trying their luck on the *Capitana* the moment he left the site. This was no real problem, until after 1950 when scuba gear became more widely available. Here now was a simple, portable, inexpensive diving rig that no longer needed a backup air compressor on a surface craft. The diver was free and untethered to dive where he wished. All he needed was a boat in which to throw his air tank, regulator, mask, and fins and he was in the diving business.

Quite quickly, scuba divers were also in the treasure-hunting business, and that was the domain McKee had handled virtually single-handedly with his 1733 shipwrecks. Now, even he had switched over to the new kind of diving gear and was daily aware that the growing competition was anxious to move in on his operation. One example of how extreme the situation became occurred in 1960.

Mickey Spillane, a good friend of McKee's, had come down to Plantation Key to visit him. To kill time, he went out to the *Capitana* with McKee to help clean it up, restore some of the cannon into their proper position, and get the whole site ready for the Colonel John Craig movie.

"I knew Craig from earlier times," McKee later told me. "He and I designed a bangstick together. It was a 6-foot-long pole on the end of which was a chamber for a 12-gauge shotgun shell set up with a spring. When you hit something with it, boom! Boy, she made a heck of a racket. You had to hold it tight, or when she went off the stick would go the other way."

Craig had told McKee, "I want you to hit a shark with it, if you can."

That was the idea of the thing. Something to keep off the sharks. But since they couldn't find anything to test it on, they had settled on a big moray eel. It blew him in half.

Finally, Spillane and others helped get the wreck cleaned up for the film. Sand was jetted away. Two of the cannon he had in his harbor were put back on the ballast pile, and it was all set to be filmed.

At about that time, McKee heard some ugly rumors. He learned that a group of rival treasure hunters calling themselves the River Rats, comprised of Tim Watkins, Olin Frick, and a bunch of his divers, planned to give McKee some trouble about the *Capitana*.

McKee had no idea what they were going to do, but he planned to keep a sharp eye on his lease holdings.

One day, a navy photographer and McKee's son, Rick, joined him on a trip to the wreck aboard McKee's 54-foot converted shrimper, the *Jolly Roger*, which he had rigged with gin pole, airlift compressor, and everything necessary for light salvage.

As the *Jolly Roger* sped the 3½ miles offshore toward the *Capitana*, another vessel suddenly appeared from behind nearby Tavernier Key, headed in the same direction.

It was the *Buccaneer* with Olin Frick, Tim Watkins, and his men.

"The closer we got to the site, the more it looked like our two boats were on a collision course," McKee told me. "We figured they were heading for the wreck too, so we really put on the steam. Later I learned that they had been to the wreck before us, stolen our two cannon, and taken my concrete marker with the metal plaque on it that read, 'Posted by the State of Florida,' with our lease number, and 'McKee's Museum of Sunken Treasure, Agent,' and, according to them, they threw it out into the middle of the Gulf Stream."

Despite McKee's burst of speed, the *Buccaneer* reached the wreck site first and threw out a marker buoy.

"When I saw their float, I knew it was no crawfish trap float," said McKee. "They beat us to the wreck, but they overshot it. I slowed down, and before they could get back to their float, I had dropped my anchor right where I always did, in the middle of the ballast pile. I was anchored smack over my wreck when they came up."

Aboard the *Buccaneer* the River Rats circled McKee's *Jolly Roger* like a bunch of Indians around a wagon train. As the *Buccaneer* kicked up a big wake, the River Rats shook their fists at the *Jolly Roger*.

"We just laughed," said McKee. "Then Olin Frick came out on deck carrying a .30-.30 rifle. He cocked it and said, 'This is loaded and I'll blow your butt out of the water, McKee!' "

In a voice loud enough for everyone to hear, McKee replied, "Rick, call the Coast Guard!"

The *Buccaneer* drew alongside and dropped anchor.

McKee said to them: "If a diver is down it's illegal for you to be within 500 feet of us. I'm asking you to please go off. This is our wreck, and we're going to do a movie on it. If you want to come back and look at it another time, that's all right. I know you've been working on the *El Infante*, and that's in our leased area too."

"Your lease, hell," said Frick. "The state has no business giving you a lease and we're going to fight it. We'll see you in court."

"Well it just might be that way, too." McKee started putting on his diving gear. He told the navy photographer, "Get some pictures of that guy over there with the rifle."

The photographer took the pictures and the next day they appeared in the newspapers. The *Herald* took one side of the controversy and the *News* the other. It was a big squabble over a shipwreck.

Finally, McKee went over the side and took the bangstick down to the wreck. To keep sand out of the mechanism he tied a Bull Durham tobacco pouch over the end of it. Being a walking diver, he had a lot of weight on to stay down on the bottom.

Looking over the *Capitana*, he saw that the cannon and the marker were missing. Before he could notice anything else, however, five scuba divers—the whole crew of the *Buccaneer*—were coming down on him.

As they fanned out and approached, McKee backed up until he was against a huge mahogany timber he had put on the wreck to dress it up for the movies.

Thinking that they were going to pull off his mask and rough him up a bit, McKee did the first thing that came to mind.

He put up his hand like a traffic cop.

The menacing divers stopped in their tracks.

McKee didn't want to use his bangstick on any of them, but he patted it. He turned around and as he explained to me: "Like a damn fool, instead of getting 6 feet away, I choked the pole down to 3 feet and hit that damn timber as hard as I could with it. It went *whoom!* Jammed my mask down and bloodied my nose!"

When McKee looked around, just one diver was left. All he saw were the fins of the others heading back to their boat.

"I looked back at this guy and he was still there, crouched down like this, see, and I could see a big question mark over his head you might say, wondering . . .

"So I patted this bangstick again. I only had one shot, but he didn't know that. I started toward him and he took off fast. So there I was. I had all the confidence in the world, walking on down that wreck."

McKee stalked around his site, checking it over. His 55-gallon drums, filled with artifacts that he had placed back out there with the cannon to recover for Craig's cameras, were tipped over. McKee suspected they had taken the things the day before.

Periodically, he looked up at them hanging on the drive shaft of their boat, shaking their fists at him, and he responded by patting his bangstick. Of course, the only other shell he had for his weapon was up in his own boat, but they didn't know that. McKee had bluffed and it had worked.

Later, after he came ashore, he heard one of them say, "Hell, we were scared you were gonna take that other shell and hole the boat!"

But McKee only laughed. "You're lucky it wasn't a double-barreled bangstick," he said.

Topside, the River Rats regained some of their courage. Frick got out his rifle again and the air turned blue with their blustering.

Meanwhile, Rick whispered to his dad that he couldn't reach the Coast Guard. The radio was dead.

But the River Rats didn't know that. McKee got the phone

and jerked the wire right out of the set, so he could get out the door and it would look like he was talking and calling the Coast Guard.

The bluff worked. While he was going through the charade, the *Buccaneer* and its cursing crew hoisted anchor and took off.

Back on the beach, McKee reported the incident to Dan Ferguson, who was in charge of this for the state.

Ferguson said, "Have them arrested."

McKee contacted Charlie Vocelle, a representative of the attorney general's office in Miami. Vocelle told McKee that he had been advised to tell the treasure hunter to see a judge in Miami, in order to swear out warrants for their arrest and confiscation of their vessel. It appeared that the state was really going to do something.

McKee's lease read, "from the low water mark to the edge of the Gulf Stream or the 10-fathom line." He paid $100 a year for it. The state received 12½ percent of whatever he found. As a result, McKee looked after the shipwrecks as best he could. But everyone was poaching on them. Now he was ready to take those characters to court.

Suddenly, the state backed down!

"Boy, it was embarrassing," McKee remembered. "I got the warrants all ready. The judge appointed me as an agent for the state to deliver them in Dade County, where they could be served by the Dade County constable. So I went all the way to Miami, found the constable, and they were ready to be served at nine o'clock that night, when Tim Watkins, who owned the *Buccaneer* with Jimmy Green and a little corporation they had, came home."

While they waited, McKee phoned his wife and learned he had had a call earlier from Tallahassee. When he returned, Vocelle told McKee, "I hope you haven't served those warrants yet. I'm sorry, but I've got orders from Tallahassee to withdraw them."

Finally, it came out. McKee had been paying for a lease on the shipwreck each year, spending money and time for over eight years with the assumption that the state would protect them. Now he learned that the state would protect them no more than 3 miles offshore. Florida had been taking his money illegally for eight years, because it had no jurisdiction over shipwrecks beyond the 3-mile limit. And the *Capitana* was 3½ miles offshore!

Once he learned that, McKee tried to get his money back. But the state never did reimburse his eight hundred dollars. To make matters worse, they threatened to sue his corporation for the remaining two years at one hundred dollars a year.

Rather than get into a hassle with them, McKee said, "All right, we'll keep all the relics. We'll pay you the money, and let's forget the whole thing."

After learning that the state had no jurisdiction over the shipwrecks more than 3 miles offshore, McKee quit working the Florida wrecks and struck out for the Caribbean, looking for shipwrecks on those banks. From then on, he expanded his treasure-hunting operations to such places as Jamaica, where he explored the sunken city of Port Royal. Thus, McKee learned to benefit from the second most important rule of professional treasure hunting: *find investors willing to finance your treasure hunting.*

# Chapter 5

# Going for the Goodies

Although McKee's underwater explorations along the Florida coast located nine of the twenty-two ships lost in the 1733 hurricane, thanks to the chart he received from the Spanish archives, McKee largely lost interest in salvaging them for treasure after his problem with the state.

Having achieved a certain amount of fame and popularity as a successful treasure hunter, he had already made invaluable contacts who would assist him now that he was taking his search farther afield. Moreover, people sought after him to go treasure hunting.

All it required was for McKee to get together enough of those with sufficient money to enable them to charter a large enough boat and crew to sustain themselves during their sea hunt. Some backers came with preconceived ideas about where they wanted to look for treasure. Others offered the funding and hoped that McKee would take them to one of his favored treasure hot spots.

McKee did everything he could to discourage investors in believing that they surely would find a sunken *El Dorado*. He told them that if they had money to go to the horse races, then they could afford treasure hunting, and would come back feeling that they had got a lot more for their money than if they had lost it on the horses.

"Nothing in this treasure-hunting business is a sure thing," McKee always said. "You go, you hunt, and you hope. With any luck, you'll find treasure. With a lot more luck, you get to keep it. But more often than not, you won't find a thing."

Naturally, the more often he told people this, the less they believed him. One fellow was so certain that he would be coming back from one of McKee's expeditions loaded with money that he bought himself a brand new Cadillac before he left.

Nothing was more intriguing, more seductive, than the thought of finding treasure on the bottom of the ocean. All were smitten men. They too had read Rieseberg's books and were anxious to have a go at the gold. Let McKee tell how he first found gold on the bottom of the sea, and anyone with a speck of adventure in his soul within hearing was willing to mortgage his home, sink his savings into the project, and set sail with McKee for that distant Caribbean reef to do likewise. You can be sure that when McKee told the tale, he left nothing out. Here's more or less how it goes:

> Back in the days when McKee was diving helmet and hose repairman for the waterline to Key West, he was approached by a man who had a map of a Caribbean shipwreck that promised to produce treasure.
>
> Showing it to McKee, he said, "I'll pay you diver's wages for a ten-day job, if you go with me there and we see what we can find."
>
> McKee had nothing to lose. The man with the map did just what McKee later did—chartered a fully crewed vessel, shared his expenses with several others who wanted to go treasure hunting, and off they went, with McKee and his Miller-Dunn helmet and compressor stowed in the hold.
>
> Without difficulty, they found the wreck site. It was in clear, shallow water beside a coral reef. McKee donned his helmet, cranked up his compressor, and went down into the warm tropical seas to look around.
>
> The first thing he found were several large iron cannon. He thought that perhaps some large ship had run aground on the reef, then

jettisoned their cannon to lighten the vessel and get off again. But he was wrong.

For a whole day he poked around that reef, trying to find something of value, without success. As he returned to the dive vessel, he looked down through the clear depths and noticed that more cannon were strewn off into deeper water.

The next morning he followed the cannon trail, as they went over the edge of the reef. There he found a large number of them lying on the sandy bottom in 80 feet of water. Approaching what appeared to be a large clump of coral whose odd shape looked unnatural, McKee knocked off a chunk with his small pick.

Where the piece broke off, he saw a cavity containing rotted barrel staves.

"Now ain't that interesting," he murmured to himself.

He gave the chunk a couple more hard whacks with his pick. This time he exposed what appeared to be hard pitch or tar. Suddenly his heart began beating double-time, as he realized that several gold coins protruded from the black mass.

Cracking off a larger chunk of it, he dropped it into a lift basket and had them haul it up to the boat.

Later, over his dive phone came the good news. 'You hit it, McKee! We found eighteen gold coins in that chunk! Send up some more!'

"Man, was I ever excited after that!" McKee always told his listeners. "Until then, I'd never actually seen gold on the ocean floor. I was so excited I couldn't knock that encrusted barrel of pitch apart fast enough! But finally, I smashed the whole thing into manageable pieces and sent it topside."

Frantically pulverizing the rocklike pitch on deck, we found that it had contained over sixteen hundred gold coins.

"Of course we all wondered what they were doing stuck in that barrel of pitch," explained McKee. "Later I learned that it was common in the early days to hide contraband treasure that way, so that it could be smuggled into Spain to avoid paying import duties on it. Also, it was a good way to hide treasure so pirates could not find it. That's why treasure that is never declared on a manifest list often turns up hidden among the ballast rocks in the very bowels of the ship.

"That was my first real treasure," McKee would add, "but all I got out of it was a few coins my employers gave me as souvenirs. After all, I was only being paid to dive."

Over the years, McKee ran treasure-hunting expeditions back to that same site at least fifty times and failed to find any more treasure. Yet, the unsuccessful efforts never quenched his thirst for more expeditions, more treasure hunts. What McKee's expeditions often lacked in treasure, they usually made up for in adventure. Few trips ever went as smoothly as he planned. Things happened. They happened with such regularity that it was almost as if McKee was as addicted to the unknown adventure as he was to the overwhelming odds of finding no treasure. Once the quest began, nothing prevented him from following it to the end, no matter how bitter that ending.

For example, Roatán is a tropical island off the coast of Honduras. Legend has it that the island was a frequent pirate stronghold. Both fiction and fact about their presence there have tantalized generations of treasure hunters. When McKee learned that an Englishman had found pirate treasure in a cave on Roatán, he promptly lined up some fellow adventurers with funds, and they all flew down there to seek their fortunes.

When Roatán authorities learned that there were treasure hunters bent on making off with what the locals considered their national historical artifacts, the adventurers were placed under house arrest in a local hotel. After several days of boredom, the group slipped out of the hotel and went to a nearby beach for a swim. McKee and the others were sunning themselves on the beach, when from out of the ocean roared a Honduran naval landing barge. In front of the Americans' startled eyes, it dropped its ramp and disgorged a whole gang of angry soldiers armed to the teeth. They rushed ashore brandishing their weapons. As one of the soldiers menacingly approached McKee, he grinned and said in English, "Have a mango."

The soldier promptly whacked him over the head with his rifle butt. McKee's companions were similarly roughed up. Then, bleeding and unconscious, they were dragged back to their hotel jail, where they remained for several weeks. Eventually, the American embassy learned of their plight and secured their release.

After that, McKee vowed to confine his treasure hunting to the sea, but he didn't. It was the land hunts that almost did him in. But then, the sea hunts weren't too kind to him either.

Draw a line on a chart 135 miles south of Kingston, Jamaica, and it will end at Banner's Reef on the Pedro Bank.

For some reason McKee was obsessed with Banner's Reef. It began the first time he heard that a fisherman in 1906 had found gold bars there. McKee sampled the site with Ed Link of aviation fame, after the group exploded some fictional myths concerning the sunken city of old Port Royal, Jamaica, in 1956. But Banner was his nemesis.

Using Link's towed magnetometer, a device one might say is a supersensitive underwater metal detector, they located some shipwrecks on the Pedro Bank. Several historical artifacts were found, but no significant treasure. Bad weather blew them out of the area, but the sample was enough to make McKee believe they had just missed finding the big payoff.

What he was hunting was the wreck of the *Genovés*, (or *Genovesa*) spelled by some as it is pronounced, "Genovays." That was a nickname of a 1730 Genoa-built fifty-four-gun frigate loaded with 3 million pesos of gold and silver that shipped out of Havana in August of the same year. As she neared the channel between Serranilla and Pedro Shoals, a hurricane did her in. Her hulk ended up on Banner Reef, where a variety of salvagers began helping themselves. By year's end she had been reduced to little more than her bilge and ballast; the seas were fast covering her with sand.

Banner Reef is like a five-toothed saw. Each indentation is a deep blue pocket of water. A half-mile from the reef's southwest end, a shipwreck in one of these blue holes was reported to have produced six thousand dollars in gold for Cayman Island salvagers in the early 1900s. It might have been from the *Genovés*. In any case, nothing else had ever turned up, but McKee felt more was there, if he could just find it.

In 1962 he rounded up eighteen eager would-be treasure hunters, charged them one thousand dollars each as their share of expenses, then chartered a 136-foot vessel with crew to carry them all to Banner Reef to find the *Genovés*. As they sailed past Cuba, they were stopped by a Cuban gunboat. After questioning, the Cubans realized the group was not planning to attack the island; they were only treasure hunting. They were released and continued on to Grand Cayman Island to take on an islander who claimed to know the exact location of the wreck.

Using a glass-bottom bucket, the native spotted them over the same shipwreck McKee had worked earlier with the Link expedition. Eagerly, his companions began working the site. They found some thirty iron cannon, ship's timbers, and anchors. But no treasure.

In the days that followed, however, their finds became more interesting. Using several airlifts that suctioned sand off the bottom, they began to turn up such things as several ivory combs, ship's rigging, a brass sailmaker's palm, clay smoking pipes with engraved stems, a silver spoon, and thousands of cocoa beans. Literally tons of the beans were uncovered, to such an extent that they dubbed the site, "The cocoa bean wreck."

Still, there was scant treasure. After three weeks of hard work, all the group had to show for it was a few gold medallions, a gold crucifix, and a gold key.

Eventually, McKee decided it was not the *Genovés;* not the wreck where the fisherman had found the gold bars. He decided to locate another wreck in the area, when he had trouble with the charter vessel's captain. Throughout the trip, he had not been the friendliest type. Now he insisted that the vessel return to Grand Cayman to refuel, rather than look for another shipwreck.

To avoid any trouble, McKee agreed. But once they reached Grand Cayman, he learned that the captain planned to double-cross them. As soon as they refueled, he intended to sail to Roatan, where he had arranged with a crooked official there to share in all the equipment and "treasure" McKee had aboard. The equipment alone was valued at over twenty thousand dollars.

McKee decided the best thing he could do was get it off the boat as quickly as possible. When he attempted to do so, a drunken first mate shoved a pistol into his belly and said he would kill McKee if he took anything off the vessel.

One of McKee's divers summoned the police, and the mate

was arrested. McKee's group promptly got its gear ashore, then everyone flew home.

Several years later, McKee returned to Banner Reef with another group of eager treasure divers, this time aboard his own vessel—a 110-foot wooden salvage boat named *Rosalie*. *Rosalie* had made so many maiden voyages in her time that she now looked like a dishevelled dowager in dire need of care and repair. But no longer did McKee have to rely on charter boats and sometimes crooked crews. He outfitted *Rosalie* with everything he needed for serious salvage work. Despite the lady's appearance, *Rosalie* provided McKee with just the kind of floating salvage base he needed.

Six weeks of hard diving and living aboard the vessel over the reef brought the treasure hunters only a few silver coins. To help defray expedition expenses, McKee arranged with Jamaica's Reef Club Hotel to provide enough shipwreck material to give them a waterfront display that tourists could dive on.

Subsequently, his divers hoisted five iron cannon and related shipwreck artifacts, which were then sold to the hotel. Among his divers on this expedition was Burt Webber, a longtime avid treasure hunter, who would later gain fame as the discoverer of a long-sought legendary Spanish galleon laden with treasure.

At Jamaica, McKee's group decided it had had its fill of treasure hunting on Banner Reef. They caught flights home, leaving McKee with his 110-foot-long *Rosalie* to bring home by himself. It was a memorable voyage.

# Chapter 6

# Ordeal by Sea

McKee tried to find a crew to help him bring the boat back to Miami by way of Grand Cayman Island. Four Jamaicans agreed to go, but the government wanted McKee to pay a one thousand dollar bond for each man. McKee knew he would never get the money back again, so he decided to take *Rosalie* home by himself, a journey of almost 1200 miles.

He provisioned her with sardines and baked beans, put a screwdriver in one hip pocket, a crescent wrench in the other, checked all his equipment, and plotted a course for the Cayman Islands, some 300 miles away. After refueling up, he took on twenty stems of bananas, thinking that once he reached Grand Cayman, he would sell them to help defray his costs.

Hardly had he left Kingston, when a storm kicked up. It was no ordinary downpour. It was a flood. "Boy, I bet they haven't had this much rain since the earthquake of 1692!" he thought. At least so it seemed, as he manned the wheel of the big lumbering vessel, sending it crashing over the top of the big gray waves and slewing heavily down their sides into valleys of foam, while sheets of rain fell so fiercely, he was unable to see from one foaming crest to another.

The *Rosalie* had been so long in the sun, her deck seams were cracked. Below decks, McKee found it raining almost as hard as it was above decks. Worse, his Loran, the navigational instrument he had counted on to keep him on course with his automatic pilot, had gotten wet and had stopped working. Now, he had to manually steer the vessel, unless he could repair the instrument.

Looking astern, he saw the Montego Bay light. "If I'm going back," he thought, "now's the time to do it." Finally, he turned his back on the light and looked straight ahead. He made up his mind to go.

As both the storm and the seas worsened a few hours later, McKee wondered if he had made the right decision. "Good gosh. Here I am by myself on a 110-foot ex-navy sub chaser that normally has a skeleton crew of eighteen. I must be crazy!"

Yet he had spent so many years at sea, he felt sure he could handle whatever came up. His greatest danger would be falling asleep for too long a time, during which things could happen. To make sure he did not oversleep he had brought along two alarm clocks set to go off every thirty minutes.

Finally the storm abated. McKee lashed the ship's wheel, so the *Rosalie* cruised in slow circles while he dried out the Loran. He got it working again and brought his vessel back on course. After that, he went below to make sure everything was all right, checked his engines, cleaned the fuel filters, saw that the bilge pumps were handling the flood that had leaked in, then went topside and glassed the horizon. From this point he had almost 200 miles to go. At his present rate of speed it would take him over seventy-two hours.

When he grew tired, he slept on a mattress beside the helm. Every half-hour he awakened, as the two alarm clocks went off. McKee jumped up, reset them for another half-hour, checked his vessel, scanned the horizon for other ships, then caught another catnap.

Slowly the days passed without mishap. Then, on his last night at sea before reaching the Caymans, another storm materialized. It raged intermittently through the black night. Sometime during the early morning hours, McKee sighted a ship's light ahead of him. He changed course to avoid the oncoming vessel.

It appeared that the ship did the same thing, in the same direction as the *Rosalie*. McKee brought the *Rosalie* back on her original course. Maybe it was his imagination, but he would have sworn that the oncoming vessel did precisely the same thing.

By McKee's calculations he was approaching his estimated time of arrival in the Cayman Islands. But there was no glow of light on the horizon, no signs of any island. If he missed the group, he would be out in the wide open reaches of the sea again, and it stretched all the way across the Caribbean to Mexico. McKee didn't even dare guess what missing the small islands would mean.

The large ship with all its lights approached closer. Again McKee realized it was on a collision course with him. Quickly, he took evasive action. He tried to radio the ship, but got no response. Grabbing his signal light, he blinked out a labored Morse code that said, "Where . . . is . . . Cayman . . . ?"

From the bridge of the big ship came a snappy reply. "Blinkety-blink, blinkety-blink."

McKee was never too good at reading the stuff. This didn't make a bit of sense to him. "Oh, to hell with it," he said and just kept on going.

About 5 A.M. he spotted what appeared to be a light on the horizon. "That might be Little Cayman," he thought. It was within 100 miles of Grand Cayman. "If I'm right, at least I'm in the ballpark!"

He had plotted his course to run between Grand Cayman and the smaller island, Little Cayman. Looking up, he saw the constellation Orion above the light. Even if things clouded in on the horizon he would have some idea of which direction he had seen the light.

It was a good thing he established this range, because the light soon disappeared behind a passing rain squall. McKee reduced his speed by half. Reefs reached far out from the islands and he had no wish to find them the hard way. Finally, he decided not to go any closer until he had better light.

In the gray light of dawn he was glad he had waited. In the distance he saw waves pounding on an iron shore that lay directly ahead. Swinging wide of the reef, he brought the *Rosalie* around the obstacle and continued until he was sure of being off Grand Cayman.

As he approached the harbor entrance flanked by dangerous reefs, the wind, waves, and the tide were against him.

As he started in, one of his generators quit. Then, one of his two engines sputtered into silence. Since the seas dropped off deep beyond the reefs, there was no way he could anchor to repair the problem.

Instead, he limped a safe distance away, lashed the wheel to cruise in a circle, then went below to do what he could. Correcting the trouble, he got underway again. This time, as he started toward the treacherous passage, his second engine failed.

Again he retreated and went below to correct the problem. Finally, on his third try, a generator failed as he started in. McKee said "to hell with it" and kept on until he had negotiated the narrow passageway into the harbor.

With a sigh of relief, he shut down both engines, kicked the anchor over, and set it. Then he sagged down onto a hatch cover and slept like he had never slept before.

A few days later, after selling his bananas, reprovisioning, cleaning out his fuel tanks, and refueling, McKee was ready to head for Miami with the *Rosalie*. His destination was 800 miles away.

This time he located a Cayman Islander to go with him. His name was Rolli. He was supposed to be a great navigator and a great engineer. McKee also soon found out that he was the greatest boozer he had ever had aboard his boat.

McKee had given Rolli money ahead of time. What he didn't know until later was that, while he was away from the

*Rosalie,* Rolli bought himself some sea stores—enough rum to last him indefinitely. He hid the bottles of booze all over the boat.

The next afternoon the two seamen powered the *Rosalie* out through the pass and into the open ocean. Rolli was drunk and McKee's Loran was not working again,.

McKee put the boat in circles and repaired his navigational instrument. Once again he got it to working and put the boat on course. By midnight Rolli was still working on a bottle of rum. McKee put the boat on automatic pilot and went below.

"By gosh, are you still drinking?" he asked Rolli.

"Yessir," said Rolli. "It's the last bottle I got."

McKee snatched it away from him and threw it out a porthole. Then he went back to the helm.

Sometime later when he went below, he found his engineer nursing another bottle. Despite Rolli's complaints, it too went flying out the porthole. After that, McKee searched the ship for other bottles. He found an armful.

Despite Rolli's moaning and protesting, McKee dumped them all overboard.

At noon the next day in high seas, with a sobering Rolli manning the wheel, trying to keep the bow into the waves, McKee came aft with his radio direction finder to get a bearing on the radio signal at Cape San Antonio, the western end of Cuba. For safety sake, the decks of the *Rosalie* had so many lifelines crossing them they looked like spiderwebs. As McKee negotiated these lines, Rolli let the *Rosalie* wallow in a wave.

McKee fell, skidded smartly across the deck and over the side. Grabbing one of the lines just in time, he hauled himself back aboard. The R.D.F. had shot under the overturned Boston Whaler. McKee recovered it and was starting back to the pilothouse, when the boat made another giant lurch.

This time McKee was thrown heavily against a wooden bench, which broke three of his ribs. Holding his side, he crawled on his hands and knees back to the helm. He pounded on the cabin door until Rolli let him in.

As McKee crawled in and looked up at Rolli, the native's eyes got huge.

"Man! What happened to you? Don't you die on me! Don't you leave me out here all alone!"

It was McKee who was in agony, but it was Rolli who was doing all the moaning. McKee lay beside the helm trying to hold himself, but everytime the ship rolled, he heard the crunching of his ribs, as the broken ends rubbed together. The pain was excruciating.

Through gritted teeth he said, "Rolli, go below and bring all the aspirin and Bufferin you can find."

"Yessir, Cap'n." Rolli ducked below. Soon he was back with a handful of painkillers. As McKee chewed them up, the engineer said, "See, McKee, I tol' you, you shouldn't throwed all that liquor overboard!"

Rolli went below again and came back with all the pillows and mattresses he could find. He piled them up in the pilothouse around McKee. "There you is, Cap'n. I got you fixed up like a bird in a nest." Rollie was quite pleased with himself.

"Better bring up a sheet and tear it into strips," said McKee. "You gotta wrap me up."

"You sho that's a good idea, Cap'n?" Rolli asked. "You move around an' puncture the lungs an' we never find our way home."

McKee grimaced. "Get the sheets, for gosh sakes!"

Rolli did as he was told, tearing them into strips and wrapping McKee's chest up like a mummy.

They ran all that afternoon and into the night. By midnight, the pain was so intense that McKee was sometimes delirious. He was running a fever and cussing everything that crossed his mind, including the birds. In his more lucid moments however, he frequently asked Rolli if he was absolutely sure he was holding their course. The reply was always the same.

"Yessir, Cap'n. We's followin' the compass true."

At 5 A.M. McKee was jolted out of his delirium by the sounds of the *Rosalie*'s keel crunching into the bottom. He thought, "My God, what would we hit out in the middle of the Caribbean?"

As their boat ran aground, Rolli piped up, "Well, Cap'n, we made it to the Dry Tortugas!"

From his nest of pillows McKee said, "Look and see if you can see the big fort."

Rolli turned on the spotlight and swept its beam over the water. The only thing he could see ahead were bushes.

"It's an island, Cap'n!"

"Let me see." McKee grabbed Rolli's leg and belt and pulled himself up. He looked out to where Rolli was pointing the spotlight and saw the same desolate-looking land and bushes.

"Better go below and start the pumps. I know we must be taking on water."

They were. Rolli reported that they had plenty of water in the bow and galley.

"Better go up on the foredeck and see what you get with the lead line."

Rolli called back his findings. " 'Bout two 'n half feet of water, Cap'n."

"Holy mackerel!"

Rolli came aft and checked the depth off the stern. " 'Bout 8 feet here, Cap'n."

"Okay, Rolli. Put the engines in slow reverse. If the tide is coming in, it should help us get off."

About 8:30 in the morning the bottom slowly released its hold on the *Rosalie*. She backed into deeper water. As she did, McKee spotted a boat in the distance with five men aboard.

"Head on over toward them, Rolli. We'll find out where the devil we are."

As the big *Rosalie* bore down on the five men in the boat, McKee saw them rapidly pull in fishing lines, hoist their sail, and try to make a run for it.

With the ship's siren going full blast, McKee and Rolli chased them down and finally cornered the panicked fishermen.

In reply to Rolli's question in Spanish as to where they were, McKee caught the words "Cabo Real, Cuba."

"Good gosh! Rolli get us out of here quick! Pull down that American flag and hoist the British Jack for the Caymans."

Then seaward they went as fast as they could. When they were about 3 miles out, three Migs roared down on them.

Rolli leaped down the companionway, spraining his ankle. McKee, already too bunged up to take any serious evasive action, looked up and waved.

The Migs made a second pass, flying low over them. McKee waved nonchalantly, trying to grin. As the fighters roared back over the horizon, he kept the *Rosalie* heading out to sea.

They repaired each others damaged parts. Rolli wrapped more bedsheets around McKee so tight he could hardly breathe. McKee bound his ankle. Now, both staggered.

McKee's high fever soon had him seeing things. It came and went. About then they ran into another severe storm off the Cape. As they wallowed through it to the other side, McKee thought he saw the distant mountains of Cuba. Were they real, or was it his delirium? Were they headed toward shore, or out to sea? He was never too sure.

Realizing they had taken on a lot of water from both the grounding and the storm, he had no idea how bad it was until he heard the *Rosalie*'s twin propellers start running fast and erratic. They were cavitating. Looking forward, he saw the bow was dangerously low. It was so heavy with water, it lifted the stern high enough for the propellers to churn air!

"If you can't fix those bilge pumps," McKee told his engineer, "we're going down right here!"

Rolli went below. Moments later, McKee heard him making all too familiar sounds. His engineer was seasick. McKee called him back up.

"Rolli, you're going to have to rig me up in a block and tackle and lower me down there to do the job. Haul me up and down."

"Cap'n, don' you go down der. De water already up to my knees. You drown!"

"Well, if I stay up here we're both gonna drown anyway, so I better get down there and get those damn pumps fixed."

Rolli rigged up the block and tackle and lowered McKee into the sloshing hold. McKee went to work on the bilge pumps and finally got them going again. When Rolli hauled him back out of the hold, his eyes widened at the spectacle of the water-soaked, grease-begrimed McKee looking like a tarred mummy.

"Lordy, lordy, Cap'n. We ain't never gonna get you clean!"

"That's okay," said McKee. "At least we won't sink right away."

But their troubles were far from over. The bow lifted a little, but then one of the pumps failed again. Finally, McKee got the generator going and the radio operating.

"Mayday . . . mayday . . . mayday . . ." he radioed to all ships at sea. "WD0866. This is the motor vessel *Rosalie*. We need help!"

McKee repeated the call several times. Finally, he got an answer. "This is the tanker, *Joan*. This is the tanker *Joan*. We're coming to your rescue. Do you read?"

McKee acknowledged them. Then he heard the Coast Guard talking to the tanker, but he could not reach the Coast Guard.

Finally, a big four-engine Coast Guard airplane came out of the blue toward them. In his on-again, off-again delirium, McKee was trying to remember what he wanted the Coast Guard for. He turned to his engineer and said, "Rolli, you're just going to have to talk to them."

Apparently, his explanation was all right. The plane bore down on them again and dropped a parachute attached to a half-gallon drum. Somehow the two of them managed to block and tackle it aboard. The drum contained a Briggs and Stratton pump and a gallon of gasoline.

"Good golly," wheezed McKee. A *gallon* of gas!"

Fortunately, they had plenty of fuel in 55-gallon drums lashed in the stern. Once the pump got rid of some of the water, they picked up a line from the tanker *Joan* that came alongside, and in due course, were being towed toward Key West.

McKee was so totally exhausted by now, he sagged down on the pillows and slept. Next thing he knew, they were loading him into an ambulance at Key West. Cameras were flashing and reporters were asking, "Did the Cubans shoot you up like that?"

And no wonder. The *Rosalie* looked like she had just returned from a major naval engagement. Her canvas awning was torn to shreds, the flag and after deck was so black from diesel smoke, they were unrecognizable. Moreover, both Rolli and McKee, swathed in bandages and equally begrimed, looked like wartime casualties.

When the story appeared in the newspaper, it was apparent to McKee that Rolli had been interviewed and got carried away with the drama. He had the *Rosalie* being chased by Cuban gunboats and attacked by Russian fighters. All McKee could do from his hospital bed was plead for the customs, immigration, and other officials to please read his log. At McKee's request, Rolli had wrapped it and McKee's watch in bedstrip bandages and bound them to his chest, when it looked like they might be caught in Cuba.

"If you want the truth, it's in the log. I reckon some nurse has got it by now," McKee told the authorities questioning him.

In time they repaired him and turned him loose. The *Rosalie* had been put in drydock. Rolli had stayed with her, as he had promised McKee he would. After the ordeal, his medication was a well-hidden bottle of rum McKee had failed to find. With the *Rosalie* undergoing repairs of her own in drydock, Rolli returned to Grand Cayman, ready to retire from lengthy sea voyages.

When the *Rosalie* was once again shipshape, McKee brought her up to Plantation Key. Waiting for a full moon and high tide to get her into his harbor, he anchored for the night not far from Hen and Chickens Light.

In the middle of the night, McKee was awakened by the banging of a locker below. He went to secure it. Seeing there was water in the bilge and evidence of spilled diesel fuel, he decided to pump the bilges with the small Coast Guard furnished Briggs and Stratton pump that sat on a low table with a raised edge around it. Beside it was a 5-gallon tank of fuel. McKee started up the engine and went topside to lie down on the mattress in the pilothouse.

Sometime in the hours before dawn he was awakened by a loud *whoosh*.

Leaping up, he was appalled to see flames licking up out of the companionway from below. Immediately, he grabbed a fire extinguisher and started shooting the carbon dioxide down into the hold. When it was nearly exhausted, he tied down the handle and tossed the extinguisher into the flames. By the time he ran to get another one, the flames were as high as ever.

For the next couple hours, McKee fought the fire as best he could. He ended up throwing all nine fire extinguishers down there with their handles tied open spewing carbon dioxide, but nothing helped.

He raced to the afterdeck and shot off all the flares and rockets he could find. "Jesus, I was losing my ship, but it looked like a regular Fourth of July celebration back there," he said later.

He kicked over the vessel's ten-man rubber raft, tied on a 75-foot line that he threaded through the afterdeck fitting, and climbed down into the boat. There he sat, huddled under *Rosalie*'s counter, watching her name flickering in the firelight.

"I guess this is it, ol' girl," he thought. "What a way to bring you home!"

About then, McKee remembered the drums of fuel lashed around the stern. They could blow him to kingdom come. He let out the line so the raft would drift away from the fire. He didn't want to get too far off, for fear of drifting away in the dark.

He was coughing and exhausted from fighting the fire, but where he now was proved to be equally dangerous. Flaming embers were showering around him. Now, it was a real case of being caught between the frying pan and the fire. All he could do was hang on and hope that help would come.

Since he was a mile and a half offshore, the large fire and rockets McKee had sent up were sighted on shore. The Coast Guard was alerted and, in a short while, their large vessel came up and circled the conflagration.

Through a bullhorn, one of the guardsmen asked, "Is there anyone aboard?"

From the darkness McKee called, "Nope. Just me and I'm over here."

"That thing's ready to blow at any minute, so be ready," they told him. "We'll make a pass at the raft and get you."

They came by the raft and snatched McKee out of it and over the side of their boat so roughly, they broke his ribs again.

Next thing he knew, he was being put into an ambulance and on his way to a hospital again. "But what about the ship?" he asked.

"There's nothing we can do," they told him. "She's a gonner."

After dawn, the Coast Guard towed the hulk into shallow water, where she finished burning.

After McKee's ribs healed, he went out and looked at her. It was a sad sight. She was a blackened, gutted hulk. He guessed that in the night she had turned sideways and taken a beam wave from a passing tanker that dumped the pump and fuel onto the deck. Then it caught fire.

In the days that followed McKee salvaged what was left of the *Rosalie*—her large propellers, her two 700-pound manganese bronze rudders, along with her 4-inch monel shafts. That was it.

It had been a rough trip for all concerned. But at least, after the treasure hunt and this ordeal by sea, McKee had escaped with his life. On his next treasure-hunting expedition, the fates were not to be so gentle with him.

# Chapter 7

# Tortuga's Treasure

As such things so often do, it began with a mysterious telephone call to McKee in the middle of the night.

"I can't tell you any of the details over the phone, Mr. McKee, but I have some old Spanish documents I think you will be extremely interested in seeing. They tell about treasure I think we can find, if you are willing to undertake a search with me."

"Well," laughed McKee, "all I can tell you is that I'm willing to look at what you have. After that, we can decide what to do."

"Fair enough," replied the caller.

A meeting was arranged. McKee was contacted by two men from Venezuela who wanted him to look over some old documents found in the walls of an old house that was torn down in their country. As best as McKee could translate them the items seemed to be part of a collection describing different treasure sites. Most were written on leather, contained strange symbols, and some were dated as early as 1557. One document indicated that an old pirate fort had existed on the island of Tortuga, located in the Caribbean, about 110 miles off the coast of

Venezuela. Like so many other islands along the coast from Panama to the Orinoco—the infamous Spanish Main—it had a history of being a hangout for pirates, buccaneers, and freebooters preying on the heavy traffic of Spanish treasure ships operating in this part of the Caribbean. Indeed, in the heyday of the sixteenth and seventeenth centuries, they raped, robbed, pillaged, and plundered Spanish holdings along the entire coast for hundreds of miles. It was assumed that much of this plunder was hidden away in these notorious pirate strongholds.

The two Venezuelans figured that, if Tortuga contained a pirate fort, then hidden treasure had to be nearby. Would McKee help them mount an expedition to find it?

This was exactly the kind of quest that fired McKee's imagination. According to a translation of the leather documents, the fort on Tortuga had been built by pirates in the late 1500s and had been in the hands of rival pirate groups operating on the Spanish Main. One such group was called the "Organization of the Doble Cruz." Their sign of the double-cross appeared invariably along with their signatures on the old documents.

Members of the Doble Cruz included such infamous figures as Henry Morgan, F. Carmou, Borin, the Machui Brothers, and others. Mentioned on one of the documents was this statement:

"In Tortuga can be found the treasure of Mexico 1635, the cargo of *La Magdalena,* the cargo of gold which was taken from Montezuma to Islas Canaries. The one of Brazil was not buried in Tortuga, because the guides had to take refuge in the Islas de Juanacoco. They hid it and after were sacrificed by the English fleet. It is lost, but there is documentation of the other treasures . . ."

Another leather letter addressed to Senoa Cte of the Doble Cruz, is translated to read:

"As you know, I left Chagre the thirteenth to do as you told me, but the sixteenth at noon, I saw three ships coming not far from mine. We were close to *Los Testigos* [a small island group 150 miles northeast of Tortuga]. I recognized that one of the ships was the

*Magdalena* and the son of a dog of Gramon. You know that he does not like to waste his time, so I wanted him to take his dinner [fall into my trap.] I prepared his dinner carefully. Before he knew it, he lost his teeth [lost his advantage], because he did not know that for eating [conquering] Tortuga, he must be very hungry [desperate to conquer] and needed good teeth [fighting strength] also. We had the bad luck of sinking his *Magdalena*. The new sailors behaved as good soldiers. The son of a dog was very well punished. Everything is safe in the island. Waiting for your order.

(signed) F. Carmau

According to other leather documents that McKee examined, the Spanish crown and the church organized a fleet of warships to seek out and destroy the pirates at their fortress hideaway on Tortuga. Plans for the fort showed several rooms and four watchtowers. The fleet converged on Tortuga and, after a devastating battle, the Spanish marines landed and massacred all but two pirates who managed to escape to the mainland. The fort was leveled and nothing remained but the record of destruction of "Forte la Tortuga."

Succumbing to the lure of yet another treasure hunt, another adventure, on May 14, 1976, McKee flew to Maracaibo, Venezuela, where he was met by Professor Alberto Cribeiro Valiente and his son—the two who had furnished McKee with the old documents.

They immediately made plans for an expedition to Tortuga to find and search the area of the old pirate fort. Supposedly, there were some marks on a rock slab near the fort that would lead them to some "very valuable loot" cached by the pirates prior to the fort's destruction.

The men prepared a list of their expedition's needs. Since there was no habitation on the island, they planned to fly in enough supplies to last them at least ten days at which time they would be picked up by their helicopter.

All the things they needed were assembled at the airport. But just hours before they were to take off, McKee received an urgent cable from Miami advising him that his aged mother was critically ill in the hospital and not expected to live.

The expedition was postponed. The helicopter was unloaded and all the equipment stored in a hangar until McKee could return to Venezuela. McKee made an itemized list of everything and put it in his briefcase.

He arrived in Miami on May 27th, just an hour and a half before his mother passed away.

Returning to Maracaibo the next month, he arrived at the helioport to find that all their equipment had already been loaded aboard the helicopter. Even his briefcase with its list was buried beneath boxes of supplies.

"Are you absolutely sure that everything is in and nothing has been overlooked?" McKee asked Professor Cribeiro.

"Yes, yes, everything has been put aboard, McKee."

"You sure we got enough water for ten days?"

"Yes, it's all there," the professor assured him.

Before they left, they discussed their plans with a friend of the professor, a senior officer in the Venezuelan air force, Colonel Torrelles Paiva, who was assigned to the helicopter service.

"If we don't turn up in about a week, you better come looking for us," quipped McKee laughing, as he climbed aboard the helicopter with Professor Cribeiro, his son, José Valdes, and the pilot.

"If you find the ruins of the fort," called Colonel Torreles, "I'll send ten guards and four workmen to help you excavate. Good luck! Hasta luego!" He waved them off.

Following the coast and jungle-covered steeps of the Cordillera de Merida Mountains, it was 310 air miles to Caracas. Another 110 miles northeast of Caracas, brought them over the 30-mile-long by 12-mile-wide chunk of sun-scorched, fractured volcanic rock called Isla la Tortuga. As they made an aerial survey of the island, hoping to pinpoint an area that might contain ruins, their enthusiasm waned.

"Boy-o-boy," murmured McKee, as he relayed the story to me. "I can't ever remember seeing any place that looked quite so desolate." From 2,000-foot altitude, the sun-cracked slabs of rock comprising the upper layers of the island looked like pieces of a giant jigsaw puzzle. Dense cacti growth covered most of its rugged surface. A reddish orange sand comprised the only few flat areas of the desert island. A white beach extended well into the sea at its western end, and its iron shore exposed to the wide stretches of the open Caribbean was constantly pounded by huge waves.

Descending to 800 feet, they made repeated passes over one spot of the island designated on the old document as being the site of the pirate fort. Seeing no sign of ruins, they thought perhaps the extensive cactus growth might be covering them.

Finally, the pilot set the helicopter down on one of the flat reddish orange sandy sites on the interior of the island. As they touched down, McKee said, "Maybe we'd be better off if we set up camp closer to the coast."

"I'm already low on fuel," said the pilot.

McKee shrugged. "Okay. This place will be all right."

They started unloading their gear. As McKee got out of the helicopter, he stepped on a shovel handle and twisted his left knee badly. It was the same one he had injured playing football in high school, but it did not appear to be too serious at the time.

The helicopter pilot was instructed to return and pick them up seven days later at 4 P.M. He then took off for his base at Caracas.

McKee and the others set up camp. It was easily seen from the air by their large orange and blue tent. They cut a 20-foot-long pole and tied a red shirt on it, thereby establishing their base of operations on *La Tortuga*.

As McKee looked over their pile of equipment, he suddenly asked, "Where are the canteens?"

The equipment list they had made out at Caracus had included three half-gallon canteens, which were now missing. Also missing was a fine ninety dollar compass they had purchased just before leaving.

Their main water supply was in three plastic 5-gallon containers, but the only canteen they had was a 1-quart container that McKee had carried with him.

"Well, I guess we just have to make do with the one canteen," he said.

By sundown they cooked their first meal, drank a cup of water each, and turned in for the night.

In the early morning hours, McKee awakened suddenly cold. It was 4:15 A.M. and the wind was gusting cold enough to make him shiver.

"What strange weather," he thought. "Fry you by day and freeze you by night."

At daybreak, after breakfast, Professor Cribeiro suggested that they take a look at the seacoast. "It's only a short walk and we can search for the fort on the way."

McKee checked his small pocket compass and noted that they were heading north. He made sure that their one canteen was full and, after everyone took a big drink from their main supply, they started for the coast. McKee knew that, as soon as the sun appeared, their day of intense heat would begin.

The patches of cacti were thicker than they had seemed from the air. Where they could they went around them. Where it was impossible to go around, they chopped their way through with machetes, on a course that took them over extremely treacherous rock ridges. Cracks in the foot-thick cap of volcanic rock were often several feet wide and deep enough to lie in. Traversing this cracked, rocky landscape through tall spine-covered cacti was extremely difficult.

After hiking a couple miles, McKee's injured knee was paining him. It was beginning to swell, so they stopped for a while to rest under a small shrub.

Finally, after four hours of beating their way through a jungle of cacti and cracked rocks, they reached the coast. It was delightfully refreshing. The seas were high and breaking over the rocks, sending a cool, misty spray over the sweaty men.

Quickly, they stripped off and followed a sandy beach out into the cool water to swim.

They spent some time exploring this coastal area, until it began to grow late. They decided it best to start back to camp. McKee discovered that there was now less than a pint of water remaining in his canteen. From then on they would have to ration their drinks to one canteen capful each. It was already late in the afternoon and they knew it would be impossible to find safe footing after dark. They had to get back to their camp site as soon as possible.

On the way to the coast they passed a pelican nesting area. McKee wanted to photograph them on the way back and had planned to stop. When they missed the area, however, he re-checked his compass and found the needle acting strangely. Whenever the compass was moved, the needle would spin. He figured they were in an area of magnetic rock.

Getting his bearings from the sun's position, he led them south toward camp.

By now, his injured knee was severely swollen and he was in almost unbearable pain. "We better rest here for a few minutes," he said.

They stopped for a five-minute break. Each had a capful of water from McKee's canteen.

After resting, McKee tried walking a few steps. It was virtually impossible for him to step over the rocks. In fact, any weight on his leg at all was terribly painful.

"Listen," he told the others. "I'm just slowing you fellows down. We're about an hour and a half from the campsite. Take my compass and what's left of the water and leave me here to rest overnight. You can bring back food and water tomorrow morning, when you come back to get me."

"You can't stay out here all night, McKee."

"Well, I damn sure can't go on," he said. "It'll be all right. Just watch the sun and the compass. When you reach camp, fire two pistol shots. I'll answer with two shots, which will let you know that I heard you. You get a good night's rest and bring me some supplies in the morning. My knee will probably be all right again."

"Okay, McKee. If you insist, we'll go. We'll signal you in a little while, then get back here just as fast as we can tomorrow morning."

"Good," said McKee.

Reluctantly, the professor and his son started for the base camp without McKee. As soon as they were gone, McKee curled up under the only low, scrubby tree in the area that had any leaves and waited for the signal shots.

Two hours passed without a signal.

McKee rationalized that they might have been slow along the way. Four hours passed and still no signal.

"Whew! What am I doing getting caught in this kind of thing again?" McKee wondered aloud. "Here I sit on a deserted island, hundreds of miles from civilization, with no food, no water, and nothing but a banged-up knee. Boy! You'd think I'd learn! It's worse than broken ribs on the *Rosalie*!"

Long after dark, he still strained his ears to hear the signal.

The shots never came.

# Chapter 8

## Ordeal by Land

Before the sun set, McKee cleared away sharp rocks from under the tree. Using a rock and a glove as a pillow, he made himself as comfortable as possible. Finally, he fell asleep. Sometime later, he was suddenly awakened by a lizard running over his face. It was gone in a flash, and McKee immediately went back to sleep again.

He slept fitfully until 4 A.M., when the cold blast of wind blew across the island. After that, sleep was out of the question. He shivered until the sun came up.

At dawn, his mouth felt dry as cotton. All morning he waited, hoping to hear his friends' signal. But none came. As the morning wore on and they too failed to appear, McKee suspected something serious had happened to them.

He took stock of his scanty possessions. His clothing consisted of undershorts, long pants, long-sleeved shirt, and shoes. His large towel could be used as a flag. With the string from his tennis shoes, he tied the flag to a long pole that he propped up in the branches of his tree. He also had a .38 caliber pistol with twelve rounds of ammunition, his wristwatch, a machete, an 8-inch knife, one glove, a sombrero, and an empty camera, which the professor's son had left with him.

Searching his pockets carefully, McKee found two medi-cated throat lozenges and a tube of sun-screen ointment with a coconut oil base. That was the sum of his survival gear.

During the night, the swelling in his knee had somewhat subsided. Walking a short distance from his sheltering tree, McKee investigated his surroundings for something to eat and drink. Other than the lizards there seemed to be no other animal life around.

With his knife, he cut off a chunk of cactus. It contained a milky sap. Cautiously, he tasted it. It burned his lips. Returning to his tree, McKee applied some of the sun-screen ointment to his lips.

Cutting one of the larger cactus stalks, he found a few drops of green juice in the pulp. Thinking it might be poisonous, he was afraid to taste it. Instead, he sat down gloomily and watched the lizards catch flies off the rocks. Wondering where they got their drinking water, he squeezed a few drops of cactus juice on a rock and was elated when one of the lizards ran out, extended its tongue, and lapped up the juice.

McKee watched the lizard carefully to see if it was suddenly going to flip over on its back and die. When the lizard went back to feeding on the flies, McKee cut a fresh cactus and squeezed the juice into the palm of his hand. By then, his thirst was so intense that it easily overcame his reluctance to taste the juice.

First he wet his lips with it, then he swallowed some of the moisture, expecting to become sick from it. It tasted bitter, but that was all. He waited two hours before trying any more to see what would happen. Meanwhile, he put a few more drops of juice on the rocks for the lizards and dabbed it on his parched lips.

As the day lengthened, the blazing sun reflected such intense heat from the hot rocks that McKee felt as though he was being baked in an oven. Nearby, he located another small tree with leaves and cut off a few branches to add to his tree for more shade. The effort made his mouth go dry again. His throat felt as if he had swallowed sawdust. Seeing that the lizards still darted about in as lively a fashion as ever, McKee knew the cactus juice was not poisonous. It would have to supply his only source of liquid.

He cut more of it, chewing the pulp and letting the bitter drops trickle down his parched throat. It was the first liquid of any consequence he had had in two days. Drop by drop, it relieved the worst of his thirst.

Realizing that it would be impossible to handle the needle-spiked cactus in the dark, he cut extra chunks for use at night.

The next morning, after squeezing cactus juice for over two hours, McKee felt he had enough water in his system to make it through the day. He soon learned to save the well-chewed cactus pulp and place it on a flat rock. The large temperature change that occurred at night produced enough condensation to fill the pulp with almost sweet water by morning. He thanked God for this discovery. It meant that he had won round one in his fight for survival.

He was soon to learn that there was a bad side-effect to the cactus juice. After satisfying his immediate thirst, he had taken slabs of the pulp and rubbed the comparatively cool, moist pulp over his face and neck. Some of the juice got into his eyes. When he awakened the next morning, both his eyes and mouth were dry-sealed shut. After that, each time he awoke from a sleep of any duration, he had to unseal his lips and eyes. His mouth soon became sore and his gums bled constantly. It would take him two days to remove the scale that formed on his eyelashes. Oddly enough, though he had nothing to eat, he felt no hunger pangs. Probably, he suspected, it was because he was too thirsty all the time.

McKee realized he had to have some way to keep track of the passing days. With his knife he carved his name and the date in the bark of his shade tree limb. After that he made a notch for each day.

"All I've got to do," he told himself, "is hold off past that seventh notch when the helicopter will be coming back for us."

He used the medicated throat lozenges to curb the bitterness of the cactus juice. After each use, he would put them back in their wrapper. One day he became greatly disturbed when, after carefully unwrapping his last little bit of lozenge, he accidentally dropped it amongst the rocks. By then, it was too dark to find, but at daylight the next morning, he searched and found it. It was covered with black ants. McKee tried brushing them off, but gave up and finally popped the piece in his mouth, ants and all. In spite of its medication, no candy ever tasted better.

Day after day, he listened for the sound of a helicopter motor, but all he heard were two or three jets that flew over the island each day, too high to see him. As he dozed during the heat of the day, he thought he heard an airline stewardess asking him if he cared for a cold drink.

"Mr. McKee, would you like a Sprite? A Coke?"

Each time, he eagerly answered and abruptly woke up before he could be rewarded with his dream beverage. Frequently now he dreamed of all kinds of cool situations—snow melting, ice cubes, ice skating—and each time he woke up parched from thirst. Had it not been for the cactus juice, he would have gone out of his mind.

At night, he tried counting stars. When it was perfectly still, he yelled as loud as he could, calling his companions' names. Not even an echo responded.

Gradually, McKee began experiencing dizzy spells. He had to hold onto tree limbs to get to his feet. Sometimes he found himself singing. He started remembering cheers from the bleachers at his hometown football and track meets. He yelled cheers until he grew hoarse. He tried remembering back to the earliest days of his childhood. He passed the time in a million different ways and often fell asleep only to awaken in the heat of the sun or in the cold of the 4 A.M. breeze. He knew that he was getting weaker every day. The daily heat that soared to well over 120 degrees and the predawn hours of cold were getting to him, gradually sapping him of all his remaining strength.

McKee found that the big, flat volcanic rocks around him would absorb the heat of the sun until they were hot enough to fry an egg if he'd had one. He took advantage of this condition to try and maintain his body heat as long as possible, to make it through the night.

As soon as the sun started to go down, McKee would test the heat in the rock with his hand. When it was bearable, he would stretch out on the rock and enjoy its warmth. The rock's heat lasted well into the night, but then the cold breeze began. McKee curled up into a ball on his hard rock bed, trying to conserve his body heat. Several times he was tempted to take down his flag/towel and wrap himself in it, but he thought better of it when he realized that he was now so weak, he could probably not put the flag pole back up again.

Constantly, he wondered what had happened to his companions. Several times a day, he counted the notches on his calendar tree. This became so confusing, he often lost count and would have to begin all over again.

Then he was invaded by ants attracted to the cactus juice and fresh cut pulp. McKee set up his cactus-juice-processing area away from his shade tree, but still they came. Finally, he cut some cactus pulp and let the ants swarm over it. Then he picked up the pulp and threw it as far away from his camp as he could. By doing this repeatedly, he finally managed to move the local ant population.

Whenever a stray ant bit him, however, it always made him do a midday or midnight strip act. "By golly," he said, "if these ants were as big as crickets, one bite would require stitches!"

Gnats or ants were constantly getting into his ears. To get any sleep without being bothered by these pests, McKee inserted a .38 caliber shell casing in each ear. After that, he slept as soundly as he could.

Late one afternoon, a small beady-eyed brown mouse came out of the brush and peered curiously at McKee. "Better get out of here, buddy, or I might eat you!"

At the sound of his voice the mouse scampered away.

McKee spent each afternoon waiting for him to come back. He wished he hadn't frightened him off.

The lizards around him became tame. He soon had them lapping up cactus juice from everywhere but the palm of his hand. They must have sensed his intentions. However, McKee doubted that he could have closed his hand quickly enough to catch one. After that, he felt bad about the trick he planned to pull on the poor lizards. After all, they had showed him that the cactus juice was safe to drink. He even felt sorry for the ants he had killed. This was their territory. The whole place belonged to the ants and the lizards. McKee really had no business here. Indeed, he soon began to envy the lizards and the ants, because they were safe at home.

He began thinking of what a wonderful life-saving beverage cactus juice was. He wondered if he could sell the idea to Coca-Cola. He could see the advertising blurb now, "Pure Cactus Juice. Sure to Quench the Thirst." He wished for a pencil and paper to write down the ideas. He dreamed up an entire package deal to sell to Coca-Cola when he got home. And there was no doubt in his mind whatsoever that he would eventually get home.

"When I'm rescued, I'm going to take one of these cactus plants with me," he vowed. "I'll have it analyzed and find out how the water gets into it in this dry hot-and-cold hell."

He began thinking of condensation and air conditioners, comparing the vents and riblike structure of the cactus to the radiator cooling system on automobiles and air conditioners. His mind reeled with ideas. He purposely kept it occupied, for he always believed he would be rescued.

"Doctors should test the body chemistry of someone who has existed on nothing but cactus juice for seven days," he thought. "*Seven days!* Could that be?" Hastily, he counted the notches in his tree calendar. It was indeed the seventh day, the day the helicopter was to return and pick them up!

"God, I wonder what happened to those other guys." He wondered if they were dead or were somehow still alive like he was.

Excitedly, McKee checked his flag to make sure it was flying in the breeze. He looked at his watch. It was 3 P.M. Was the time right? If so, in less than two hours he would drink water again, wonderfully sweet cold water. As much of it as he wanted! His mouth was dry, but he chewed no cactus during that long hour's wait. His gums bled easily now, and it was almost too painful to chew the pulp.

In anticipation of this moment, McKee had polished his machete blade with gravel, until the metal shined bright in the late afternoon sun. He practiced holding his wristwatch so that the bright back would reflect like a mirror. He figured that, if the helicopter pilot saw just one flash coming from where McKee was, he would certainly search the area.

Standing atop the rocks in the sun, with his watch and shirt in one hand, his bright bladed machete in the other, he counted the minutes to zero hour.

Suddenly, McKee heard a distant hum. As it got closer, he recognized the pulsing chop of helicopter blades. His heart began pounding just as hard. Then McKee saw the helicopter!

It was on a south-to-north course, but too far east of McKee to see him or his flag. McKee waved his shirt and flashed his machete, but the sun was in the wrong direction.

The sound grew fainter and fainter. McKee figured he must have reached the island's northern coast. Were his two companions there? Was he landing to pick them up? Would he come back?

Once more, he heard the sound of the helicopter. Then he saw it. McKee's heart raced excitedly. The helicopter was headed directly for him and his flag. Despite his injured knee, McKee jumped up and down, waving his shirt with one hand and his machete with the other.

Sitting in the big plastic blister on the nose of his helicopter, the pilot had to see him. He was on a beeline course, straight for McKee!

Suddenly, the helicopter veered to the right. McKee figured he was maneuvering for a landing. He continued to wave and shout, but the helicopter never altered its course.

"No! No! You've *got* to see me!" yelled McKee. But it made no difference.

The sound of the helicopter faded in the distance, leaving him standing forlornly on the hot rocks, holding his shirt and machete. He had been swinging the machete like a wild man. Now he wondered if he had scared off the helicopter pilot. Or was he going for help?

As it grew dark, gnats began getting into McKee's ears. He had to put up with them, because he was afraid to plug his ears with the cartridges for fear he might not hear the helicopter if it returned.

After sunset, he cut a cactus and painfully chewed the pulp for juice. He sat up most of the night, listening for the helicopter to return. Finally, from pure physical and mental exhaustion, he fell asleep, dreaming that when the rescuers came, they found only his clothing and a pile of bones that had once been him.

# Chapter 9

## Out of the Frying Pan

When he awakened, shivering in the 4 A.M. cold, he thought about the blazing sun soon to be endured. He cut another notch in the tree. It was the eighth day. Did the helicopter pilot find their camp, and the others? Was he flying them to Caracas? Or did his friends never make it back to camp and the pilot was flying to Caracas to report them missing?

By the tenth day, McKee did not know what to think. Had he known what happened to the helicopter pilot, he would have been even more perplexed. For the man never reported them missing. Indeed, he never again reported for work at the helicopter service!

Having not eaten food now for well over a week and knowing that the cactus juice would not sustain him much longer, McKee made a decision. He decided he had to find the pelican's nesting area. If he could find it, he might catch one in its nest and be able to eat it raw.

Knowing that this might be his last bid for life, he cut a large supply of cactus pulp into sections to fit in his pockets. After gathering his few things, he took pieces of volcanic rock and laid them on the ground in the position of an arrow pointing in the direction he planned to go. The rocks, sun-blackened on their surface, were almost white underneath. Turning them bottom side up, McKee figured they might show up well from the air should the helicopter return.

The rising ball of fire was just appearing on the eastern horizon as he prepared to leave. He looked up at his towel flag waving in the early morning breeze. Again he counted the notches on his tree calendar, then took his machete and cut off a branch of the tree that had shaded him through the nine days of blistering heat. As he did so, he felt a pang of remorse for having to cut off one of the tree's few limbs.

On its bark he cut a message which read, "Will try to get to sea. Follow arrow." Then he carved the date.

Was he doing the right thing? Or was he merely jumping out of the frying pan into the fire?

After staggering about a hundred yards from his protective tree, McKee almost changed his mind. Looking back, he saw the flag. "It's still in sight," he thought. But his legs were like rubber. Still, he was determined to try and make it to the beach.

As he lurched through the broken rock, he suddenly stumbled and fell headlong into a thornbush whose leaves were as viral as poison ivy. Vainly, he tried to get up, but was entangled in the thorny vines.

By rolling over, he finally got clear of the entanglement. Immediately, red welts appeared on his arms and he burned all over.

Somehow he managed to get to his feet and stagger on. Then he fell again. Regaining his feet once more, he tried again. But again he fell. This time proved to be especially serious. As he landed on a large rock, he heard the ribs in his right side crunch. He had broken them again!

Severe vertigo swept over him and he mercifully passed out.

According to McKee, how long he lay unconscious is a mystery. Vaguely, however, he remembered how he awakened with the intensely bright sun in his face. Forcing open his eyes, he thought he was blind. He turned his head aside, then realized he was lying in the open, fully exposed to the blazing sun. His mouth was dry as dust.

He tried to get up. A pain shot through his right side, so sharp that he almost fainted.

"God," he thought. "I've got to get some shade!"

Fumbling in his pocket, he found a piece of cactus pulp. He pushed it into his mouth. He tried to chew it, but his gums bled and his teeth felt as if they would fall out. All his teeth had now loosened from the effects of severe dehydration.

McKee tried crawling, but every move was unbearably painful. Holding some of the pulp over his mouth, he squeezed a few drops of moisture between his cracked, parched lips. For an instant his head cleared a little, and he found he was only a few feet from a tree with some shade.

How long it took him to reach that tree, he couldn't say, but when he got there, he passed out.

Later that day, a search party found his body. So sure were the men he was dead, that they were putting him into a body bag when Colonel Torreles Paiva saw McKee's hand move.

"Stop!" he shouted. "That man's still alive! Give him water!"

McKee felt drops of cool water falling on his face and lips. Then he realized that someone was trying to open his dry-sealed mouth. He choked on the first drops of water and then passed out.

He never heard the helicopter taking off but, during the flight, he was vaguely aware of the voice of Professor Cribeiro saying, "We're both okay, McKee. And you're going to be all right, too."

They flew him to a hospital in Caracas and immediately set about trying to keep him alive. For the next two days he was only semiconscious and incoherently reliving his last days on Tortuga. X-rays showed that McKee had three broken ribs as a result of his last fall. He was coughing up blood. A blood clot had broken loose in his injured knee, passed through his heart, and lodged in the right lung. During his ordeal he had lost 41 pounds in ten days!

A few days later, when his condition permitted, he was airlifted to a hospital in Maracaibo. After two more weeks of intensive treatment, he was taken to Professor Cribeiro's home for several days and then placed aboard a plane for Miami.

Only after McKee became more lucid did he learn what had happened to his companions.

After leaving McKee, Professor Cribeiro and his son missed the base camp. For five days they wandered, existing only on cactus pulp. Finally, reaching the sea, they found and ate shellfish and snails. They also found half of a large dead fish, which they ate raw, and later became sick. On the afternoon of the fifth day, they sighted a small boat from Caracas. The boat responded to their frantic signals, but refused to take them aboard. Instead, they were given water from a jug that had recently held kerosene. Again they became sick.

Continuing up the rocky coast, they survived off sea creatures they found in the rocks, which provided them with the fresh water they needed. Again they sighted a small boat, and it responded to their frantic waving. Their would-be rescuers were fishermen, who were camped at the extreme east end of the island. The fishermen gave them food and water. They explained that they had left an American under a tree in the island's interior, but the fishermen refused to go in search of him, despite the fact that Professor Cribeiro offered them five thousand dollars. They considered the island haunted.

Taking the professor and his son with them, the fishermen returned to their camp, where a message was radioed to Caracas.

The next day, newspapers carried the story in large red headlines, announcing that three men, including Professor Alberto Cribeiro had been lost on Tortuga and that an American was presumed dead.

Headed by Colonel Torreles Paiva, a search and rescue team fueled up two large helicopters and alerted other units of the Venezuelan Air Force to bring back Professor Cribeiro, his son, and the remains of Arthur McKee. Taking off early on their mission, the helicopters were soon in sight of Tortuga. Upon landing, search parties spread out looking for McKee.

Leading his team, Colonel Torreles and his men soon found McKee's flag tree. Though they could not read the English message crudely cut in the bark, they saw the arrow and continued in the direction it pointed.

It led them to McKee, more dead than alive. But he *was* alive.

Back in Florida, under his doctor's care at a hospital in Coral Gables, he was far from well. His ribs still ached, his feet were swollen, both lungs had fluid in them, and on his flight to Miami, another blood clot passed into his left lung. Complete recovery was a long way off.

I stopped to visit McKee the summer after his ordeal. He was still weak and underweight, but his spirit was in no way diminished. He talked of future expeditions he had in mind. I was glad to hear that none of them were land expeditions. He had had his fill of those. I encouraged him to finish his book about his adventures, which he had been writing for many years.

The next time I heard from McKee was after his friend, Burt Webber, had invited him to the Dominican Republic to see and evaluate the treasure of the *Concepcion*, Webber's fabulous find that had been tantalizing treasure hunters for centuries. McKee's postcard came at Christmastime, and I could tell by the tone of it that Art was having the time of his life. At the end of the card he wrote: "P.S. I'm still writing on my book."

That was the last I heard from Art.

But it was not the last of his treasure hunting. It was with particular sadness that I learned, sometime later, he had died.

A letter from his wife, Gay, whom McKee had met and married at Grand Cayman in the 1950s, said it all:

"I don't know whether you are aware that, nine months prior to his death, Art found the wreck of the *Genovés* on Pedro Bank, south of Jamaica, and in only three days of diving on the wreck (the weather is always bad in that area), he and his crew found one 70-pound silver bar, twenty-two small bars, ranging in weight from 11 ounces to 3 pounds, four *tejos*, and a brass pot of some kind. He had also worked in Santo Domingo, doing the appraisal of the *Concepcion* coins for Burt Webber.

"He was very active right up to the day he had the heart attack here in Grand Cayman. He seemed to take a turn for the better and was making plans to finish his book, while he was recuperating, but died three-quarters of an hour after leaving the hospital."

If there is anyone I can think of who did it "his way," it is Art McKee, Jr. Complications from some of his more harrowing treasure hunts were surely what finally caught up with him. Still, no matter where McKee's spirit is, you can bet that it's enjoying the adventure. Throughout his entire life, adventure was the real treasure Art was seeking.

He always found it.

# PART II

## Kip Wagner:
## Beachcomber's Reward

# Chapter 10

# Cannon's Cannon

What first brought me to Sebastian Inlet were sharks.

Large sharks, in the 12-foot category. In those days our sport was fighting big game sharks from the beach. I was involved in a shark fishing tournament north of Cape Canaveral one Fourth of July weekend, when a friend from Melbourne, Florida, made a special trip up there to tell us that a pilot had spotted large sharks lying like logs just off the mouth of Sebastian Inlet.

Narrow, swift Sebastian Inlet, about 40 miles south of Cape Canaveral, on Florida's east coast, is perhaps one of the most treacherous of the entire seaboard. Its waters are invariably murky. When the tide changes, a torrent of water rushes seaward through the narrow pass with the long, jagged rock jetty on one side and the shallow limestone reef and ledges on the other. Boats trying to negotiate this natural flushing crab their way in. Those going out are briskly ejected. And when the Atlantic winds howl directly into the out-rushing flood of Sebastian Inlet, the resulting chaos is a nightmare for any yachtsman foolish enough to be caught in these narrows at such a time.

Naturally, all the inlet's bad characteristics made it a popular place for coastal roving sharks. All they had to do was lie in the outflow of this torrent and food would be swept to them. It was a self-activated chow line that cranked up a couple of times a day, and you can bet that the recipients were well conditioned to the feeding times.

This feature was highly appealing to such anglers as ourselves. We promptly hastened to Sebastian Inlet, used a canoe to carry out our 10-pound bloody bonito baits, and promptly caught sharks. Overnight we bested an 8-foot-long lemon shark, a 10-foot bull shark, and three tiger sharks up to 12 feet long. After that, my companion and I had both our reels stripped by even larger sharks.

Knowing what was in those murky brown agitated waters, I had no desire whatsoever to dive there. Just south of the inlet, however, sat a 40-foot-long converted liberty launch named *Sampan* that rolled and yawed in the large waves streaming in from the Atlantic to churn the inshore waters between the inner and outer bars. No one appeared to be aboard the heavily rolling vessel. Its crew was crabbing along the bottom underwater, trying to keep from being somersaulted by the surge.

We knew about the *Sampan* and why her crew was there, being mauled on the bottom in these sharky waters. Knowing what we know about the kind and size of critters there, I could not help but admire the courage it took to do what they were doing. Whatever they found, I hoped it was worth it.

Only later did I learn what was happening on the bottom and the nature of their magnetic attraction to this unlikely piece of underwater real estate. It had happened earlier that year, in the spring of 1960.

All winter long, the seas had been high and heavy along this coast. In a small beach house nearby, a group of grim-faced men waited out the weather, far more anxious than most men to get their vessel out though the pass, to see if what they believed could possibly be true. They believed that in the area of ocean bottom where they planned to look just a few hundred feet offshore, a fortune in sunken gold and silver waited for them.

Was it there? Or was it all just a figment of someone's overworked imagination?

"Let's give it a try, Kip," Harry Cannon pleaded, as he and the others stared out the window at the rampaging surf. "Hell, the water's clear out there and once we get past the inlet we'll be all right," Cannon insisted. "We can wait for high tide, then nudge her through easy like."

The older, full-featured, white-haired man beside him might have been just as anxious, but more cautious. He knew that many a vessel had run aground trying to navigate through narrow Sebastian Inlet in seas a lot calmer than those they were looking at. But Kip Wagner also knew from looking at the others—Dan Thompson, Del Long, Lou Ullian, and Erv Taylor—that they sided with Cannon. They were anxious to have a try at it, to get out there and see for themselves what was on that bottom.

Wagner could think of a lot of reasons why they shouldn't go, but he also knew that they deserved to go. He owed them that much. They had all worked extremely hard the season before, diving on an old shipwreck that contained little but ballast rocks—tons of it. They moved those rocks by hand all season long to recover a relatively small amount of treasure—no more than a dozen wedges of silver.

"Okay," he said. "We'll go."

It was one of the best decisions Kip Wagner ever made in his life.

Around 8:30 that morning, the big old converted liberty launch rocked and rolled her way through Sebastian Inlet, then turned south and chugged over the large sea swells for about a mile and a half before heading in, taking the large swells on her stern. Wagner fretted constantly about the possibility of the vessel getting caught in the trough between waves and grounded on the limestone ridges paralleling the beach.

A cold January wind swept the *Sampan*'s wet decks. Everyone shivered, but most shivered more from the anticipation of the moment than from the bone-chilling gusts off the Atlantic.

Arriving over the area that Wagner thought was the best site to be searched, they dropped anchor and eased well back on the chain. The *Sampan* wallowed sickeningly in the heaving seas.

That time of year everyone knew the Atlantic waters would be icy cold. Only Harry Cannon and Dan Thompson had rubber wet suits. So they volunteered to don scuba gear and see what they could find on the bottom.

As the divers splashed overboard, the others stared at their clouds of bursting bubbles. Wagner noticed the bursts moved quickly southward. A strong bottom current was apparently moving that way. He hoped he had not made a mistake bringing them there before conditions were better.

Time moved like molasses for the men at the rail. After a while, they tried busying themselves about the boat, but kept darting glances at the water. More than one was saying to himself, "Why the hell don't they come up and tell us something? They know we're waiting!"

Ten minutes dragged past before a diver burst through the surface and shouted, "Cannon!"

Dive masks hide identities. The first thought to flash through Kip's mind was that Harry Cannon was in trouble. But an instant later, he realized it was Cannon himself yelling. He had apparently found a *cannon* below.

"Bring the boat," gasped Cannon between breaths. "There's more here!"

Ullian and Long scrambled to get in the anchor and in their excitement had more trouble than usual. The others tried to help, which added to the momentary chaos.

Underwater, Dan Thompson was a little behind on the excitement. He had all he could do to keep from being somersaulted over the bottom each time a big comber came crashing through. Still a novice diver and not too sure of himself in this alien environment, even when it was not topsy-turvy, Thomson tried to keep Cannon in sight, while both were being buffeted about.

They swam a crisscross search pattern when possible. Visibility was bad, but better than usual. At least each could still see his own hand in front of his mask. Most times out there you couldn't.

Suddenly, Thompson saw Cannon head for the surface. He thought maybe he was in trouble, and surfaced nearby in time to hear the excitement about the cannon. Thompson quickly descended, and when he did, almost swam right into the shadowy muzzle of a 9-foot-long iron cannon lying on the bottom. Behind it were two more half-buried, radiating out like giant spokes of a wheel.

In the excitement and the physical effort of trying to keep upright in that churning water, Thompson realized he was breathing faster than he should. "Calm down," he told himself. "You damn sure don't want to run out of air now!"

The bottom looked as if it had been vacuumed clean. The sand was so smooth it struck Thompson as looking strange. He guessed the winter storms had scoured it that way. Whatever had happened, it left solid objects sticking up prominently. They all looked like rocks, but not the kind usually seen along this coast.

Thompson finned down for a closer look at one of the objects and saw it was a greenish black clump about a foot and a half across. Another about the same size lay nearby. But what got Thompson to gulping big breaths were the pockets of silver coins scattered all around the lumps. Then he suddenly realized, the lumps themselves were coins, thousands of silver coins fused together in a solid mass!

First he shouted wildly into his mouthpiece. The yell roared past his ears in a rumble of expelled bubbles. He bent down and tried lifting the chunks. They felt heavy as iron. He could barely budge them.

"I need the boat," he thought. "With the boat above, we can rope them up."

Then, in a panic, he realized that to summon the boat he had to leave the coins. How would he find them again in so much current? What if he lost them outright and they never found them! If anyone ever broke out in a sweat while diving frigid water, Thompson did.

Still he couldn't stand there guarding the damn things until all his air ran out. He had to *do* something. Finally, he made up his mind that he had to surface and call the boat.

As soon as he broke through the waves, he saw that the *Sampan* was still where it was before. They were having trouble with the anchor. "Wow! What a time to screw up!"

Thompson spat out his mouthpiece and waved. "Hey, you guys! Come quick!" He didn't waste any more time on the surface, but popped his regulator back in his mouth and dived back to the bottom.

Suddenly, he almost panicked. *The clumps were gone*! Frantically, he swam about. He had lost them! For a wild moment he finned back and forth over the bottom, then thankfully spotted the dark masses again.

This experience convinced him it would be too risky to leave the clumps again.

He waited for what seemed an endlessly long time, but the boat failed to come.

"Maybe they're still having trouble," he thought. "Well, if they can't come to me, maybe I can go to them." He decided to try and carry the clumps underwater to where the boat was.

He made it with a clump under each arm for maybe 50 feet. By then, he was huffing and puffing so hard, he had to stop. The combined weight of the two chunks were about 135 pounds. The water lessened that load, but not much.

"I can't make it," Thompson thought. In desperation he dropped one of the chunks and carried the other to a mast strap he had spotted earlier. It would serve as his marker. Then he returned for the chunk he had dropped.

Again, panic surged over him with the realization that he couldn't find it. He swam in circles trying to find it, but failed. Finally, when the *Sampan* came up and dropped its anchor, Thompson scooped up a handful of loose coins and surfaced to hand them up to the others.

"They're all over the bottom," he blurted. "If I had a garden rake, I could rake them into a pile! Let me have a line."

He lashed the line about the large clump, and between those in the boat hauling, and Thompson pushing, they finally got the thing aboard. Thompson followed right behind it.

No one had even heard of a coin clump this size before. And when they all saw that the black corroded mass was actually made up of thousands of odd-shaped pieces of metal stuck together, and that these were indeed silver pieces of eight that they had dreamed about, there was no holding back their emotions. Everyone pounded each other on the back and yelled at the same time. The whole bunch was bug-eyed with excitement. "We're rich!" they shouted.

If this was pandemonium, it was nothing compared to what happened after Thompson caught his breath and told them: "I lost another clump on the bottom just like it. Couldn't find where I dropped it!"

With a whoop, divers grabbed gear from every direction and leaped off the boat. It made no difference if air tanks were only half on or that fins were clutched in hands when they went, or that most had no protection whatsoever against the bone-chilling water. They were in the high heat of frenzy when they bailed overboard, hot to find that other clump of coins.

How that first plunge snapped them back to reality, made their teeth clamp onto their rubber mouthpieces, made them hyperventilate in their mad scramble for the bottom, arms outstretched to embrace a fortune, eyes bugged wide! The fever was on them and there was no denying it. Only the hefty feel of silver coins in their eager hands and the cold grip of the Atlantic would in time provide any surcease to the kind of fever they felt.

Soon they started popping to the surface like corks. Tight-fisted, arms high out of water, wide grins behind their masks. They came to the boat with hands clenched over coins and handed them up to Wagner. Then down they went again, like children gleefully picking dandelions in a grassy glade and hurrying back to shower them on their beaming parents.

And beaming Wagner was. He could not remember a happier moment. Here they had just come out to scout the site and had stumbled over the pot at the end of the rainbow. They didn't even have any dredging gear! It was just there, scattered all over the bottom, for the taking. Wagner couldn't believe their good luck. He might not be down there on the bottom scrabbling it up, but he was getting just as much of a thrill out of it as they were.

But where was the elusive clump? Nobody had found it yet!

"It's gotta be so close to us that someone's passed just a few feet from it," Thompson insisted, as he hung breathless for a moment on the anchor chain.

"You guys better figure out something," Wagner called to him. "Or I'll get on my gear and come down and find it for you!" he threatened.

Some of the divers linked hands and finned themselves along the bottom searching. But all they found were more loose coins. Not bad, but each of them thought about that cluster with maybe *a couple thousand* coins in it.

Finally, Harry Acres, a friend of Wagner's just along for the ride, found it. They had hunted forty-five minutes, and there it was, sitting right where Thompson had dropped it!

They got a line on it and hauled it aboard. Again merriment rang out from the wallowing old *Sampan*.

After that, it was all over but for the cheering. Their fevered fires were finally cooled. One by one they climbed aboard with teeth chattering so hard they couldn't have held a regulator in their mouth for one moment more. To a man they were totally exhausted—numbingly so—but so happy, they could hardly talk.

Talk is what they did later back on the beach in Wagner's place, with a roaring fire for warmth and snifters of Kip's brandy to celebrate and to toast their good fortune. Wagner phoned two other members of the group, Dr. Kip Kelso and Libe Futch, who shortly arrived to see the find.

They dumped their booty on the floor and sat around it grinning. They had found about five hundred loose silver coins, which together with the two large clumps would run the total to what they guessed would be around four thousand pieces of eight, Spanish coins dating around 1714 and worth what they estimated then to be a small fortune.

Even in their wildest imagining, whether influenced by the brandy or not, not one man there . . . not even Kip Wagner . . . could have guessed that what they had found that day was a mere pittance to what was about to be found. Before they would finish, it would amount to literally *tons* of silver coins.

# Chapter 11

# Seek and Ye Shall Find

"When I was a youngster growing up in Miamisburg, Ohio," Kip Wagner said, "nothing was farther from my mind than the thought of becoming a professional treasure hunter." His biggest ambition had been to become a good house builder like his father. He admits, however, that his imagination did ramble somewhat as he read through the pages of Robert Louis Stevenson's *Treasure Island*. Young Kip had no trouble whatsoever hearing the screeching cry of Long John Silver's parrot, "Pieces of eight, pieces of eight!"

His first trip to Florida was in the winter of 1921. He was fifteen and accompanying his older brother in a shiny new Model T Ford. Interestingly, a coincidence, or act of fate, that occurred on this trip was to put Wagner on a trail of treasure that would result in rewards far grander than any Robert Louis Stevenson ever envisioned for his hero of *Treasure Island*.

It began when the new Ford broke down. Some rivets popped loose from the Model T's differential. One can imagine the brothers' comments, as the shiny car lurched to a noisy halt and they coasted sadly into someone's front yard.

"Gosh, why'd this have to happen to us in the middle of

nowhere?" Kip's brother growled. "Another 12 miles and we'd a made it to Vero Beach and a garage."

"What's this place called?" asked Kip.

"Wabasso. Doubt if it's got a garage. It's just a little hamlet."

Almost directly opposite this small community on the Florida east coast, about 160 miles north of Miami, were the sites where a Spanish treasure fleet had perished—the fleet that would one day make Wagner's name famous.

They hiked the 12 miles to Vero Beach for the parts to repair their car. The delay required them to spend several days at Wabasso. While there, they met Earl Wellborn, who happened to be from their home town of Miamisburg, Ohio. The Wellborns and local folks showed the boys so much neighborly hospitality, that both the Wellborns and Wabasso made a lasting impression on them.

Even in the years that followed, as Kip built up his construction business, every opportunity that presented itself, he headed south to the friendly town of Wabasso. Before long, he was bringing with him his wife, Alice, and their young son, Tom.

Finally, as World War II was ending, the Wagners moved to Florida permanently, settling into a frame house near the new job he was contracted to do—build the Penn-Wood Motel in Wabasso. The family could not have been happier.

One day a severe rainstorm blew up. Being unable to work, the construction man repaired to a local tavern. While they were sipping beer, one of Wagner's new friends, who was also in the construction business, made a chance remark that intrigued Wagner. The man's name was Captain Steadman Parker. And the remark he made was:

"This would be a great day to be at the beach looking for coins."

"What coins?" asked Wagner.

"Silver coins. Spanish pieces of eight. I thought you knew about them!"

"Nope. Not a word."

"Well then, let me tell you . . ." Captain Parker leaned back, took a breath, and laid on Wagner a tale of shipwreck, treasure, and coins on the beach that hardly fazed him. It made a good tale for a stormy afternoon while the suds flowed, but that was all he considered it.

Captain Parker was a colorful character in the community. He talked a lot about treasure and shipwrecks along the coast and promised everyone within hearing that he would one day find the fortune that lay somewhere out there in the sea.

Wagner thought no more about the story until later, when bit by bit, he learned from others that they, too, knew someone or other who had indeed found Spanish silver coins along certain stretches of the beach between Wabasso and the next little town of Sebastian.

In fact, Wagner heard enough about them to crank up his curiosity to the point of actually driving to the beach to see for himself. Wagner was not normally a beach goer. He had no time to lay around on the beach. Consequently, on this afternoon he was highly self-conscious of being there, especially for such an unlikely reason.

"For crying out loud," he thought to himself, looking suspiciously over his shoulder, as he ankled through the soft sand. "What if somebody sees me out here? Damn. I shoulda had sense enough to bring a fishing pole. I coulda told them then that I was surf fishing."

No matter. He'd get it over with as quickly as possible. Wagner hurried to the hard-packed white sand bordering the water's edge and hiked briskly along it, darting his eyes from side to side.

He spent no more than a few minutes before giving up the search with a well-I-told-you-so sigh. As he hustled back toward his car, he was almost relieved that his fool's mission was over. There were no coins. There weren't even any pretty shells to see.

Wagner became a dedicated treasure scoffer. That's a guy

who, when he hears a tale of treasure trove, he scoffs at it. The results were always the same. The tale teller would dig in his heels and pour on the facts to substantiate his tale.

As a result, Wagner's scoffing led to him hearing a lot of tales. Some of them were fairly lofty, but some had the ring of truth to them. No matter, Wagner maintained his staunch disbelief and simply filed away the facts that might be true— like the one told by the coastal mail carrier of Indian River, who swore he once spied cannon lying on the bottom near Sebastian Inlet, just north of where they lived.

One old-timer Wagner had befriended had no coins to show, despite the fact that he had walked the beachfront for a large part of his eighty years. "I don't know anything about coins," he told Wagner, "but I found lots of those flat odd-shaped chunks of black scrap metal that always wash up. I fingered many of them," he said. "They always made fine skipping stones!"

"*Skipping stones*!" Wagner exclaimed. "You mean you threw them back into the water?"

"Yep. I reckon over the years I maybe skipped back around two thousand of them. But I never seen no coins."

The man's response floored Wagner. More and more he was beginning to believe there was something to all these tales about old coins. If he could just see one. . . .

The revelation he yearned for came from an unexpected quarter. We'll call him Duffy Ludlow. He was one of Wagner's workers. He knew construction and he was a hard worker. Wagner had employed him on several jobs and they had become friends. Duffy's only drawback was that he often drank as hard as he worked. And sometimes he showed up for work too drunk to do his job.

One morning, during just such a time, Wagner heard Duffy arguing with another worker. He could tell the way Duffy's words slurred that he was having one of his days. Rather than fire his friend, Wagner thought it best to try to sober him up.

Thinking a little sea breeze might do the trick, Wagner

drove Duffy to the beach. As they were wheeling along, Duffy, slumped against the passenger door, lifted his head, glanced out the window, then turned bleary, bloodshot eyes on Wagner.

"Whoa!" he blurted out. "Stop the car!"

Wagner stomped the brakes, believing Duffy was on the brink of a queasy situation requiring immediate attention. The car skidded onto the shoulder and stopped.

Duffy lurched out. "C'mon, Kip."

"Huh?"

"C'mon, c'mon, c'mon," Duffy grinned crookedly over his shoulder and tottered off into the palmettos. Wagner thought it best to keep up with him in case he fell and hurt himself.

Onto the beach careened Duffy, bobbing and reeling drunkenly. He weaved all over a patch of sand near the water, hardly able to stand. Then he bent down and picked up something.

"There ya are." He flipped it to Wagner. "It's one of them coins."

Wagner stared at the blackened piece of rectangular metal and saw the design stamped on it. "Well, I'll be—So that's what they look like!"

"Yeah, and here's another." He was holding up yet another coin.

In the next half-hour Wagner and Duffy probably would have appeared to any passerby as a pair of drunks, staggering around the beach together, sometimes managing to stay upright, but mostly on their knees, at which time they played in the sand, or so it seemed.

Later, as they drove back to town, they stopped at the first place they came to, so Duffy could slack his thirst. Being a gregarious fellow, Duffy showed the patrons his newly found coins—all seven of them. When everyone oohed and ahhed over them, the generous Duffy gave everyone a coin—all except Wagner, whom he had forgotten about.

Wagner had looked just as hard as ever in the same stretch of sand as Duffy, but he had found no coin. He did, however, learn one lesson that he never forgot. He saw how a man with vision so dimmed by alcohol that he could hardly see, let alone hardly talk or stand, found coins, while he, Wagner, stone sober, found nothing. Duffy did it, pure and simple, because he knew exactly what to look for, and Wagner didn't.

Wagner had been looking for shiny round coins. These were blackened chunks too thick sometimes to even vaguely resemble a coin, as he had known them. And no two were the same size or shape. Some were elongated; most had sharp corners. And from their immersion in the sea, they had turned black. No wonder his old friend had skipped so many of the things back into the sea! They surely didn't look like they were worth keeping. Chunks of old scrap metal were more like it. Wagner remembered seeing such things before.

"Dammit," he said to himself. "I've walked right past some of them being uncovered by the rain!"

From that moment on, he was hooked. The fever had him and he knew it.

Wagner stepped up his beachcombing, but oddly enough, failed to find any more of the intriguing coins. But that did not deter him. When Steadman Parker mentioned that he had located such a wreck in the surf and wouldn't mind some help salvaging it, the idea really appealed to the beach-bound treasure hunter.

He wasn't the only one. Before the idea was barely born, five others were involved in it, chipping in funds, equipment, and time in all-out salvage effort to find out what was hidden under those coastal sands in 4 feet of water.

Surely, Wagner must have believed it to be the source of the coastal coins. In any event, he quit his job and joined Captain Steadman and the others with gusto.

It was quite an operation—the kind that just the thought of today makes modern underwater archaeologists froth at the mouth. The hunters pushed a huge pile of sand into the ocean with heavy equipment, then steered a powerful piece of earth-gouging gear, called a dragline, out the sand pier. From the end of it, the scoop shovel dipped into the Atlantic, dug up a chunk of the bottom, and deposited it on the beach, where Wagner and the others sifted it for artifacts. Each time the tide washed away the sand pier, they had to start anew.

All they got for their efforts, an approximate twelve thousand dollar investment and time, were a few ship spikes, rotted timbers, and a single copper Spanish coin dated 1649.

No matter. The fever was high. By summer's end, after they dissolved their operation, the partners went their own ways. Wagner went back to his building business and midweek beachcombing.

He borrowed an old World War II metal detector and started looking along the wave-washed beach with a vengeance.

All he found were rusty tin cans. At least that was his take for several months. Then one day, out of the blue, he found his first piece of eight—a large odd-shaped silver coin. After that, his luck changed.

From Sebastian to Wabasso, the lonely beach began revealing its hidden treasures to the eager hunter—not speedily, but begrudgingly. Just enough to keep Wagner hot on the trail of the blackened metal pieces.

Finally he had some forty of them. Then he began finding gold coins. All were dated prior to 1715. The finer pieces he squirreled away, not too sure whether the federal government would approve of him having them or not. Others, almost devoid of markings, he fashioned into pendants and bracelets for the local children. With gold running then around thirty-five dollars an ounce, he appreciated the value of those pieces, but the silver coins seemed hardly worth considering, then.

"I'm going out to take a look at my money beach," he often told his wife, as he left with his trusty metal detector. And more often than not, he returned by day's end with a few more of the odd-shaped silver coins. His money beach was the 8-mile stretch from Sebastian to Wabasso. Why were the coins there? Did they come from under the sand, where high tides often washed all the way to the dunes? Or was there a shipwreck somewhere offshore from which the coins were gradually washing ashore?

Wagner believed the latter. To test his theory he often swam offshore and tried to see what was on the bottom there. One day he met a fellow beachcomber who showed him how to make a diver's face mask from a window pane and inner tube. Together they boated along shore, looking underwater but finding nothing.

The clue to what lay offshore was to come from an unexpected source.

# Chapter 12

# The Old Map

His name was Kelso, Kip Kelso—a practicing physician who had moved to the Sebastian area just a few days after Wagner and set up his practice. Doc Kelso was a remarkable man. Not only was he the family physician for the entire area, but he possessed an insatiable interest in everything. Blessed with an almost photographic memory, Doc Kelso never forgot a name nor a face. Moreover, his interests in matters historical provided him with an incredible knowledge of historical facts that he could delve into at will with instant recall. It was this unique ability that was to help Wagner in his quest for information about the mysterious beach coins.

The two men met one night when Doc Kelso came to Wagner's house to give him a physical for an insurance policy. Wagner and Alice were engrossed in examining several old Florida east coast charts when the doctor arrived. Before the evening was out, Doc Kelso was on his hands and knees on the floor with Wagner, pouring just as intently over the old charts and discussing possible answers to the riddle. Wagner told his new-found friend about his beach finds, and Doc Kelso was instantly fascinated by the whole idea of treasure wrecks and lost fortunes waiting to be found.

Doc Kelso was a walking encyclopedia of Spanish colonial history. Still, he and Wagner differed on their opinions of where the coins actually came from. Doc Kelso believed they had been buried on the beach and were gradually appearing as tides scoured away the coastal sands. His scientific background made it difficult for him to believe that such things as heavy gold and silver coins were actually being moved laterally along the soft, sandy bottom of the ocean by currents and washing ashore in this manner. It made more sense to him that, being heavy, they would only sink deeper into the sand.

To try and solve this mystery, the two hired a ditch-digging machine for a day and drove it to one portion of Wagner's money beach that had been especially prolific in coins.

There the machine dug several long 2-foot-deep trenches that crisscrossed the beach. Wagner and Doc Kelso carefully sifted through the diggings, but found no coins.

In Wagner's mind at least this supported his belief that the coins were being washed ashore.

In their search for information the two men visited all the local libraries and read whatever books they could find on treasure or Spanish history. When they exhausted these sources, they began searching through other more distant libraries. Somewhere Wagner learned that a large fleet of Spanish ships carrying 14 million pesos of treasure had foundered along that part of the Florida coast. But there were conflicting stories about exactly where the wrecks were. After sending some of the coins to Mendel Peterson, a historian and self-made authority on such subjects at the Smithsonian Institute, the treasure hunter learned that the 1715 fleet had foundered some 150 miles farther south and that Peterson was writing a book on the subject.

The only intriguing part of all this was that the incident of the lost fleet supposedly occurred in 1715 and all of the coins Wagner had found were dated no later than 1714. If Peterson was right, what were coins from that treasure shipment doing up near Sebastian Inlet?

So eager was Doc Kelso to find more historical information on the subject that he bundled his wife, mother-in-law, and seven children into the family car, bought a house-trailer, and went to Washington D.C. While the family made the most of their vacation in the capital, Doc Kelso spent his days going through historical documents in the Library of Congress.

Gradually, from several sources, he began picking up valuable clues. One led to another, and eventually, one book in particular provided a key clue. It was *A Concise Natural History of East and West Florida*, written by English cartographer, Bernard Romans, and published in 1775. In the book's endpapers was a detailed fold-out map of the old Florida coastline. As Doc Kelso carefully unfolded the crisp brown deeply creased fragile document, his heart began beating faster.

Romans had written various notations on the chart. Kelso's eyes reached the area of the map that would be where Sebastian Inlet is located today, and his excitement soared when he read this notation: "Opposite this River perished the Admiral, commanding the Plate Fleet of 1715. The rest of the fleet, fourteen in number, between this and Ye Bleech-yard." Nearby were the words *El Palmar*, followed by tiny drawings of five palm trees. In the book Kelso read this statement by Romans:

> Directly opposite the mouth of San Sebastian River, happened the shipwreck of the Spanish Admiral, who was the northernmost wreck of fourteen galleons and a hired Dutch ship, all laden with specie and plate, which by [undistinguishable word] of northeast winds, were drove ashore and lost on this coast, between this place and the bleech-yard, in 1715. A hired Frenchman, fortunately escaped by having steered half a point more east than the others. The people employed during the course of our survey, while walking the strand after strong eastern gales, have repeatedly found pistereens and double pistereens, which kinds of money probably yet remaining in the wrecks. This lagoon stretches parallel to the sea, until the latitude 27:20, where it has an outwatering, or mouth. Directly before this mouth, in 3-fathom water, lie the remains of the Dutch wreck. The banks of this lagoon are not fruitful."

When Wagner learned of Doc Kelso's lucky find, he too was overjoyed. Here at last was substantiation of the tale he had heard about the long lost 1715 fleet. At least they had an idea where one of the ships was, if they could believe Romans's map. Wagner felt sure that this Admiral's ship was the source of the coins in the Sebastian Inlet area. But they still needed more definite information.

From his wide reading on sunken treasure, Wagner realized that many writers seeking historical information about the old Spanish fleets had gone straight to the source itself—the General Archives of the Indies at Seville, Spain. Supposedly, in this richest repository of old Spanish American documents in the world, there existed the complete story of the 1715 fleet and its tragic history. But how to obtain it? That was the question.

Wagner began by writing a letter to the archives explaining that he wanted some historical information about the 1715 fleet. A long time elapsed before he received a reply. At best, it was sketchy. It gave him nothing to work with.

By chance, one of Wagner's friends planned to vacation in Spain and asked him if she could do anything for him while there.

"You sure can!" Wagner said. "I'll write another letter for you to take to the Archives of Seville. See if you can possibly find out something about that 1715 fleet." He also gave her a few shiny silver coins from that period to take with her as evidence of his finds.

When his friend visited the archives, she met the man who had corresponded with Wagner. Through a translator, she learned that the man had some historical information for Wagner, but for political reasons, was unable to release it to her at that time. He indicated that perhaps later he would be able to mail it to him.

When Wagner learned of this turn of events, he felt sure that he would never again hear from the archives that held the historical key to his questions. But hardly had his friend been home a few days from Spain, when Wagner received a large package from the archives.

Not believing his good fortune, he unwrapped the package with trembling hands. In it he was amazed to find 3000 feet of microfilm detailing the history and loss of the 1715 fleet. For this material, he was charged twenty-five dollars!

But Wagner's and Kelso's elation turned to tears of frustration when they projected the material and found it all written in indecipherable archaic Spanish script.

Here they had it all right in their hands—the history of where the treasure fleet was lost and how much treasure lay on the bottom of the sea—and they could not read the text!

Despite the fact that both Wagner and Kelso could read and understand modern Spanish, the words traced in almost illegible letters on this ancient document totally baffled them.

It took them a year to painstakingly translate what few Spanish words they recognized and piece together bits of the story revealed to them by language experts, who helped translate the archaic Spanish. Gradually, they learned the whole story— that the lost fleet had perished between Sebastian Inlet and Fort Pierce to the south, scattering fourteen million pesos of silver and gold along that portion of the Florida east coast. They learned what happened to individual ships, how much of the treasure had been salvaged, and how much remained. Also, for the first time, they read about a Spanish salvager's camp on the beach opposite one of the shipwrecks.

After that, it was time for the treasure hunters to leave their documents and try to locate the sites themselves.

# Chapter 13

## Silver Wedges and Real Eights

Wagner decided his first target would be the Spanish salvage camp.

"Find that and it should be almost opposite the Admiral's wreck with all the treasure," he told Doc Kelso.

With that in mind, his first major purchase was an old U.S. Army metal detector, a World War II relic he bought for twenty-five dollars. With this scientific innovation on his side, he couldn't lose.

In high spirits, the wily treasure hunter set off to search the sandy strand south of Sebastian in a way he had never searched it before. Up and down the beach he roamed, then well above the tide mark, ranging into the dunes with his trusty instrument and heavy head phones.

"Click-click-click," chattered the instrument in Wagner's ears, and he was like a dog digging up a cherished long-hidden bone. Oh, how he made the sand fly! Down he dug, with hands scooping furiously, flinging the silica in showers behind his splayed legs.

His first major find was a Model T Ford's coil spring.

Wagner stared at the artifact, then glanced over his shoulder to see if anyone was watching him. Disgusted, he flung it aside and went on with his search.

Many, many rusty tin cans, bits of metal, more springs, and a mountain of metallic junk he had collected within a couple months pointed up the fact that this treasure-hunting business wasn't going to be as easy as he thought. In all the time he had worked with his detector, he had accumulated enough discarded metal to open a junk business.

Tiring of this, he leased an airplane and sought the site from on high. Besides being a lot easier on the back, it gave him a chance to get a good bird's-eye view of both the coast and the coastal waters where the shipwrecks surely lay.

But this too ended in failure. He saw nothing out of the ordinary.

Back he went to his ground attack. One day, high on a palmetto-covered bluff, he came upon a small clearing. It showed signs of having recently been dug, at least within the last few years. Moreover, an old hound, who had taken up the daily search with Wagner, suddenly stopped to drink from a puddle in the depression.

Since it had not rained recently, it flashed through Wagner's mind that this might be a crude man-made well—the kind that just might have been made by Spaniards occupying a campsite where freshwater was not readily available. As luck would have it, he was without his metal detector that day. But taking a range on the spot, he hustled home and got it.

Moving carefully over the clearing with his detector, Wagner got the familiar series of rapid clicks in his earphones indicating the presence of metal.

Feverishly, he dug down through the soft sand. And this time, instead of a rusty tin can or old water pipe, he pulled out a blackened ship's spike.

Minutes later, he found a cannonball. After that, wherever he tried the detector, it went wild, clicking madly. The whole place was littered with pieces of rusty metal. Best of all, there wasn't a piece of modern junk in the batch!

Wagner was jubilant. He hardly doubted that he had found

the old Spanish salvage camp he had been seeking. But what to do now?

Trying to establish just how wide an area of high metal content he had to contend with, he ran the detector in all directions, until he figured the area of most interest covered about a half-acre.

Hoping that he wasn't about to pour a lot of effort into something that was not what he thought it was, he phoned a Florida historian and described his finding to him. Interested, the man himself came to view the site. He quickly told Wagner that he was on the right track. From all the evidence he saw, it was a period site from the era of interest to the treasure hunter.

That was all the encouragement Wagner needed. He promptly leased the site, hired a bulldozer to clear it, and went to work with shovel and screen to see what the sands contained.

Months later, after much back-breaking work, he had his answer. It was in the form of his findings—three blackened rectangular pieces of silver, clusters of cannonballs, bricks, broken pottery shards, thirteen pieces of eight, a pair of cutlasses lying as if they had been in a case, and a crudely made gold ring holding a 2½-carat diamond surrounded by six tiny diamonds.

For once, Wagner's efforts were paying off. To break the monotony of digging, he built a homemade surfboard with a window in it and searched the offshore areas. One day, he was amazed to find five iron cannon lying on the bottom, where they had been recently uncovered by currents. All were about 8 feet long. Wagner had guessed correctly. The campsite was close to a shipwreck. On shore he hastily bulldozed a giant arrow through the undergrowth from the camp dig that pointed straight at the offshore wreck. Now he had his ranges. He could find the spot from the land, sea, or air.

He hired an airplane and scouted the coast again for signs of shipwreck. When he spotted something unusual he dropped a marker, had the plane land on the beach, and swam out to see what he had marked.

The effort proved unproductive. There were just too many

pieces of shipwreck—both old and modern—scrambled along the coast. The wreck he sought was probably buried, and that meant more men and equipment were needed for any kind of successful recovery effort.

Wagner heard of another shipwreck near Fort Pierce. Doc Kelso had gifted him with a complete scuba diving rig and he eagerly tried it out on this shipwreck. Again, there was lots of ballast rock and little than that to be seen. Other divers had been on it before. Wagner wondered what might lay beneath those tons of rocks. Again, it would take manpower to find out.

All in all, he realized that from this point on, his treasure hunting efforts were going to require three things—money, men, and machinery.

To protect whatever he might find, Wagner applied to the state of Florida for a nonexclusive salvage lease for a 50-mile area from Sebastian Inlet to a point near Stuart, Florida. The state would receive 25 percent of whatever he found. It was one of the wisest moves Wagner ever made. His sites and finds would now be legally protected. All he had to do now was to get the three things he needed to move on with the project.

By Florida standards, the winter of 1959 was cold. Divers with common interests often spent nights near warm fireplaces talking about the treasure hunting they planned to do when the weather warmed. Those who talked to Wagner of such things were instantly appraised as possible associates in his treasure-hunting activities. Wagner was in no rush to find the kind of fellows he could trust and work well with. That's why he took his time and talked little about how much he knew about the subject.

Gradually, however, before the winter was out, he had selected a small group that would form the nucleus of his operation. The part-time treasure hunters were Lou Ullian, Delphine Long, Ervin Taylor, Colonel Dan F. Thompson and Lieutenant Colonel Harry Cannon, the latter two from the installation at Cape Canaveral.

The group, which would eventually grow to eight members

and call itself the Real Eight Company, scrounged diving equipment, built what they required in dredging equipment, bought a dilapidated 40-foot liberty launch, which they patched, painted, and named the *Sampan*, then went into the treasure-hunting business.

Rather than tip his hand to the site he had found offshore near Sebastian, Wagner led the group southward toward the old wreck and its mountain of ballast stones there. He wanted primarily to see how the men worked together, whether they could stick it out under fairly rough conditions in which they worked lots, but got little in return. In fact, Wagner suspected that from the already worked wreck they would find little at all.

Much to his surprise, they in fact did rather well. Weekends were spent laboring on the bottom, moving hundreds of ballast rock from one part of the wreck to the other, then sifting the sands underneath in search of goodies. For a while, they were teased by finding just enough shipwreck artifacts to keep everyone interested. Then suddenly, they struck treasure in a big way. They began finding silver wedges, large ones the size of a wedge one might expect served from a two-layer cake. Finally, they had eight wedges that when fitted together formed a pie. Each wedge was then believed to be worth about six-hundred dollars.

After that, Wagner felt the men were ready to dive on his site off Sebastian. He primed them for it for it with the tales of his efforts both on the salvage site and offshore. It was this first trip there aboard the *Sampan* on that wintery cold day in January, 1961, that paid off so successfully in silver coins. The party that night, which included faithful Doc Kelso, celebrated their first big success, which had already gone beyond their wildest expectations this early in the game. Thompson's corroded coin cluster, weighing 77 pounds, contained an estimated two thousand silver coins clumped together like a rock. No rock was ever toasted so much.

High spirited as they were the next morning, the weather prevented them from returning to the site for a repeat performance. Indeed, the seas raged for the next few weeks, leaving them frustrated.

Finally, when a break came, they shot out the inlet and dived on the site. To their amazement, everything had changed. The whole place was covered again with sand. Even the cannon were buried. But they unlimbered their dredging gear and soon turned up scattered pieces of eight. Lou Ullian found a clump of coins similar to what Thompson had recovered earlier. The hunters estimated its worth to be from twenty to thirty thousand dollars. The find was cause for another exuberant celebration. Anyone within hearing may have well wondered what it was all about. Not one of them dared breathe a word of what they had found or why they were celebrating. It all had to be kept secret, at least for the time being.

It was at this time that the group formed itself into a corporation named Real Eight, after the Spanish term for a piece of eight coin—*ocho reales*. The eight members elected Kip Wagner president.

That winter the group bore down on building sand-moving equipment. Several of them had read about the injection dredges used by western divers to separate overburden from hidden nuggets, so they used the same idea. Only they enlarged upon it, until they had a device aptly nicknamed the *Hungry Beast*. It consisted of a 9-foot-long aluminum pipe, 6 inches in diameter. When compressed air was injected into it near its nozzle, the suction literally ate holes in the soft sand bottom. With this they hoped to eat into the bottom and uncover the treasure.

Moderating weather that spring brought them swiftly to the site. To their amazement it was uncovered again. The fickle tides and currents had done their work for them!

For four days they jubilantly picked up goodies lying virtually uncovered all over the bottom. Then, Mother Nature did her thing and deposited tons of sand on the site again.

That summer the Hungry Beast ate into the overburden and spit out everything, from blackened silver coins to pieces of broken pottery and ship spikes. It uncovered twenty iron cannon and several thousand pieces of eight, before northern gales finally closed down the operation for 1962.

Wagner, however, never closed down. When the seas were too rough to dive, he worked the beaches. One cold November day he and young nephew, Rex Stocker, were doing just that with the trusty metal detector, when the boy found something unexpected on the beach.

When Wagner saw Rex running toward him from the dunes, he thought at first the boy was yelling excitedly about a snake he had found. Instead, the narrow yellow object in his hands was a length of a gold chain connected to an odd-looking pendant.

"It was half-covered up near the dunes," gasped wide-eyed Stocker. "When I pulled, *all this* came out of the sand!"

"All this," proved to be an elaborately wrought heavy gold chain, 11 feet 4½ inches long. The pendant was a 3-inch-long dragon. Hurrying home to inspect the find more closely, the two got out a magnifying glass and found they had even more surprises to contemplate. The chain itself was four-sided, made up of intricately linked flower blossoms. The pendant was finely carved in minute detail showing each scale. Blowing through the dragon's mouth produced a shrill whistle. Its back swivelled to present a curved toothpick on one end and tiny ear scoop on the other. Later appraisal by museum experts placed the dragon and chain necklace at a value between forty and sixty thousand dollars. The piece later sold at an auction for fifty-thousand dollars, making it the single most valuable find of the 1715 treasure recovered up to that time. Since it was found on the beach, the artifact was considered treasure trove, or finders keepers. Florida received no portion of monetary returns from this item.

Wagner's spirits soared. He felt that the finding of the dragon was a sign that, from then on, their luck was destined to become better than ever. But 1964 started slowly for the salvagers. For the first four months all they found were scattered silver coins. No more gold.

By June, however, the Hungry Beast began uncovering the silver coins in clusters. The first, weighing 70 pounds, contained about fourteen hundred pieces of eight. Several days later, five more valuable clusters, weighing between 50 and 75 pounds each, turned up, and, as always, when burrowing into the sand with the airlift, divers found many fragments of pottery.

Wagner remembered finding similar fragments of the blue and white ceramics in the site he had excavated on shore. They were all pieces of K'ang Hsi pottery dating from 1662 to 1722. One day, as the divers continued uncovering an endless number of fragments, they were suddenly amazed when the sucking maw of the Hungry Beast uncovered stacks of intact cups, bowls, and saucers of the same fragile china. Incredible as it seems, each piece was completely intact. In fact, many were still stacked, as they had been shipped in their original packing clay.

It was later learned that the pieces had originated in the Orient. They had crossed the Pacific on the Manila galleon, undergone a trade fair at Acapulco, and crossed the mountains on mule back to Veracruz. There they were loaded aboard ships of the flota, and then transshipped to Cuba, where they were being sailed up the Florida Straits aboard the 1715 fleet, which was struck down by hurricane. The fragile pottery had somehow managed to survive the hurricane and over two centuries of burial on the ocean floor before being recovered intact by Real Eight's divers.

Not long after finding the porcelain, a diver noted a yellow gleam beside a cannon muzzle and fanned up another elaborately linked gold chain. This one attached to a small pendant once containing two miniature oil paintings. Unfortunately, under their long immersion, only a faint trace of paint still remained.

Although the divers had been turning up literally thousands of silver coins, this was the first gold found on the wrecks. It somehow broke the jinx, because a few days later, as Thompson and Long were watching the Hungry Beast devour sand in 9 feet of water, its cone-shaped sand hole in the bottom suddenly seemed to sprout gold coins. The divers swiftly plucked up twenty-three four- and eight escudo gold coins. Beneath them, Long found a gold ring with an expansion band.

Surprisingly enough, throughout all this treasure-hunting activity, except for a couple of state officials, no one else knew the men were making these finds.

They kept their secret well. Naturally, the waterfront locals knew that Wagner and his men were engaged in treasure hunting, but no one suspected just how successful they were. Each time the *Sampan* came back to its marina mooring, some of the crewmen engaged the curious dockside crowd in conversation, while the others quietly transferred the heavy bags of silver coins from their boat to the trunk of their car. Such was the covert operation that was turning up thousands of coins in the surf just off the beach opposite the heavily trafficked highway U.S. A1A, and hardly more than the people doing the recovery knew what was happening right under the public's nose. No one was the wiser.

Treasure hunters are an uncommon breed. The successful ones are generally quite close-mouthed about their activities. Understandably so. Especially during the heat of the hunt. Only later, after the search, does their story usually appear. Then outsiders learn whether they were successful or unsuccessful in their endeavors. Interestingly, though they may never have met, all within the fraternity pretty much know what the others are doing. They find out by word of mouth through the diver grapevine. Divers talk to other divers and the word spreads, which is the reason Real Eight member Lou Ullian walked into a skin-diving shop in Los Angeles and happened to meet Mel Fisher.

Even then, in the winter of 1962, Fisher was something of a celebrity in California. Caught up early in the adventure of scuba diving, he was already marketing his underwater diving adventure films to a weekly Hollywood television station to help defray expenses for his many far-reaching treasure-hunting expeditions. Until then, none had been too successful. He and his diver friends had found an occasional coin and plenty of shipwreck artifacts, but it was his films, dive shop, and shared expenses with his other would-be fellow treasure divers that helped pay the bill for these activities.

Fisher had the reputation and some far-reaching experiences, which made Lou Ullian feel he was talking to a kindred soul. He told the diver about Real Eight's finds on the Florida east coast. With that, the die was cast.

On a subsequent trip to California, when Ullian learned that Fisher and his friends were about to embark on an expedition off the coast of the Dominican Republic in search of the legendary treasure of fabled Silver Shoals, Ullian suggested that Fisher stop by Wagner's home on his way there.

"I think you two would have a lot in common," said Ullian.

"Yeah," replied Fisher. "I think we would, too."

That common denominator, coupled with a few new twists Fisher would bring with him, would soon revolutionize treasure hunting and catapult everyone concerned from their small covert operation into a booming treasure salvage business that would make headlines around the world.

# Chapter 14

# Carpet of Gold

When Fisher met Wagner, the two talked shipwrecks and treasure-hunting for hours. Fisher was much impressed when Wagner
showed him some of their recovered coins. And when the west
coast treasure hunter left for Silver Shoals, Wagner gave him an
old chart he had of the area.

As others before him have done for centuries, Fisher
probed the maze of reefs north of the Dominican Republic,
searching for the lost galleon of Silver Shoals, but finding
nothing but the remnants of more modern-day shipwrecks.

Back at Wagner's home again, that March, Fisher suggested
an arrangement that Wagner found appealing.

"You fellows are into something really big," said Fisher.
"But since you only work on weekends diving the wreck, it'll
take an eternity for you to recover all the treasure that is there.
How about me forming a hard-core team of experienced professional divers who would pay their own way and provide their
own equipment in return for diving on your lease sites? Everything that we bring up will be split fifty-fifty down the middle,
after the state takes its quarter share off the top. Anything Real
Eight has already recovered is still yours."

Wagner thought it sounded like a pretty square deal.

"I'll tell you what, Mel. We'll kick it around at our next board meeting, while you see if you can find the divers willing to get involved in this kind of thing."

It made sense to Wagner that since they had already worked two years on the Cabin Wreck, the 1715 shipwreck he had found near Sebastian Inlet, they had hardly scratched the surface of the site. At this rate, it would take them years to realize any profit from their efforts. There were more wrecks to the south and supposedly more treasure. None of them were getting any younger, especially Wagner.

A few weeks later, Fisher wrote from California that he had found his dedicated crew. They were willing to work a year without pay on the chance that during that time they would strike it big.

Shortly thereafter, Fisher sold all of his west coast holdings and moved his family and fellow divers, who called themselves, Treasure Salvors Incorporated, to Florida, ready to dive on Real Eight's shipwrecks. Besides Fisher's wife, Dolores, and their four children, he had five experienced divers—Rupert Gates, Walt Holzworth, Fay Feild, Demostines Molinar, and Dick Williams.

In addition to being experienced divers, all of the people had in some way participated in various kinds of treasure hunting. The one thing they all shared in common was a single-minded dedication to finding treasure. One of the key figures among them, who would later be responsible for their spectacular success, was Fay Feild, an electronic expert whose hobby of hunting iron shipwrecks (because they were a special habitat for the rare spiny oyster *Spondylus Americanus*) led this shell collector to build a unique device. It was a supersensitive underwater detector called a magnetometer that, when towed behind a boat, detected deviations in the earth's magnetic field, caused by concentrations of iron such as those that usually have occurred on shipwrecks. Such a device would prove invaluable to treasure hunters seeking iron concentrations, such as cannon and ship spikes associated with old shipwrecks. Well aware of this, Fisher had made a special effort to persuade Fay Feild to join their group.

Thinking that he would give the newcomers some experience working a typical wreck site, Wagner directed them to the Wedge wreck, one of the 1715 fleet shipwrecks near Fort Pierce. He had no idea that they would find anything and was surprised when the well-picked-over wreck yielded another pie-shaped wedge of silver to Fisher's divers.

As time passed, however, it largely proved to be an unprofitable year for Treasure Salvors. They found nothing of any consequence and, as the year they had gambled on gradually drew to a close, they were a disheartened crew. A sudden turn of events, however, spared them the final fate of many unsuccessful treasure hunters.

Strolling along the beach just south of Fort Pierce, two young men, Bruce Ward and Don Neiman, found some perfectly struck gold coins in the sand. Immediately, they contacted Frank Allen, and the trio, believing that they were about to stumble on a fortune just offshore, formed a company.

Several months of searching the coastal area, however, failed to produce the hoped-for shipwreck. Realizing that they lacked all the necessary ingredients required for a full-scale salvage effort on the site, the three decided to try another tact.

They contacted Kip Wagner, showed him their gold coins, and offered to strike a deal with Real Eight that would put Real Eight and Treasure Salvors on the site in exchange for a percentage of all future finds.

Wagner and his company found this arrangement agreeable and drew up a contract. He then sent Fisher and his men south to survey the site.

During the next four months, the divers tried to locate the treasure wreck with no success. Finally, fed up, Fisher told Wagner that Treasure Salvors's percentage was too small; that, after all their work, if something was found, their reward would be far too small.

"Either we draw up different terms, or we don't work the site," said Fisher.

Wagner told the trio Fisher's ultimatum and they grudgingly agreed to terms giving Treasure Salvors a larger slice of the pie, when and if it was found.

Back Fisher went to Fort Pierce, armed now with another innovation, a device that was to revolutionize treasure hunting from then on.

Called a "mailbox" by the treasure hunters, because it resembled those that often sit on street corners, it consisted of a metal box that, when lowered over the salvage vessel's propeller, forced the prop wash to go at a right angle toward the bottom. Initially the idea was to divert clear surface water to the bottom for better diver visibility. But when the device was tried, everyone was astonished to find they had created a unique piece of excavation equipment, for the swirling water dug deep holes in the bottom. All divers had to do was hover beside this invisible column of water and watch for artifacts to appear from the deepening excavation.

Three months of magnetometer probes and punching holes in the bottom with the mailbox resulted in a large pile of junk, none of it from any treasure wreck. Then, one day in April, a half-mile north and more seaward of where they had formerly searched, they uncovered ballast rock. Then a single iron cannon. By month's end they had some one hundred silver coins. Then their luck suddenly improved.

Spotting a dull yellow gleam in the sand, Panamanian diver Moe Molinar dug his hands into the fine coral particles and came up with a pair of heavy objects. They were solid gold disc-shaped ingots weighing about 7 pounds apiece. Nothing like them had ever been found before on the wrecks. Some idea of their value can be realized by the fact that Fisher later sold a similar disc of 22½-karat gold bearing a Mexican mint mark for 17,500 dollars. And that was long before the value of gold skyrocketed!

Several days after the celebration party and a spate of foul weather, they returned to the site, hopeful of finding more treasures. But all they found was poor visibility; the bottom was muddy.

"Let's go further out and punch a hole," Fisher suggested enthusiastically. But the other divers were ready to call it quits.

"C'mon," urged Fisher. "I gotta hunch it's right over there!" The others shrugged, hoisted anchor, and moved the boat about 50 feet to the east. They dropped anchor and Molinar went over the side to look around.

Seconds later he was up, grinning broadly, a gold coin clutched in his fingers.

"See, I told you!" laughed Fisher. "I had a feeling!"

The coin was a beautiful gold eight-escudo dated 1698. It was just the beginning. A few more turned up that day, and on May 21st, things really brightened. With the mailbox going full blast, the divers uncovered over two-hundred four- and eight-escudo gold coins.

Then, as Kip Wagner later reported, "Three days later, on May 24th, the big haul was made. Mel's blaster cut a hole about 15 feet long and 5 to 6 feet wide down a ridge between two rocks. Moe, Walt, and Lou down to see how it looked, and they were blinded by a bright yellow glow. There, in its magnificent splendor, was a veritable carpet of gold, the likes of which modern man had probably never seen before. The divers burned up almost a full tank of air just staring in awe at the sight. Then Moe grabbed a double handful and surfaced."

After that, it was a mad free-for-all, a coin grab that wasn't quite as easy as one might imagine. Being heavier than any of the other metals they had handled, a coin dropped was a possible coin lost, for it slipped beneath a disguising cover of sand that instantly looked like all the rest of the bottom.

The blower was still going, which helped send out a shower of disturbed sand to rain down on the already exposed coins. Divers finned hard to stay near the bottom against the mailbox's swirling currents, while frantically plucking coins before they disappeared.

To avoid losing their finds, they shoved them inside the wrist band of their gloves, surfacing only after they had bulged the glove with some sixty or seventy coins, which were then deposited swiftly on the boat deck. Then they hurried back to the bottom for more.

All day long that went on, everyone fearing that a storm might suddenly appear and make them leave their honey hole. Frantically, they worked, not even breaking for coffee, just hustling gold coins from bottom to top, then returning to the bottom again. They paused only long enough to switch air tanks when necessary. And you can bet that more than one of the divers were hyperventilating a bit from the excitement. Lou Ullian exhausted six tanks of air working five hours plucking gold coins off the bottom. Never in his life had he done such profitable work!

By day's end the divers' wrists were rubbed raw from gold coins being pushed into gloves. But it was worth it. Their find totaled 1,033 pieces of gold!

# Chapter 15

# Sampling the Royal Treasury

Mel Fisher was beginning to believe the bottom was paved with gold. All you had to do was uncover the right spot.

Wagner and his Real Eight people were beginning to believe the same thing. They shifted work from the Sebastian Inlet wreck to the Fort Pierce site, which was first called the "Colored Beach Wreck," and later for obvious reasons, the "Gold Wreck."

The day after their big find, the divers returned to the site and picked up nine-hundred more doubloons. In a week's time they had collected nearly twenty-five hundred of them! Some called it a king's ransom. In truth, they were just picking their way haphazardly through a king's treasury—one that never got to where it was going.

A few days later, the golden bubble burst. The gold stopped coming. Kip Wagner and Doc Kelso got out their pencils and did some hasty figuring. They calculated that they had found what was probably the contents of a single chestful of gold. It was great while it lasted and sad when it stopped. There had to be other such chests. But where?

"That's an awfully big ocean out there," said Fisher. From the top or the bottom, it all looked alike. It was obvious that they had to devise some kind of practical search pattern or they would be merely digging in the same old holes over and over again. Finally, they hit upon the idea of marking all their spots with bleach jugs on weighted lines. This worked well for a while, until the elements wiped them out. Then, it was anyone's guess where they had dug!

That August's hurricanes and associated storms wiped out their diving season. Counting up their finds, the treasure hunters decided to go to market. It was high time they realized some kind of reward for all their accumulated debts and hard efforts.

After a division with Florida, the treasure hunters set up a coin auction in New Jersey. Selecting about one hundred coins, mostly gold, they let the world bid on them for the first time. When all the hue and cry was over, the treasure hunters came away twenty-nine thousand dollars richer. One choice 1711 four-escudo gold piece had stolen the show. It brought thirty-six hundred dollars for its rarity, the highest price paid for any single coin at the auction. By the time all the treasure hunters paid their bills, bought equipment replacements, and divided the remaining loot, few of them had much more than a thousand dollars or so to show for their work.

"Seems ironic as hell," said Kip Wagner. "We find a fortune in treasure estimated to be in the millions, but these few thousand dollars are all we're able to stuff into our pockets!"

The cost of uncovering a fortune was becoming all too clear to them.

With the news of their finds now public knowledge, Real Eight and Treasure Salvors were suddenly thrust into the hot glare of public attention. Immediately, their covert operation was no longer so. Divers by the hundreds scurried to Florida to scavenge the beaches for overlooked coins and to see if they could dive up some treasure of their own on the lease sites when no one was looking. Everyone got so treasure conscious that would-be coin hunters and con artists almost outnumbered the annual tourist crop flocking to Florida. Chamber of Commerce sharpies with an eye out for focusing some of that interest on their areas quickly came up with such names as "The Gold Coast," and "The Treasure Coast." The "Great Florida Treasure Find," created the Klondike gold rush days all over again.

Even Florida officialdom got shook up over all the excitement. New rules and regulations came out, putting more restrictions on the treasure hunters. New people were hired to keep an eye on Florida's share of the loot before any division occurred, and new voices were heard decrying the fact that Florida was actually contracting treasure hunters to pillage what some were now touting as "the public's historical heritage."

The first real valuable treasure finds triggered it all, including all the bureaucratic nightmares that went with it. While these battles and intrigues ebbed and flowed around the now famous—or infamous—treasure hunters, they blundered on as best they could with their business of looking for more lost loot.

By now, Real Eight's hard-pressed workboat, the *Sampan*, was in such a dilapidated condition that Wagner often feared for their lives whenever they took it through the rampaging inlet. For all concerned, it seemed wise to get rid of her before she did it to them first.

The company got a "new" salvage boat. Though little more than an open hull, they planned to rebuild the 50-foot-long by 15-foot beam vessel from the hull up to suit their salvage needs.

"I nearly cried when I saw it for the first time," was the way Del Long expressed his opinion of the new boat.

"I have to admit it has a ringing resemblance to a garbage scow," said Wagner. "But it belongs to us now, for better or worse."

On her maiden voyage for the company, belching billowing clouds of black diesel oil smoke from her exhaust, it looked like the boat was going to perform at its worse. Hardly away from shore, it broke down and had to be towed back by the faithful *Sampan*. The company dubbed the tub the *Derelict* and pitched in one and all to make it into a proper salvage vessel.

By the beginning of the 1965 season, Real Eight was into

the business of treasure hunting full time. With their vessel finally ready, Real Eight moved it between the Cabin Wreck near Sebastian Inlet and the Colored Beach Wreck south of Fort Pierce, working the sites interchangeably.

What made everything so uncertain was how widely scattered everything was. What it came down to was picking your patch of ocean, digging the bottom, and hoping for the best.

Certain ones of the combined groups soon developed a reputation for being able to foretell finds. Some thought that Fisher had this ability. The same was true for Real Eight member, Del Long. One day, toward the end of a trip, Long pointed to the south and said, "I've got a feeling, fellas."

Everyone gathered around him, waiting for the prophetic pearls to spill. "I've got a feeling that we're going to hit it big again soon, right over there." Everyone estimated the spot to be about 900 feet south of where they were working.

"Yep," drawled Long. "If we go over there, we'll find a heap of gold."

Reporting the incident later, Wagner said, "Sure enough, and may I be struck on the spot, if it's not the gospel. Bob and the boys motored over to the location in the next couple of days, and on May 30th, found 130 gold coins 4 fathoms down, not 50 feet from the site Del had pinpointed! It was phenomenal. How can you explain it?"

It was the kind of strike they had all been waiting for. Next day, the *Derelict* was overflowing with company divers anxious to try their luck at the new honey hole. Even Wagner was there. Here's how he described it:

"I hadn't been diving lately, because of a bad back, but I couldn't resist the temptation and down I went. It was a beautiful day, and the waters were as clear as any I could remember. Visibility was 40 or 50 feet in all directions. Conditions were perfect. The sands were so white, it looked as if the surf had scrubbed the grains with detergent.
"And then I saw it—a sight every man should see just once in his life. The blaster had cut a hole about 30 feet in diameter, and there, in this vast pocket of the ocean floor, lay a carpet of gold! Believe me, a carpet of gold! It was the most glorious picture one can imagine. Not even Hollywood could have upstaged this natural

underwater scene. Off to one side, against a rock-coral formation, the coins, so help me, were even lying in neat stacks of three and four. The water magnification made it seem as though the entire bottom was lined with gold."

The sight stunned the divers—even the hard-core guys who had been at it for more than five years. They were all spellbound, staring at the incredibly beautiful scene. Wagner even surfaced to make sure that everyone on board got a chance to get down and see the wondrous sight before they began picking up the coins.

After that, it was a replay of Fisher's "carpet of gold" find, as the divers moved in literally scooping up the coins by the double-handsful and loading buckets to the brim with them. Besides being plentiful, the gold pieces were all in mint condition. And they were large coins, many of them eight-escudo pieces the size of American silver dollars.

Before it was all picked up, they called to Fisher's group to come over and join in the gold-plucking operation, just for the fun of it. Everyone joined in the orgy of salvaging samples of a Spanish king's long lost royal treasury, sending a steady cascade of gold pouring out over the rough-hewn decks of the *Derelict*.

Late that afternoon, they knocked off and carried their collection home with them, where they separated, assessed, counted, and stacked their find until the early hours of the morning. In the final count, they had found 1,128 gold coins that day. Almost half were eight-escudo pieces, which were then valued up to three thousand dollars apiece. One was a 1711 perfectly struck four-escudo royal, estimated to be worth up to five thousand dollars. The least current value of any of the gold coins was probably three hundred dollars. All considered, it had been a most profitable day!

Foul weather prevented them from returning to the hot spot for several days. Then when they did, all they found were a half-dozen more gold coins. Apparently, once again they had found the contents of a single chest of gold coins, the wooden part rotted away, and the contents spilled over the spot where it had rested.

Once again Real Eight returned to the Cabin Wreck off Sebastian Inlet and began searching in deeper water for shipwreck remains with Fay Feild's magnetometer. First they found some cannon. Then the divers recovered three pie-shaped wedges of silver. Nine more wedges were recovered later, along with three silver coin clumps, several hundred loose pieces of eight, and ten big round discs weighing from 44 to 105 pounds each. These odd discs were later found to be part silver and part gold, platinum, and copper. They were lying under 4 feet of sand.

The more they dug on the site, the more they found. In the next couple of days, it proved to be more productive than any similar area they had sampled in the last two seasons. They ended up recovering several thousand loose silver coins in one afternoon, and before they finished, they had 665 pounds of silver coins, or nearly ten thousand of them! A dozen more silver wedges turned up, eight more of the strange metal discs, two biscuit-shaped silver ingots, and a clump of coins.

After a week of that kind of activity, they learned that they had brought up nearly *a ton* of pieces of eight!

As the days went on, their find increased to a 125-pound clump of coins, a pair of silver plates, 60 pounds of loose coins, an old apothecary mortar, rings, pendants, necklaces, and an onion-shaped bottle with liquid in it. They thought they had seen it all. Then one day, Wagner's nephew, Rex Stocker, surfaced and shouted: "Hey! There's a chest of silver down there!"

Nobody aboard the *Derelict* believed him. Everyone knew that the only times you found treasure chests full of silver and gold were in Hollywood movies. Real wood treasure chests are quickly consumed by teredo worms and other boring marine organisms not long after they sink to the ocean floor.

But Rex insisted, begging someone to just go back down with him and see for himself. Del Long obliged, to put an end to the joke.

Seconds later, he was on the surface shouting that the boy was 100 percent right. "There *is* a treasure chest down there, sitting on the bottom just as pretty as you please," he told them.

There was no need to say more. Divers grabbed tanks and rolled over the side to see it for themselves.

On the bottom sat a blackish-colored wooden container about 3 feet long, 1 foot wide, and 1 foot deep. One end and the top were missing. The rest was remarkably intact. Since this might well be the only chest of silver ever found intact anywhere in the world, they did not want to damage it.

Everyone surfaced and plotted how best to recover it. Best guess was that it weighed around 200 pounds. They decided to construct a plywood platform to slip under it to support the fragile pieces of wood, which had survived simply because, for the last couple of centuries, the chest was at least partially buried in the protective sand.

When all was ready, the divers shoved the platform through the sand beneath the chest and secured it to the object. Then with divers lifting and lines hoisting, the whole thing was carefully brought to the surface.

Once aboard, it was quickly submerged in a large tub of water to prevent the wood from drying out and rapidly deteriorating in the air.

Florida underwater archaeologists later determined that the packing case was made of cedar and that the coins inside, in clumps resembling the bags they once had been in, comprised over three thousand pieces of eight. From impressions in the encrustations on the coin clumps, experts were even able to determine what kind of cloth and weave were used for the money bags.

By the end of the 1964 salvage season, Wagner estimated that they had recovered from the 1715 wreck sites a treasure valued in excess of $3 million in gold, silver, jewelry, and artifacts. Others have believed the amount lost and still recoverable to be in excess of $14 million dollars.

After dividing with the state of Florida and paying their taxes, what was left was divided among members of Real Eight and Treasure Salvors. Wagner and his associates built a large treasure museum near Cape Canaveral that was popular with the public until it burned down years later. In time, Real Eight sold its holdings and went out of business. Other companies under contract to the state came in to work the shipwrecks. Though still receiving percentages of finds from certain sites, Fisher's Treasure Salvors group contracted them out to other salvors; Mel Fisher moved his company to Key West and used his share of the 1715 treasure to help finance his search for another long lost legendary treasure galleon, one named, *Nuestra Señora de Atocha*.

Other members of the original eight who started the company with Wagner used their portion of returns to go into businesses of their own. Wagner's nephew, Rex Stocker, whom many a youngster would envy for having been able to grow up living the real adventure of treasure hunting, is still in the business, working with a salvage firm, still successfully recovering treasure from one of the 1715 sites.

After achieving his dream of finding treasure, Kip Wagner went on to enjoy some of the spin-offs of his fame and fortune before he died in the 1970s. Much of the treasure has gone into private collections. Wisely maintaining an intact collection of the gold coins, Fisher was able to repeatedly use it as collateral for bank loans for his future treasure hunt.

Perhaps the largest collection of all that still remains is that held by the state of Florida. The most interesting pieces are on public display at the Museum of Florida History at Tallahassee. Other small exhibits may be seen at a few other state museums in southern Florida.

Meanwhile, Wagner's money beach, stretching from Sebastian Inlet to south of Fort Pierce, still provides beachcombers with a steady trickle of blackened silver coins, especially after a northern gale scours the beaches opposite the wreck sites. Sport divers looking for lobsters along the inshore reefs still occasionally find a golden goblet or some other suddenly revealed evidence of the widely scattered treasure from the 1715 shipwrecks, a treasure that will undoubtedly long outlive anyone who has ever been involved with it.

# PART III

Robert Marx:
Incorrigible Adventurer

# Chapter 16

# Sea Fever

On January 1, 1656, a combined armada of twenty-two Spanish merchant ships and galleons sailed out of Havana harbor on its voyage back to Spain. Each of the fleet's two heaviest armed war galleons—the *Capitana* and the *Almiranta*—carried over 5 million pesos in treasure. Much of it was in the form of bar silver, gold and silver coins, exotic jewelry, uncut emeralds with other precious stones, and pearls. Along with its share of treasure the *Almiranta, Nuesta Señora de la Maravilla* (Our Lady of the Miracle), carried a solid gold statue of the Madonna and Child. It was the lead ship.

Four days sail from Havana, near midnight, the lookout aboard the *Maravilla* suddenly sighted breaking seas ahead. As a warning to the other vessels to veer off, the ship fired her cannon.

Caught unaware, because the pilots thought the fleet had already cleared the dreaded shoals of the Bahama Channel and were in open ocean, several ships continued on course, while others, heeding the warning, swerved westward into deeper water.

One of the first of the fleet to get into trouble was the

galleon *Jesus Maria*. She struck a coral reef that tore off her rudder. Disabled, the vessel anchored in 4 fathoms of water.

The instant she fired her cannon, pandemonium broke out among the passengers aboard the *Maravilla*. Many thought they were being attacked by enemy ships, and changed course immediately in an effort to sail off the shoals. In the confusion, the *Maravilla* collided with the fleet's *Capitana*, which had continued sailing northward toward the shoals.

The two ships were locked together for almost a half-hour, while their crews worked desperately to separate them, clearing away entangled rigging and sails.

Finally, the two vessels disengaged, the *Capitana* sustaining only minor damages. She continued sailing into the night. The *Maravilla*, however, was mortally wounded, her bow below the waterline severely damaged. The vessel immediately began taking on large amounts of water and sinking by her bow.

Despite all efforts to man her pumps and try to keep her afloat, it soon was apparent that she was going down. In a valiant effort to save as many lives and as much treasure as possible, her admiral managed to run her aground on the shoals that had threatened the fleet in the first place.

A half-hour after the vessels had separated, the *Maravilla* struck bottom violently about six times before finally coming to rest on a sand bank in 30 feet of water. Hardly had she reached this resting place with both her fore and stern castles out of water, when a strong northerly wind began blowing. Soon, giant seas built and began smashing the ship to pieces. Of her 650 panic-strickened passengers, some fought their way into the ship's two longboats and drifted off into the darkness, clinging to floating wreckage. Some 150 still clung to the main part of the galleon that was above water. Then it too began to disintegrate. The ship broke in two—the bow remaining waterlogged and in place, while the main after section was carried away. All who clung to this part of the wreck were never seen again.

By dawn, only about forty-five pathetic survivors still clung to the bow section. Eventually, by late afternoon, as the seas began to subside, they were rescued by a longboat from the anchored *Jesus Maria*. Both bow and stern sections of the *Maravilla* wreck were marked by buoys, and six days later, after finally repairing their rudder, the *Jesus Maria* made it into deeper water and set sail southward. Contrary winds, however, kept them at sea until March 10th, when the survivors finally reached Cartagena.

Meanwhile, believing that the two ships had returned to Havana, the Spanish fleet sailed on for Spain. As soon as word got out about the *Maravilla*, a salvage effort was launched from Cartagena to recover her five million pesos worth of treasure.

The salvors located her bow section, but were unable to find the main portion of the wreck that had contained the main treasure, including the Madonna and Child. In time, the Spanish salvors recovered over six-hundred-and-fifty thousand pesos in treasure, along with several of the vessel's bronze cannon from the bow section.

Periodically over the next few years, the Spanish tried to find the main bulk of the wreck, but failed. In 1677, after using casks of gunpowder to blast away an overburden of sand covering the site, the Spanish salvaged another 1½ tons of silver bullion and specie. The next year, they returned to take 2 more tons of silver and about 40 pounds of small gold bars from the site. After that, all efforts by the Spanish to recover more ceased, the last salvor reporting that the rest of the wreck was buried too deeply in sand.

In 1680, an October hurricane that swept across the Caribbean, taking fifty thousands lives on the island of Trinidad alone, apparently scoured its way directly over the place where the *Maravilla* lay, because its timbers were laid bare by the storm.

A few months later, a Boston fishing smack, searching for ambergris along the Little Bahama Bank, spotted the galleon's timbers below the surface of the sea. Though none of the crew men could dive, they still managed to grapple up seven large silver bars and a barrelful of silver coins.

In 1681, William Phips of Boston tried his luck at the site. Phips had no success "fishing" the wreck, but a companion marked its location on an old chart, designating the site as the "Plate Wreck."

After that, every twenty or thirty years, some vessel happened upon the ship's grave and sampled some of her treasures. One inter-island trade schooner dived up what they thought was almost 3 tons of pig iron and sailed away. Only later, when the cook tried to break open a coconut on one of the bars and, in so doing knocked off the silver sulphide crust, was it discovered that their cargo consisted of silver bullion. Though they tried to return to the site, they never found the wreck again.

Over and over again, right up to modern times, this phantom galleon's still remaining riches were often glimpsed accidentally, then never seen again. All that remained in the dusty archives was the report that she was somewhere on the Little Bahama Bank.

This is the kind of tale that tingles the fingers and toes of a professional treasure hunter. But the man who was destined to find the elusive and long-sought treasure of the *Maravilla*, had not yet heard of it when he decided to dedicate his life to treasure hunting. Still, the stimulation was there. The only difference was that his fingers and toes were tingling from reading the works of a popular deep-sea diver/author who had been affecting young boys like that for generations.

"Of all the tales of sunken treasure I read," said Robert Marx, many years later, "the one that fascinated me most was that of Port Royal, the old pirate headquarters in Jamaica, which sank beneath the sea in 1692, during an earthquake, supposedly with a vast amount of treasure. The author/diver told of finding the city still standing at the bottom of the sea, of walking past houses with skeletons hanging out windows, and entering the coral-encrusted nave of the cathedral whose bell could be heard ringing when the sea was rough. I spent many a sleepless night lying in bed and thinking how exciting it would be to dive on that sunken city and search for all the treasure there my-self. . . ." The author of that book was Lieutenant Harry E. Rieseberg!

Understandably then, at the age of ten, Marx made up his mind to become a deep-sea diver. Three years later, he started on his first professional salvage job. But then, what can you expect? When you're born to the sea, you're born to the sea. But wait a minute. What's this? Robert Marx wasn't born to the sea. Far from it. He was born December 8, 1935 in Pittsburgh, Pennsylvania, before it cleaned up its act. All he knew as a child were sooty brick houses, hilly streets, and steel furnaces belching black smoke. No wonder as a youngster he always wanted to run away to the sea.

Run away he did, over and over again. His first attempted escape occurred at the age of eight. Prompted largely by the enormous difference the youngster discerned between sooty Pittsburgh and the pictures he saw in all the travel books he spent his time poring over in the school and public libraries, he got itchy feet. Money saved from his paper route bought guide books, maps, magazines (such as the *National Geographic*, which he read and reread until they fell apart), and enough food to let him hit the highway to adventure.

The key to his initially successful getaway was that he had a good set of wheels. Two wheels on a Flyer. By pedaling briskly half the night and well into the next day, they whisked him across the Ohio state line. He was heading for San Francisco, which was not too long a crayoned line on his road map. Six days of furious pedaling brought him to Chicago. By now, having run out of both food and money, he realized he either had to head home or resort to crime. Choosing the latter, he tried to swipe some change from a newsstand, got caught, was turned over to juvenile authorities, and, along with his bike, was sentenced back to Pittsburgh.

Two weeks later, itchy feet hit him again. He was stroking his Flyer past Cleveland's city limits when the law caught up with him. It was back to Pittsburgh again. After that, he changed his ways. Rereading *Huckleberry Finn* for the umpteenth time, he came to the conclusion that, if he couldn't make it by land, maybe he could by water. Besides, the powers that be had sold his faithful Flyer.

Marx and two similar-aged adventurers started collecting boxes and crates to build a raft. Then they found a burned houseboat on shore and settled for that. A week of surreptitiously sneaking small amounts of food from their homes soon stocked their escape craft. Leaving notes to their folks that they were heading for Canada, the three set sail in the opposite direction, floating down the Ohio River. Marx had carefully charted their course from the Ohio to the Mississippi, then to New Orleans, where they all hoped to sign on some ship as cabin boys and set off on a worldwide cruise to adventure.

All seemed well as their hulk got them away from Pittsburgh's sooty shores. The rain-swollen current moved them along at a spectacular clip. All went well until around noon, when navigator Marx noticed a strange drop to the river ahead of them.

"Good golly! The map didn't say anything about *waterfalls*," he moaned.

Over they went. In the wild waters below the falls the houseboat was smashed to kindling. None of the boys could swim. Men working the locks nearby leaped in to help them. Marx and one of his friends made it; the other friend drowned.

Because the escape had been his idea, Marx felt responsible. Instead of dampening his desire to get away, however, it only persuaded him that next time he had to do it alone.

The incorrigible was packed off to an aunt and uncle in Detroit, then passed onto a cousin and her husband who were spending a summer in their cottage on Lake St. Clair in Canada. As far as young Marx was concerned, that was probably the best decision the family ever made.

Marx immediately liked his life beside the lake. His cousin was a great cook; her husband, recently returned from the Pacific, where he had been serving with the marines, played platoon sergeant with him, and quickly tried to teach the boy how to swim.

To say that young Marx took to the water like a fish would be a lie. He took to the water more like a stone, invariably sinking straight to the bottom. Even after three weeks of lessons, he still bottomed out and had to be rescued. The only way he seemed able to float was from atop an inner tube.

"Thank God that uncoordinated misfit isn't from *my* side of the family!" yelled his cousin's husband.

"No way!" retorted his cousin. *"He's* got brains!"

And so it went. One day, however, his cousin returned from town with a present for him. It was a pair of swimming goggles. Marx peered through them into the marvelous under-water world, where he could clearly see fish and eels moving through the grass that grew there in the shallows. The magic changed his life.

Enraptured by the strange new world the goggles opened to him, Marx forgot his fear of the water and, within a week, had become quite proficient at swimming underwater. The new adventure soon occupied all of his time. At night, under his bed covers, by flashlight, he read such exciting books as *Twenty Thousand Leagues Under the Sea* and went to sleep dreaming that he too was part of the *Nautilus* crew and could move as freely as the fish beneath the surface of the sea.

Diving by day with his swimming goggles and reading about underwater adventures of deep-sea divers by night made that summer one of the happiest he had ever experienced.

# Chapter 17

# Montezuma's Revenge

Unfortunately, it finally came to an end. When the time came for him to return to Pittsburgh and return to school, the mere idea brought back the rebel in him. He had decided to become a deep-sea diver and could think of nothing in school that would help him in that occupation. So, he really saw no need to go.

But he did manage to put up with it in Pittsburgh for almost two years, keeping himself out of trouble at the same time. The main reason for this was his continued interest in diving. Even during the winter months he somehow managed to find an available body of water around Pittsburgh. Anything larger than a mud puddle was all he asked. He explored them all with his swimming goggles and his homemade spears. Not that he ever found anything much to spear, but he became deadly proficient at hitting old tin cans and tires littering the bottoms of some of his waterholes.

Marx reread the book about the sunken city of Port Royal so many times that it finally went the way of his disintegrated *National Geographics*.

Since he had behaved himself so well for the last two years, his mother decided he had outgrown his wanderlust. So, for his twelfth birthday, she bought him another bicycle. She was wrong.

Marx took one look at the shiny new set of wheels and the siren call of Jamaica got the better of him. Heading south over the iced roads, he pedaled furiously for the next thirty hours straight, before wheeling off the road for a few hours sleep in a barn.

Days later, numb from the cold, his legs aching, he was pedaling along the outskirts of Richmond, Virginia, when a truck sideswiped him. He wound up his trip in a hospital with a broken leg.

After that, it was a stint in a juvenile detention farm. Released on probation a year later, he got a job as a busboy, hoping to earn at least one hundred dollars for train fare to Maimi. When two older teenagers offered him a free trip to Florida in their stolen car, the temptation was too great to resist. Young Marx could almost smell the tropics, as he and his companions whizzed down the highway.

But this too ended badly—in a hail of police bullets, a smash-up, prison sentences for his friends, a broken collar-bone, and fifty facial stitches for Marx.

Once again he was in the hands of juvenile authorities when his father, whom he had not seen since his parents divorced six years earlier, read about his experiences in the newspaper, came forward, and convinced a sympathetic judge to give the boy another chance.

When a subsequent school incident occurred for which it appeared that Marx would be blamed, he quickly borrowed money from friends and started hitchhiking on the highway to adventure once again.

Surprisingly, his luck was better this time. When he reached Atlantic City's famous boardwalk during a spring gale, the place was devoid of tourists. Hungry, cold, and broke, he found no one anxious to give him a job. By accident, however, he met a small, wiry man named Joe Novak, who decided he could use the eager youngster on his job. Novak was a deep-sea diver with a small salvage business. He and his wife took Marx in and literally made him a member of the family.

Gradually, Novak taught the boy everything he knew about deep-sea diving, starting first with rudiments of line and hose handling, then gradually working up to familiarizing him with the heavy, cumbersome diving helmet, suit, and other equipment. Soon, Novak had Marx diving and, although it was not in the crystal clear tropical waters picking up gold bars while surrounded by colorful fish, he was learning about the underwater world from the best possible school available.

"For ten wonderful months, some days as hot as a furnace, others as cold as a deep freeze," said Marx, "we did all sorts of jobs. We installed underwater sewage pipes, blasted old pier pilings with primacord and erected new ones, raised small yachts that had foundered in rough water, and patched damaged hulls and rudders on larger vessels. When regular business was slow, we did wreck salvage, raising valuable brass propellers, brass and copper pipes and fittings, and tons of other scrap metal. We even salvaged a cargo of bootleg whisky from an old rumrunner that had sunk during the days of prohibition."

All too soon his job with Novak came to an end. Juvenile authorities had traced him to Atlantic City and were waiting at Novak's home to return him to Pittsburgh. Warned of their presence, his friendly employer promptly paid Marx five hundred dollars in back wages, put him on a bus for Bridgeport, Connecticut, and arranged for a job with another salvage diver.

The new job provided Marx with enough money to head for Los Angeles to live with an aunt. Obviously, he figured, the more distance he could put between himself and those pesky juvenile-hunters, the better off he would be. What he badly needed was some kind of proof that he was no longer a juvenile, but a full-fledged "adult." Since Marx looked a lot older than he actually was—the fifteen that he had just become—he registered with the local Selective Service Board and received a draft card stating that he was eighteen years old.

On the West Coast, Marx got his first taste of the sport of

skin diving that was then gaining popularity in California. Soon he tried his first aqualung (a device that was to revolutionize sport diving) and realized that this was the kind of equipment he had dreamed about—that it would one day let him breathe and swim underwater as free as the fish.

Though forced to return to high school, he considered the time there largely a waste, because it prevented him from spending more time diving. Summers he spent bouncing around Baja California, living along the beaches night and day, spearing fish for food, and enjoying the freedom. That abruptly ended at Long Beach in July, 1953, when FBI agents arrested him on charges of draft dodging.

Though the officials in Pittsburgh quickly verified that Marx was really seventeen years old and not twenty-two, it was a federal offense to fraudulently obtain a Selective Service card. When the FBI hinted it might not press charges against him, if he were to voluntarily join the armed forces, Marx took the hint the next day and joined the U.S. Marine Corps, hoping to see action in Korea with an underwater demolition team.

His bad luck still held. Two weeks after he signed up, the Korean Armistice was signed. Moreover, it was the navy, not the marines that had an underwater demolition team. And now he had signed up for a three-year hitch. In peacetime!

Off he went to the Halls of Montezuma.

# Chapter 18

# Road to Adventure

Instead of rebelling against the system, Marx took it in stride. Rather than run away, he pitched in, did his best, and ended up becoming a good marine.

Disappointed though he was to learn that the U.S. Marines had turned over all their underwater activities to the navy shortly after World War II, that didn't stop him from suggesting to the camp's commanding general that, to save the honor of the Corps, marines should be doing their own diving. To his surprise, the officer made him Camp Lejeune's unofficial diver. Given several quick cram courses in his duties, Marx was soon doing underwater demolitions work, body recovery, and any other job that required attention underwater.

Soon he was being loaned to other marine bases for their work. Before long, Marx set up a dive team made up of volunteers and really got into the swing of things. Soon he was teaching aqualung use to more and more marines, including the base commander.

The best part about being stationed at Camp Lejeune, North Carolina, for this long-famished, untried treasure hunting fan, was the wealth of sunken ships that lay practically at the camp's threshold. Just a few hours drive away was North Carolina's infamous Cape Hatteras, "the graveyard of the Atlantic," a coastline littered with the centuries-old remains of over two thousand ill-fated shipwrecks, including such tempting targets as legendary German submarines, whose rusting hulls were believed to carry millions of dollars worth of mercury ballast, and the long lost Civil War gunboat, the *Monitor*.

Nothing could have pleased Marx more than being plunked down in front of this smorgasbord at the government's expense and being able to sample it whenever he wished during his off-duty hours. In the next couple of years, he and his diving companions made many efforts to find some kind of treasure in some of Hatteras's old sunken hulks, but all they managed to recover was a large collection of steering wheels, portholes, cannon, bells, and crockery. That was the extent of the treasure.

When someone suggested that fame and fortune awaited anyone able to find the final resting place of the Civil War's first ironclad, called a "cheesebox on a raft," Marx was fired with the idea.

Marx began reading all the accounts he could find of the loss, only to learn that no two agreed on where the event actually took place. Broadly speaking, the *Monitor* was being towed by the steamer *Rhode Island*, some 20 miles off Cape Hatteras, when a gale came up. The ironclad broke free and sank with a loss of part of her crew. The date was December 30, 1862.

On and off for the next ninety-two years, many attempts were made to find the historical gunboat's final resting place, without success. Marx spent the better part of a year roaming the bleak Cape Hatteras beaches, visiting museums, talking to people, ferreting out old historical documents from a variety of libraries and archives. Then he actively began searching for the missing ironclad.

This time it was from the air. Piecing together information from a family that thought they had seen the "Yankee cheese-

These are gold coins from the 1715 Spanish Plate fleet valued at several thousand dollars apiece.

This early photograph shows Art McKee recovering his second bar of silver from a Bahama wreck while wearing his Miller-Dunn helmet.

*Courtesy Gay McKee*

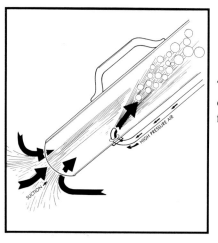

The air-lift became one of the primary excavation devices used in the search for treasure and artifacts underwater.

McKee salvages one of the *Capitana's* anchors. Note the bent fluke that gives some idea of the storm's force.

A brass inkwell with the intertwined initials "AMGR" and a candlestick holder were among artifacts McKee recovered from the *Capitana*.

McKee moved much of the *Capitana:* ribs, ballast and cannon, to his Treasure Fortress Museum on Plantation Key, Florida so the public could see it as it originally looked.

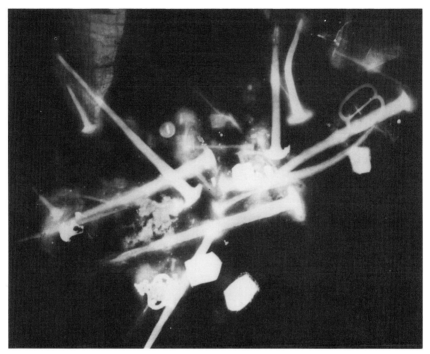

When McKee x-rayed a coral clump from one of the shipwrecks he found that it contained ship spikes, buckles and odd-shaped rectangulars of metal that are Spanish silver coins.

This 60-pound silver bar was part of the bullion from the *Maravilla* but McKee found it where a salvage boat had wrecked.

60 LB. BAR SPANISH SILVER BULLION

Besides treasure, McKee's museum contained a wide array of early diving helmets. His favorites, however, were the pair of Miller-Dunns on the right.

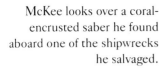

McKee looks over a coral-encrusted saber he found aboard one of the shipwrecks he salvaged.

One of three tiger sharks up to 12-feet long caught by the author and his companion fishing sharky Sebastian Inlet where Kip Wagner found his first 1715 Spanish shipwreck. Today, both treasure and sharks are still found there.

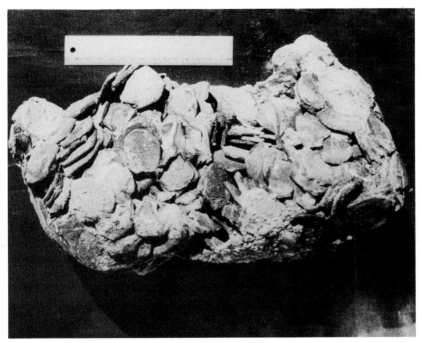

This corroded clump of Spanish silver coins is still fused in the shape of the sack that held them. At first, Real Eight divers failed to recognize them as coins.

Bernard Romans's chart spelled it out for the treasure hunters, identifying the wrecks as having belonged to the Spanish Plate Fleet of 1715.

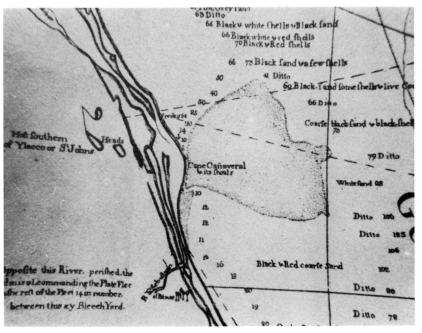

Wagner's Real Eight divers found the 1715 fleet's cannons lying so close to shore that the treasure had to be salvaged out of the churning surf.

Aboard Real Eight's salvage vessel *Sampan*, Wagner examines wedges of silver called "silver pies." He believed the silver was shaped to fit inside barrels that carried them.

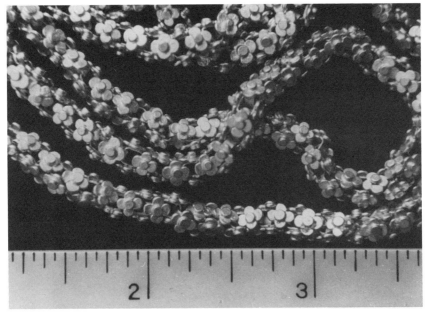

Closeup of dragon pendant's gold chain reveals four-sided gold links shaped like dogwood blossoms. The exquisite craftsmanship suggests that the artifact originated in the Orient.

This three inch long solid gold dragon with its elaborate gold chain was found on the beach opposite one of the 1715 shipwrecks. It later brought the treasure hunters $50,000 when sold at auction.

This display of Chinese K'ang Hsi period porcelain recovered from the 1715 wrecks somehow survived the centuries intact, speaking well for the oriental porcelain packing methods of the early 18th century.

The sensing element of a magnetometer is put overboard in a search for shipwrecks. This super sensitive metal detector picks up and records magnetic anomalies caused by such things as ship spikes and iron cannons.

These round, finely struck gold coins, thought by treasure hunters to have been made for Spanish royalty, were therefore called "Royals." Dated 1702 and bearing the name Philip V King of Spain, they were recovered from the Fort Pierce Gold Wreck. The presence of "Royals" on the beach suggested the source lay somewhere offshore. Such coins today may be worth as much as $40,000 apiece due to their rarity.

This gold disk typifies the so-called puddle ingots found on all Spanish treasure fleets that carried gold. Finger-sized ingots were also common. The numerals and dots signify that it has a 15¾ karat degree of gold purity. Other marks are tax stamps. This disc weighed almost five pounds.

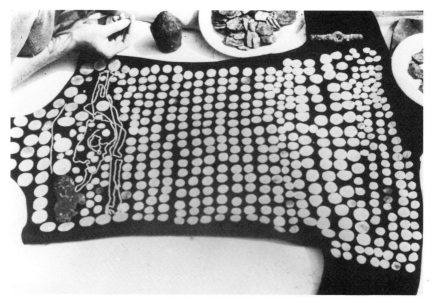

The morning's find of gold coins from the Gold Wreck lie atop a wetsuit jacket. They were recovered by Treasure Salvor divers. Also found were silver coins, gold chains and a cupcake-shaped silver ingot.

Struck by a 1715 hurricane, a Spanish Plate Fleet left its scattered wreckage and treasure from Sebastian Inlet south of Cape Canaveral to an area just north of Stuart, Florida. Its treasure is still being recovered.

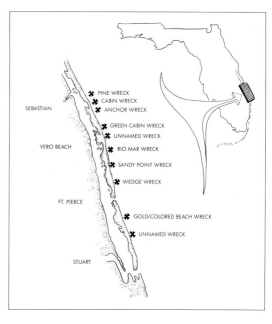

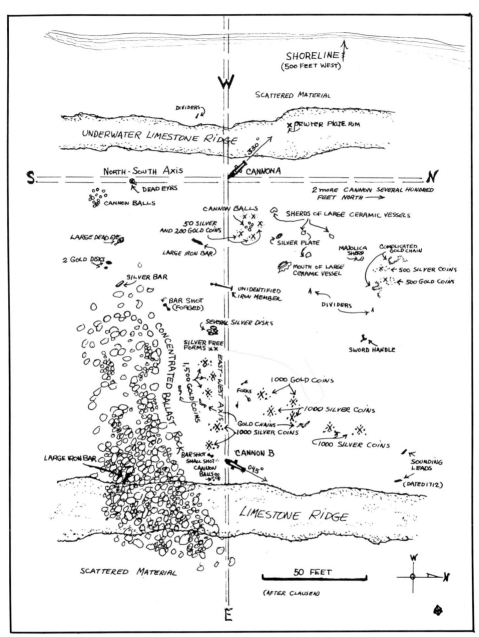

The careful work of Florida underwater archaeologist Carl J. Clausen and his assistants working with Real Eight successfully recorded where each artifact was recovered on the 1715 Cabin Wreck site near Sebastian Inlet. Their effort resulted in this overall view of the dispersal pattern. Evidence indicates the vessel split its hull on the limestone ridge resulting in the loss of ballast and treasure as the wreckage, driven by storm waves, swept shoreward in a westerly direction.

An understandably happy Rupert Gates of Treasure Salvors Inc. sorts silver coins in a vault of a Vero Beach, Florida bank.

The treasure chest found by diver Rex Stocker was one of 1,300 such cedar chests of silver coins loaded aboard the flagship of the 1715 fleet. It contained 3,000 four and eight real coins, fused into a 250-pound clump. State archaeologists used solvents to separate the coins and even duplicated weaving of the bags containing the coins from its pattern found in encrustations.

As Wagner did in the mid-1960s, treasure hunters with metal detectors are still finding coins and jewelry on beaches opposite the major shipwrecks of the 1715 fleet.

With a Whites Pulse Induction 1000 metal detector capable of use underwater, this hunter found a silver piece of eight near Vero Beach, Florida. When northern gales scour the beaches with storm tides, coin-shooters by the hundreds seek the widely scattered treasure along certain stretches of east coast beaches.

*Photo by Jim Ryan*

Diver Alex Kuze shows the elaborately designed solid gold tray he accidentally found while looking for lobsters near one of the 1715 shipwrecks. Experts believe it was fashioned by New World artisans. Kuze exchanged the tray with Florida officials for gold coins of equal value so that the one-of-a-kind artifact could be put on museum display by the state. Its early appraised value of $23,000 is today believed to be seven times more valuable.

Havana harbor was always a way-station for the homeward bound Spanish treasure fleets. This old print depicts it as it appeared in the early 17th century.

These ship models typify the kind of vessels used in the Spanish Plate fleets during the 17th and 18th centuries. Note how stern castles evolved from the high profiles of the older ships to the lower profile of those used in 1715 shown at lower right.

Searching the Caribbean for shipwrecks in 1956, Robert Marx participated in the salvage of a Spanish merchant ship, *El Matanceros,* lost off the Yucatan in 1741. These artifacts represent only a small portion of the recovered items. This vessel marked the first of his major salvage experiences with period shipwrecks.

Using a floating air compressor hooka rig, Marx found that the sunken city of old Port Royal was far different than its storybook account. During salvage operations there, the divers show some of their finds: an onion bottle, a silver plate and a clay smoking pipe.

This intact Chinese porcelain plate recovered by Marx and his divers from the sunken city of old Port Royal may have been booty of freebooters that occupied this pirate retreat at the time of the earthquake that sent part of the town into the sea.

A gold pocket watch Marx found at the sunken city of old Port Royal during his excavation for the Jamaican government. All such artifacts are currently on display at the national museum of Jamaica.

Silver pieces of eight such as this recovered from old Port Royal are of such fine quality they are valued at over $500 apiece.

Aboard his salvage vessel, *Grifon*, Marx shows some of the recently recovered treasure from the *Maravilla*.

Had these rocklike clumps been overlooked by novice treasure divers, they would have missed finding what Marx's divers discovered were 300 pounds of Spanish silver coins corroded in the shape of the bags that held them in the hold of the 1656 *Maravilla* wreck found on the Little Bahama Bank.

This old English print shows the Great Dock at Deptford that probably built the *Rose Algier,* used by Captain William Phips in his first attempt to find the *Concepcion*.

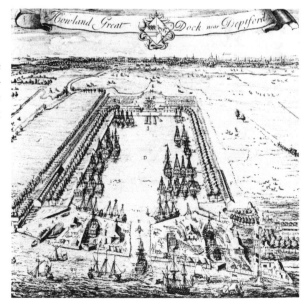

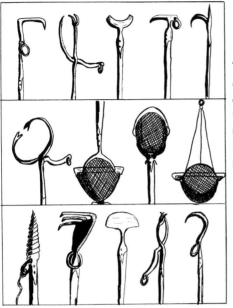

Though these may look like instruments of torture, they were the tools used by early salvagers working from surface vessels or crude underwater diving bells to salvage shipwrecked treasure. Captain Phips and others that fished the wreck site for treasure used such equipment.

Both sides of the coin struck to commemorate William Phips finding the *Concepcion* wreck.

Although this 1688 chart shows the location of the *Concepcion* wreck somewhere in the middle of the North Riff, modern day treasure hunters trying to find it realized that the complexity of coral heads there made such charts virtually useless to them.

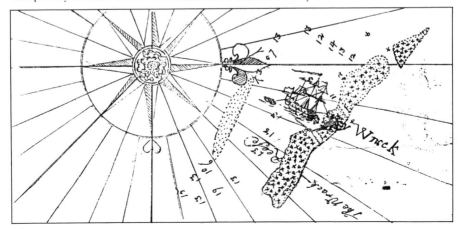

Geographer Herman Moll's notation and drawing of the lost *Concepcion* in the middle of the North Riff north of Hispaniola tantalized centuries of treasure hunters who tried unsuccessfully to find the legendary site.

Half Moon or Six Miles Reef was no stranger to shipwrecks, a fact that made targeting the *Concepcion* all the more difficult. This overview shows where Burt Webber Jr. and his men finally found the wreck.

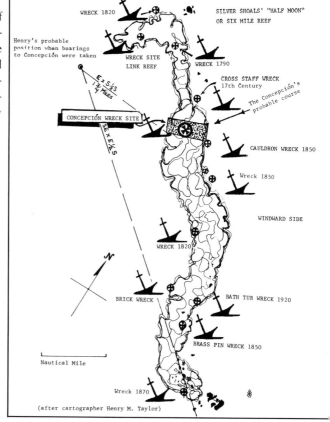

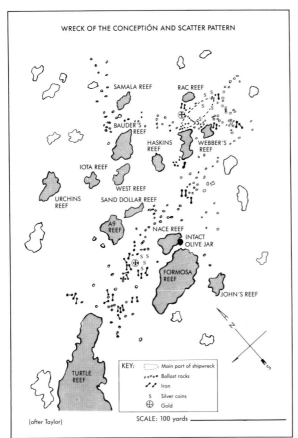

WRECK OF THE CONCEPTIÓN AND SCATTER PATTERN

SAMALA REEF
RAC REEF
BAUDER'S REEF
HASKINS REEF
WEBBER'S REEF
IOTA REEF
WEST REEF
URCHINS REEF
SAND DOLLAR REEF
A9 REEF
NACE REEF
INTACT OLIVE JAR
FORMOSA REEF
JOHN'S REEF
TURTLE REEF

KEY:
- - - - Main part of shipwreck
∘∘∘∘∘ Ballast rocks
↗↗ Iron
S Silver coins
⊕ Gold

(after Taylor)

SCALE: 100 yards

A closeup drawing of the *Concepcion* wreck site shows the scatter pattern of treasure and wreckage from the northeast to southwest.

Burt Webber Jr. (right) and diver-cartographer Duke Long compare features of their reef enlargement map to the actual reef.

*Courtesy Burt Webber Jr.*

From their detailed aerial map of the reef, Webber notes details that helped them identify coral heads at sea level.

Some of the Ming Dynasty porcelain, consisting of teacups and rice bowls, Webber's divers recovered from the *Concepcion*.

*Courtesy Burt Webber Jr.*

Spanish silver pieces of eight recovered from the *Concepcion*.

Webber poses with an intact olive jar found in the scattering of wreckage and treasure from the *Concepcion*.

This large diorama depicts ships of the 1715 Spanish treasure fleet caught in the hurricane that wrecked them all along the lower Florida east coast south of Cape Canaveral. These wrecks have attracted pirates, privateers and treasure hunters ever since.

An early artist shows pirates swarming aboard a vessel that has anchored for the night.

From *The History and Lives of Most Notorious Pirates*

Retiring to the balmy shores of Hispaniola to enjoy the fruits of their plunders, Sam Bellamy's followers may have created such a scene as shown in this old woodcut of pirates doing what they supposedly did so well.

From *Pirate's Own Book* (1837)

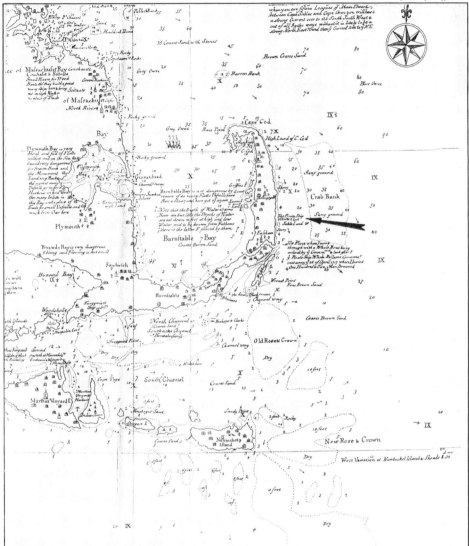

The black arrow points to the notation on Captain Cyprian Southack's Cape Cod chart where the "Pirate Ship Whido Lost." Armed with this document and pursuing other historical clues, Barry Clifford found the shipwreck almost exactly where everyone said it was.

Clifford and his crew pose with a conglomerate of iron artifacts recovered from the pirate ship's grave.

*Courtesy Barry Clifford*

Wearing a dry suit as protection against the frigid Cape waters, Clifford poses before picking up coins from the pirate treasure.

*Photo by Brent Peterson*

This silver sword hilt was found among the artifacts recovered from the pirate ship *Whyda* off Cape Cod.

*Photo by Brent Peterson*

Fulfilling a boyhood dream, Barry Clifford shows the silver coins and pieces of gold bars he and his crew recovered from the *Whyda* site.

*Photo by Brent Peterson*

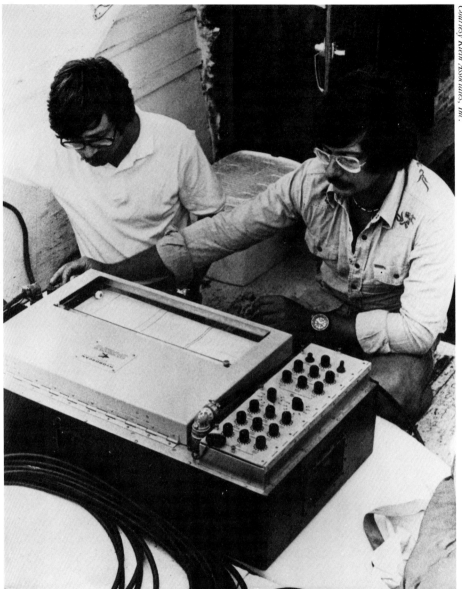

Among the scientific gear used to search for both the *Atocha* and the *Titanic* was a Klein Sidescan Sonar. Here, Garry A. Kozak (right) of Klein Associates watches a printout on a Klein Graphic Recorder.

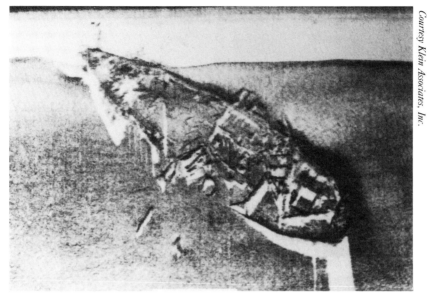

*Courtesy Klein Associates, Inc.*

Martin Klein's side-scan sonar uses sound waves from a 500 kHz towfish to scribe an almost photographic likeness of shipwrecks such as this Vineyard Sound Lightship sunk in 1944 in 75 feet of water.

This is the original "mailbox" blower developed by Treasure Salvors in 1964 to excavate holes by directing the prop wash through the elbow-shaped housing that was placed over the salvage vessel's propeller.

Translating old Spanish documents in Spain's Archives of the Indies, historian Eugene Lyon found vital information that pointed the way to the *Atocha's* final resting place. These clues sent Mel Fisher and Treasure Salvors hurrying to Key West, Florida.

Wearing the gold coin received as payment for finding the first gold chain tying their search to the 1622 shipwrecks, Don Kincaid (left) and Bleth McHaley were two of Fisher's followers who stuck with him through good times and bad until they finally reaped the successful treasure hunters' reward that marked the end of Fisher's golden dream and his 15 year quest.

During his search for the 1622 treasure Fisher's divers found the wreck of an English privateer or slaver. Mel shows some of the recovered artifacts including encrusted ankle shackles, a pewter flask, dishware, a tankard, and an ivory elephant tusk.

Moving the offices of the Treasure Salvors aboard this replica of a treasure ship moored at Key West, Fisher turned the vessel into a treasure museum to help pay for some of his treasure hunting expenses.

Underwater archaeologist R. Duncan Mathewson III, using scientific methods, sought answers to the whereabouts of the main deposit of the *Atocha* despite criticism from academic colleagues.

Two of several bronze cannons from the shipwreck added additional evidence along the trail to the *Atocha's* treasure. Since the cannons were bronze they failed to trigger a response from the searcher's magnetometer. The find was made accidentally by Dirk Fisher.

Sea turtles rubbing their backs against one of the bronze cannons wore its muzzle off at such a sharp angle it was called the "shark cannon" because it looked like a shark's profile. The site may have been a turtle roost since 1622!

A week after Treasure Salvors' vessel *Northwind* found the guns of the *Atocha*, the salvage boat sank, taking the lives of three crew members.

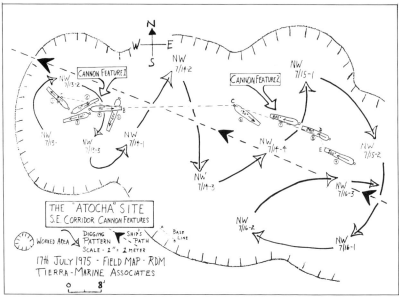

This field map by archaeologist R. Duncan Mathewson III shows each cannon position and determined the direction the *Atocha* was going at the time they were deposited. Although the ship's path indicated by the black arrows is correct, Mathewson and the others were to learn that the Mother Lode, the primary deposits of treasure and ballast, lay in the opposite direction of the arrows.

Gold "finger bars" such as this from the *Margarita* helped Fisher pay off a large part of his debt to early investors. The Roman numerals indicate that this bar has a purity of 21½ karats. Other marks are the Royal seal of King Philip IV. Since this bar lacks an assayer's "bite," a gouge of gold taken to test purity, it may have been shipped illegally as contraband, not recorded on the ship's manifest.

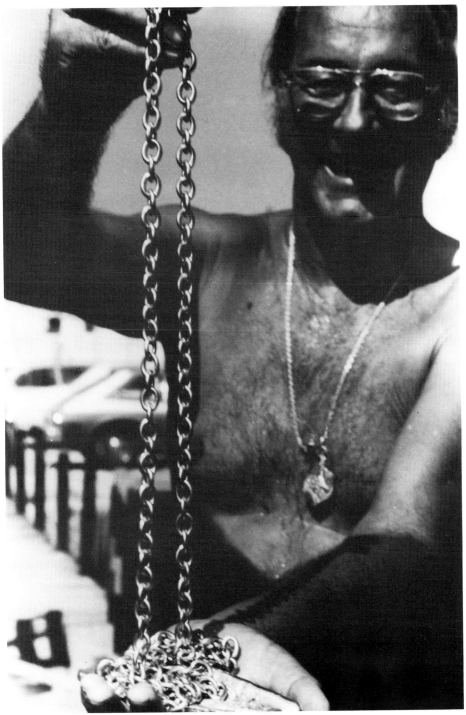

Fisher demonstrates how he enjoys slowly lowering a gold chain into someone's hand until he is adequately impressed by the weight. This too was from the fortunate discovery of treasure left behind by Spanish salvagers of the *Margarita*.

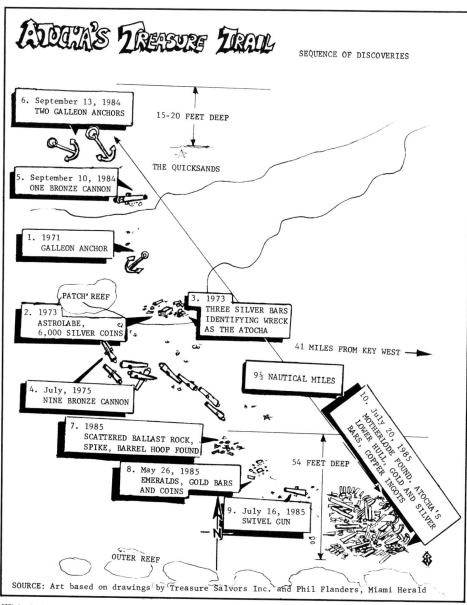

# ATOCHA'S TREASURE TRAIL

SEQUENCE OF DISCOVERIES

6. September 13, 1984
TWO GALLEON ANCHORS

15-20 FEET DEEP

THE QUICKSANDS

5. September 10, 1984
ONE BRONZE CANNON

1. 1971
GALLEON ANCHOR

PATCH' REEF

2. 1973
ASTROLABE,
6,000 SILVER COINS

3. 1973
THREE SILVER BARS
IDENTIFYING WRECK
AS THE ATOCHA

41 MILES FROM KEY WEST →

9½ NAUTICAL MILES

4. July, 1975
NINE BRONZE CANNON

10. July 20, 1985
MOTHERLODE FOUND. ATOCHA'S
LOWER HULL, GOLD AND SILVER
BARS, COPPER INGOTS

7. 1985
SCATTERED BALLAST ROCK,
SPIKE, BARREL HOOP FOUND

54 FEET DEEP

8. May 26, 1985
EMERALDS, GOLD BARS
AND COINS

9. July 16, 1985
SWIVEL GUN

N

OUTER REEF

SOURCE: Art based on drawings by Treasure Salvors Inc. and Phil Flanders, Miami Herald

This 9½ nautical mile trail of treasure and artifacts took Mel Fisher and his company over 15 years to follow. Despite the extreme cost in money and human lives, in the end, the multi-million dollar treasure was found.

Divers were bringing up gold bars from the *Atocha* as quickly as they were uncovered. The 60 and 70-pound bars of silver were not as easily lifted.

When they found the Mother Lode of the *Atocha*, there was all the ballast rocks Mathewson was looking for sitting among a veritable reef of 60 and 70-pound silver bars lying like a tumbled stack of cordwood.

The first few days of discovery of the *Atocha* were marked by a frenzy of salvage activity and catering to the demands of the media.

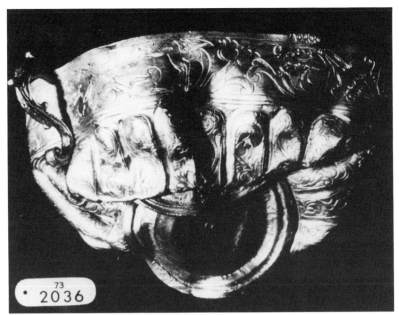

Shown crushed as it was found on the *Margarita* site in 1973 this finely made gold vessel came to be called the "poison cup" because inside was a compartment for a bezoar stone whose properties supposedly absorbed any poison that might be in the beverage, thus protecting anyone drinking from the cup.

Restored to its original form, the poison cup once held valuable jewels in the 20 cusps just below the rim. Dolphins shape the handles and a combination of flowers and mythical beasts comprise the outer etchings. Bezoar stones were found in the stomachs of goats and llamas. Belief in their magical powers apparently made them popular during Medieval times.

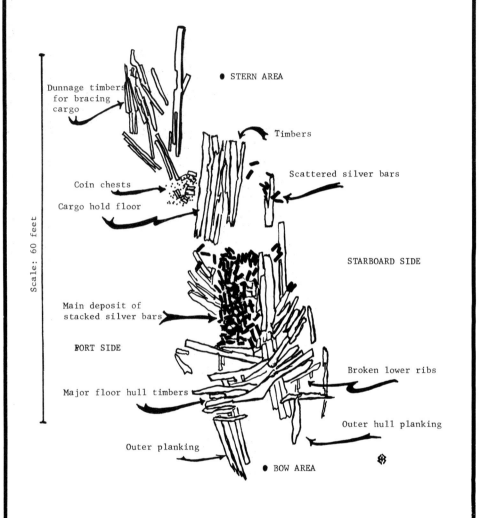

OVERVIEW OF ATOCHA'S MOTHERLODE (after Mathewson)

STERN AREA

Dunnage timbers
for bracing
cargo

Timbers

Scattered silver bars

Coin chests

Cargo hold floor

Scale: 60 feet

STARBOARD SIDE

Main deposit of
stacked silver bars

PORT SIDE

Broken lower ribs

Major floor hull timbers

Outer hull planking

Outer planking

BOW AREA

Overview of *Atocha's* Mother Lode.

This eight-inch diameter footed dish, believed to be a salver, was one of the beautifully etched treasure pieces found on the *Margarita*.

Uncut Colombian emeralds found at the site were displayed to the media in a Planter's peanut jar that held the fortune of remarkably high quality stones.

Studded with emeralds, including a 65-karat emerald from Colombia, this gold cross was found together with a large initialed gold ring set with an emerald in a silver jewelry box found on the *Atocha*. The back of the cross is engraved with religious scenes. Considering the exquisite nature of the pieces, both may have belonged to a high member of the clergy.

This plastic cuff lets visitors to Treasure Salvors' Key West treasure museum reach in and handle a bar of gold from the *Atocha*, but like the proverbial monkey trying to get his paw out of the jug while clutching a banana, it can't be done!

Like large loaves of bread, 70-pound silver ingots from the *Atocha's* Mother Lode line the walls in five bar stacks in the treasure museum at Key West.

Florida's southeast coast hosts so many old shipwrecks, including those of two major treasure fleets, that it is not uncommon today for beachgoers to find silver and gold coins on the beach opposite the wrecks.

These superbly crafted silver parts of a court sword are some of the treasure still being recovered from the Spanish treasure fleet of 1715 off Florida's east coast.

box on a raft" not far from the Hatteras lighthouse in the breakers, the young marine concentrated his efforts in this area.

Suddenly, on a seldom seen calm day, with the seas smooth as glass, Marx and his pilot buddy were making one of their many aerial surveys of area shipwrecks, when they sighted something with familar outlines.

"We flew over the area and, as I looked down, I could see at least a dozen wrecks scattered about like toy ships in the bottom of a bathtub," recalled Marx later. "I told Holland [the pilot] to fly over the spot where the *Monitor* was supposed to be, and sure enough, there she was. I could see the gun turret and the little pilothouse sticking up on the bow. The stern was half buried in sand."

They dropped markers and tried to reach the wreck by water. But a series of unfortunate events prevented it. After high seas and foul weather used all his leave time, Marx had to return to base without diving on the wreck.

Word of his find reached the ears of the press and resulted in *Life* magazine joining forces with the young marine in an effort to definitely locate the *Monitor*.

Though eventually he and a companion reached the site again, dived on it, and felt sure they had located the old Civil War gunboat, circumstances again prevented them making a positive identification. Many years later, when North Carolina's State Underwater Archaeologist, Gordon Watts, was compiling all the historical evidence he could find in trying to locate the *Monitor*, he retraced Marx's efforts.

He too wondered what the old-timers had seen in the surf near the lighthouse that made them think it was "the cheesebox on a raft." One day on a dead low tide, Watts sighted what appeared to be an armored turret. Closer observation proved it to be the vertical cylinder engine of the wooden steamer *U.S.S. Oriental* that grounded north of the shoals in 1862. Aerial photographs made of the site showed that the *Oriental*'s remains had deteriorated in a manner that did indeed make them resemble the outline of the *Monitor*.

This, or something similar, was apparently what Marx had found. The *U.S.S. Monitor*'s remains were later found by Watts and his team in 220 feet of water, about 17 miles southeast of Cape Hatteras in 1977.

The *Monitor* experience gave Marx a taste of the adventure he liked. It coupled library and archival research with the actual following of historical clues to the hoped-for site of the wreck. It really made no difference that his efforts failed to find the ironclad. What counted was the excitement of the search and the actual thrills of diving on the unknown.

Once he left the marines, Marx was free to savor diving adventures wherever he wanted, to travel as far as his mustering-out pay, his savings, and his ability to survive would take him. And he instinctively knew which direction that would be—to the Caribbean.

Having already sampled tropical sea diving, thanks to his assignment to the island of Vieques, Puerto Rico, for a short tour of duty to set up a Marine Corps diving school there, Marx lost all interest in doing any more cold water diving such as he had off Hatteras. The Caribbean offered unlimited visibility in waters so tepid one could dive in nothing but a bathing suit any month of the year.

Dive he did, almost constantly, from December, 1959, to February, 1961. He covered the Caribbean, ping-ponging from island to island, searching for shipwrecks with treasure on them. Through the years he had collected all the information he could about Caribbean wrecks and the treasures they held. Of some one hundred such wrecks, after his long Caribbean excursion, he came to the conclusion that most of them were figments of adventure writers' imaginations. Over seventy of them did not exist. Eighteen said to be in shallow waters, he later learned, had gone down well out of the reach of divers in the ocean's depths. The two he found lacked the millions in treasure they were said to contain. And *these* wrecks he had culled as the most promising from many books listing such sites.

Disgusted, Marx decided that, if he was ever going to get

any straight information, he would have to dig for it himself in the one true source of all such material, the Archives of the Indies, at Seville, Spain.

Once he glimpsed this treasure house of information it gave him a case of document fever so severe that it made his treasure-hunting fever seem like the sniffles.

Here was everything he had ever dreamed of, and more. He wondered how the Spanish ever had time to colonize an empire, because from the volume of documents left behind, they must have spent every waking minute scribbling down the details. They not only listed every ship and passenger aboard that left port, but they noted every nail in that ship and every slight detail regarding anything about that ship and what it carried—where it went, how it ended, and precisely what happened to everyone and everything aboard. And they did that for every official vessel for over 250 years! Talk about a storehouse of information! After a few weeks of trying to figure it all out by himself, Marx finally hired a number of Spanish researchers to help him. His accumulated notes filled so many packing crates and boxes that, after a few months, he was forced to move into larger quarters to accommodate it all.

In the course of his research, Marx began wondering what it must have been like to cross the oceans in a fifteenth-century ship. He had decided he would write a history of the entire Spanish fleet system. After all, there were the facts, every possible detail, just waiting to be organized into some form.

Marx thought it would make a tremendous history book. But when he mentioned his lack of understanding in exactly what it must have felt like to a fellow researcher, the latter suggested that he have someone build him a fifteenth-century ship and make the crossing himself to find out.

As farfetched as it first sounded, the idea appealed to him. He was being stifled by the book work and longed to get back to the sea again. Excitedly, he contacted individuals in the United States who might be interested in backing such an enterprise in exchange for the exclusive story. *The Saturday*

*Evening Post* agreed. Marx put his research aside and got busy on this new project.

When news of his intentions spread throughout Spain, he was soon contacted by a naval lieutenant from northern Spain who said he was building a replica of Columbus's smallest ship, the *Niña*, and wondered if Marx cared to join him on a sea voyage similar to what Marx was planning.

Marx agreed, then wondered if he had made the wrong decision, when he saw the *Niña II* and found it was only 42 feet long, instead of what historians feel was between 75 and 100 feet for the original *Niña*.

Nevertheless he signed on as pilot/navigator, along with eight others. The voyage was almost a fiasco. They had bad luck from beginning to end. Still, despite everything, using only instruments, methods, and materials available to fifteenth-century mariners, the men sailed the ungainly *Niña II* through adverse weather and depressing conditions for seventy-seven days, and covered 4,250 miles to reach San Salvador as Christopher Columbus had in 1492.

Marx felt he had accomplished what he had set out to do. He found out what it felt like to make such a crossing under primitive conditions. His articles, photographs, and lectures about the voyage helped finance his next adventures. Visiting the Mayan ruins of Yucatan, Marx saw old temple frescoes depicting European-looking men in galleylike vessels. He joined others who believed that the Americas had been visited by Old World mariners long before Columbus.

To prove this theory, he set about making another transatlantic voyage, this time aboard a replica of a Viking ship. As chance would have it, when Hollywood finished making their epic *Long Boats* film of Viking life, one of the longboats used in the film was about to be disposed of.

Persuading Columbia Pictures to donate the veseel to his venture in exchange for publicity, Marx boarded the slender ship in Yugoslavia, where the film had been made, and, with a selected crew, started sailing her down the Mediterranean.

They made it only as far as Tunisia, where heavy seas finally literally tore the boat apart. Marx managed to beach what was left, and it and his Viking voyage ended there.

Finding a ready market for his adventuresome ideas in such magazines as *The Saturday Evening Post* and *Argosy,* Marx finally decided he really wasn't cut out so much to be a sailor as he was a diver in search of shipwrecks. By 1964, he was diving the Serrano Bank in the western Caribbean in search of lost galleons, while writing features about a 1528 survivor who had Robinson-Crusoed there for eight years, living on rainwater and sea turtles. After further research at the Spanish archives, Marx armed himself with proper excavation equipment and planned some serious treasure hunting with companions along the bank. Unfortunately, however, the Colombian government opposed the idea, so Marx went to the one place where he had been going right from the beginning—Port Royal, Jamaica.

The Jamaican government agreed to let him excavate the old sunken city of Port Royal, which had tumbled into the sea during an earthquake in 1692.

Here, at last, after all those years of yearning in soot-besmirched Pittsburgh, after all those many days and nights of dreaming about sunken cities, where pirate gold littered the cobbled streets and a coral-encrusted bell tolled in the tides sweeping through the town's sunken cathedral, Marx was now about to live his dream.

Down he went in his diving gear, ready to explore the marvelous sunken city he had read about. He found it all right, but not quite the way the imaginative Lieutenant Harry E. Rieseberg who had influenced so many budding young treasure hunters, had written about it.

No cathedral bell rang; there was no cathedral. Nor were there gold-littered cobblestone streets. There was just lots of thick mud. The old tumbled-down stone walls and the few historical artifacts they enclosed, were buried beneath tons of harbor mud.

Undaunted, Marx and his small crew of Jamaican helpers

started excavating through the mud and under the walls. In the next two and a half years, their efforts produced a prodigious number of artifacts and hundreds of silver coins, all of which ended up in Jamaica's museum.

After that, Marx was ready for another adventure. The *big* one!

# Chapter 19

# Troubled Miracle

Within two months after he had terminated his Port Royal project, Marx was back in the treasure-hunting business, this time working for Kip Wagner's Real Eight Company in Florida. Although he signed a two-year contract with the company, agreeing to serve in the capacity of Director of Research and Salvage, in the back of Marx's mind was the intention of using Real Eight's salvage boat and excavation potential to locate a prize he had been researching for years—the long-sought, elusive *Nuestra Señora de la Maravilla*.

Surely it made sense that, when Real Eight's well-equipped salvage vessel, the *Grifon*, was not actively engaged in working the 1715 wrecks, he and some of the company divers could move it to the Little Bahama Bank in the northern Bahamas to see if they could spot the treasure wreck. Through his extensive research in the Spanish archives, he had obtained what the Spanish said was the shipwreck's last known location. Now he was anxious to go there and see what the *Grifon*'s supersensitive metal detector—the magnetometer—might turn up for them on the site. Surely, even if the wreck was buried deep under the sand, its cannon and other metallic parts would trigger the mag and lead them right to the spot.

For a long time, Marx thought he was the only one who knew the old coordinates to the shipwreck's location. Then he learned that others had also done their research and had also picked this key information out of the old records. But since word travels fast among treasure hunters, he knew others had visited the site, spent considerable time trying to find it with their magnetometers, and had been unsuccessful.

Shortly after he joined Real Eight, Marx was on the Little Bahama Bank with the *Grifon* and crew, systematically searching with all the electronic wizardry at their command. Weeks later, after repeatedly finding mag targets of buried metal that turned out to be modern wrecks or discarded debris, the hunters found what Marx figured were the remnants of the rudder lost by the galleon, *Jesus Maria,* which had picked up the *Maravilla*'s survivors. If he was correct, then the shipwreck was close by. Before they could continue the search, however, their invaluable underwater detector malfunctioned. They were forced to return to Florida to have the magnetometer repaired.

While there, the *Grifon* and Marx were called south, where a new pocket of silver coins had been found. For the next three months, the *Maravilla* was forgotten by everyone except Bob Marx, who resented not being able to resume the search for his ghost galleon, even though they were now recovering many thousands of dollars worth of treasure daily. But the demands of the 1715 wrecks prevented him doing much more than off-season aerial surveys of the bank in the hope of spotting evidence of the lost galleon.

When time permitted, Marx went back to Seville to dig deeper into the archives in search of more information on the *Maravilla*. On one such trip he turned up a key clue that explained why no one had found the wreck with their magnetometers. From the document he knew that the ship had carried fifty-eight cannon. That much iron should have created a big anomaly for the magnetometer.

What no one realized until now, as Marx learned from a new document, was that all those cannon were bronze, not iron, and bronze has no effect on a magnetometer!

No wonder no one found it, thought Marx excitedly. If the ship jettisoned its anchors, there might not be much of a ferrous target to detect. It was simple. Everyone was looking for a large ferrous target and probably had passed over the wreck many times without realizing it!

Getting home in mid-February, 1971, Marx itched to have another go at the *Maravilla*. Though he made several abortive attempts to prove out his theory and find the wreck exactly where the Spaniards said it was, another year would pass before he was back on the Bank with the proper combination of search and salvage equipment to do the job right.

On this occasion, Marx was contacted by oceanographer Willard Bascomb, who had interested Wall Street backers into financing a treasure hunt. With the old but reliable *Grifon* as their work boat, and an agreement with Real Eight to a 10 percent share of whatever they found in exchange for permission to work the Bahamian area already under a five-year lease to Real Eight, they headed for the Bank.

Once they reached the spot where the old Spanish documents said the *Maravilla* sank, they began a magnetometer search. This device is so sensitive to iron objects disturbing the earth's geomagnetic fields that it can detect an iron cannon or large anchor about 100 feet from the sensor. Therefore, the usual procedure when searching for such a shipwreck site was to tow the electronic instrument along parallel courses about 200 to 300 feet apart. But now that Marx knew the ship's cannon were bronze, all he might count on finding then were nails, iron cannonballs, ship fittings, and possibly an anchor. Relatively small pickings. A needle in a haystack. So instead of such wide spacings, they now made their runs just 50 feet apart. It gave them a better chance of zeroing in on a smaller target.

Still, the phantom galleon eluded them. In the next four months they covered 35 square miles of ocean this way.

"Whenever we found an anomaly," Marx said, "we checked it out by putting on a mask and sticking our heads over the side. If we saw it was a modern anchor, we kept going."

But over half the anomalies were buried beneath the sand.

After dropping buoys at the sites to mark them over a period of three or four days, the *Grifon* backtracked to each marker to dig down to see what had caused the "mag hit."

With anchors pinning the vessel in position, the searchers lowered the "L"-shaped blower over their propeller, so that its prop wash would be diverted to the bottom to blow away the sand.

Sometimes they dug down in this fashion to find the ship's chain. This meant that the ship had been modern enough to have been built after 1830, too modern to have been from the Spanish wreck. Three times they punched a hole through the bottom and found gold and silver coins. But they were from the wrong period and the wrong wreck. Marx said, "Let's go. It's not the one. There's no sense wasting time here."

Since the crew was sharing everything that was found, at times he almost had a mutiny on his hands, persuading them that they had to keep looking for the one target that would prove to be the prize worth waiting for.

And so it went, day after day, week after week, fourteen to sixteen hours a day, from the first glimmer of daylight, until the depths grew too dark to see their hands in front of their masks. And sometimes even then they went on by feel alone.

Then came their first break, and from a totally unexpected direction. In all this time Marx had been starting the search from the exact position where the Spanish said the ship had sunk, the same place from which he had started many times before. Near this spot was a modern shipwreck, one on which the mag crew would always get a small anomaly. Each day the *Grifon* passed this spot they tested their mag.

Now, after searching in all directions for 35 square miles around this spot, both with the magnetometer and with divers visually scanning the bottom for the slightest sign of wreckage, all they could do was return to this same starting point.

It was here that someone joked that maybe the *Maravilla* was buried under the modern wreck and they had been parking beside it all this time.

About then, a storm came up. Everyone had been at sea so

long they were short-tempered. Totally frustrated, Marx was ready to go home. As they hoisted anchor, there, caught in its flukes were two smooth Spanish-type ballast rocks.

"I told you! I told you! We're anchored right over the wreck!"

But Marx had already made up his mind. "Forget it!" he snapped stubbornly. "We're going home."

In retrospect, even he later realized *that* definitely was not one of his better decisions. It was more a case of being totally frustrated, completely disgusted, and ready for any kind of change. He even contemplated getting out of the business entirely. At least for the time being, Marx had hit his ebb of enthusiasm for finding the *Maravilla*.

Try as he might in the next few days, he could not shake the impression that maybe he had been a mite too hasty. After all, those were egg ballast caught in the anchor, the classic rounded river rocks commonly carried in the hold of Spanish treasure ships to give them more stability under sail. What if, in all this time, the anomaly from the modern wreck had fooled them into overlooking the one spot in all that area that they had failed to double-check? The more this possibility rankled him, the more he realized he wouldn't be content until he went back to the Bank and looked to see what was under those stones.

Four days of it was all he could take, then he was on his way back. Half his original crew had quit, but Marx had sweet-talked *Grifon*'s captain and another of the original crew members, David Edgell, a Fort Pierce teenager recently turned treasure diver, to hang in there with him. Even Marx's partner representing their financial backers was so doubtful of any success that he purchased only enough food for a couple days and refused to provide funds for taking on more than a small amount of fuel. Confidence was in short supply all around.

Early the next morning, they reached the red buoy Marx had left marking the spot. After breakfast, two divers took off in a small launch to mag the area on a fine scale, searching for small, overlooked anomalies. Marx grabbed a mask and snorkel and dropped over the side of the *Grifon*. Finning downward through the clear blue water toward the outlines of a reef, he saw what he had missed before.

"I swam through a large school of red snappers and then suddenly saw that the reef was covered with scattered ballast stones, ceramic shards, and small pieces of coral-encrusted iron objects. Grabbing a handful of ceramic shards, which included several olive jar necks, I rushed back aboard the *Grifon*, beaming with excitement."

The large jar necks from ceramic containers, typical of those used to store water, wine, and other foodstuffs aboard Spanish ships, matched the design of those from the *Maravilla* period.

*Grifon*'s skipper couldn't fathom why Marx was so excited over broken clay pots, until it was explained to him.

Back he went with scuba gear and goodie bag, loading up on more ceramics, including an intact olive jar, a big copper kettle, and a complete clay smoking pipe.

Topside, the others began catching some of the excitement, when Marx showed them his finds. The clincher was the pipe. It matched exactly the profile of a clay pipe in an artifact-dating handbook Marx always carried. The pipe he had found dated between 1680 and 1700!

Quickly they anchored the *Grifon* from three ways to hold her position, then the blaster was lowered over her prop and fired up.

In the widening hole that was gradually excavated, the divers began seeing more ballast rock and pieces of encrusted iron fittings. Hours later, after a dozen such holes in the area, they still had little more than ballast for their efforts. Then, after another move, Marx recovered more olive jar fragments and a beautiful Aztec jade ax head.

Despite all their efforts, the trail was still tantalizingly dim. They dug hole after hole, the blaster excavating 10 feet of sand in ten minutes, opening a 20-foot-wide crater that still showed nothing but occasional ballast rocks.

As first dusk, then dark, descended on the divers, only

Marx and Edgell were left on the bottom, groping through the soupy sand like blind men. The only way that one knew the other was there in the darkness was by the sound of the other's exhaled bubbles. Several times, Marx bumped into Edgell, scaring both of them.

But their determination paid off. As Marx pushed aside a ballast rock, his hand closed on a large, ornate silver tray. Just under it was a pair of silver spoons. He shoved them into Edgell's hands and signaled him to take them up.

Groping again up to his elbows in the black sand, Marx found something so strangely shaped that he had no idea what it was. Grabbing it, he headed toward the surface and the lights that the skipper had hung over the stern.

In the bright glare, everyone stared at what Marx was holding, as he climbed aboard to discover that he had found a scallop-shaped gold dish. Cemented to it by gray coral encrustations were two silver spoons, one silver fork, a silver inkwell, a silver snuff box, two pairs of brass navigational dividers, and a brass ruler.

The beauty of the find was startling enough, but Marx surprised everyone by carefully handing his find to them, then dropping back over the side into the ocean for still another attempt to find something that would positively date the wreck.

For the next fifteen minutes he moved ballast rocks, while his fingers did the feeling, probing deep into the sand in search of anything that might settle the issue one way or another.

Just moments before his air ran out, his fingers closed on a familiar shape—a flat, round object with the heft of metal. Clenching it in his fist, he shot to the surface.

Squatting on the fantail of the *Grifon,* almost too tired to move, Marx called for half of a lemon from the galley. Carefully he rubbed it against the coin. Slowly, the black silver sulphide corrosion on the piece of eight dissolved in the lemon's citric acid to reveal the coin's date—1655.

They had found the *Maravilla*!

# Chapter 20

# To Have and Have Not

That night, Marx lost sleep trying to decide where to dig next—where to put down a hole that would produce the most goodies. He was like a kid suddenly turned loose in a candy factory and told to help himself. He knew he was going to stuff himself with goodies, but he wanted to hit the best ones first.

The next morning, after repositioning the *Grifon* a couple of hundred feet east of the reef, the blaster penetrated about 18 feet of sand in fifteen minutes to reach bedrock. It was covered with ballast rock and pottery shards. Marx and Edgell were on the bottom, as the hole widened to reveal the muzzle end of a large bronze cannon.

Eagerly the divers helped the excavation project by digging away at it with their hands, until the 11-foot gun was exposed. A quick measurement of its bore diameter revealed that it probably fired an 18-pound shot. The long, heavy cannon was a type called a culverin, used as bow or stern chasers on early seventeenth-century galleons. Its ornate muzzle bore the coat of arms of Philip IV, the king of Spain. Near the gun's cascabel was its date—1651—and the maker's name, John Klep. Marx later learned that Klep was a famous gun founder who lived in Antwerp, Belgium.

Near the cannon were four ship's anchors, measuring from 5 to 25 feet in length. Next came a carpet of silver coins mixed with hundreds of small lead shots intended for pistols and muskets.

Moving the *Grifon* so they could blast a hole close to the first one, they found two more bronze cannon identical to the first. A third hole uncovered more coins and hundreds of encrusted artifacts.

By evening, as the divers climbed out of the water, bone weary from having spent more than ten hours on the bottom, Edgell suddenly complained of severe pain in his legs.

Marx suspected the worst—that the boy was bent. Normally, divers can work at depths of up to 35 feet for an unlimited time, without the danger of decompression sickness, or the bends. Anything deeper than that and they are limited to how long they can stay down without making decompression stops on the way up to breathe off residual nitrogen in their systems. All of it is clearly detailed in the U.S. Navy Dive Tables, which all scuba divers are trained to use. This time, however, in their eagerness, the tables had been overlooked.

Besides, it was a deceptive situation. Though the water depth over the Bank was only 25 feet deep, the *Grifon* was excavating down through another 25 feet of sand to reach the wreck. Therefore, the divers were actually diving to a depth of 50 feet. No one had bothered making decompression stops, and now Edgell was bent, and it could prove fatal.

They tried reaching the U.S. Coast Guard to see if a helicopter could fly him to a recompression chamber in Miami, but they were unable to get the call through due to bad reception. The only other alternative was to take Edgell back into the depths and see if his system would rid itself of the nitrogen bubbles in his joints that were causing the problem.

Marx took him down and stayed with him through the entire five-hour ordeal at different depths. The others lowered fresh scuba tanks to them each hour. When the pair finally boarded the boat around midnight, Edgell's pain was gone. But both shivered from the long exposure to the water.

Next day, it was back to the candy factory again, with Edgell restricted to only four hours of diving. Scattered among the ballast rocks now appeared several dozen human bones. With them was the lower mandible of a skull later identified as that of a male about thirty years old. Firebricks indicated they were near one of the ship's galleys. If, as Marx suspected, they were working the bow section of the wreck, then this might be one of the crew members rather than a passenger.

Among several hundred pounds of broken ceramics and coral-covered iron objects that they lifted aboard the *Grifon* that day were one finely shaped silver cup, a large silver platter, two clay smoking pipes, and several hundred silver coins including a couple twenty-coin clumps.

Most of the silver coins they found were pieces of eight or eight reales with fewer pieces of four or four reales. They had been struck at the main Spanish-American mints at Potosí and Mexico City. Nearly all were dated from 1650 to 1655, which was quite remarkable. Because of the crude way the coins ordinarily were struck, normally hardly one in a hundred was fortunate enough to bear a date. Those that did were always far more valuable to contemporary coin collectors. Marx estimated these to be worth anywhere from fifty to four hundred dollars apiece, because they were in such a fine state of preservation.

Digging just east of where they had found the four anchors, another one was uncovered. It was 16 feet long. Beneath it was a wooden pully block that still worked, along with a small 4-pound silver bar.

When Marx swam over to show Edgell his two new finds, he found him pitching ballast rocks left and right out of the excavation hole. Noticing that two of the things he had just thrown away looked different, Marx picked them up. One was a clump of encrusted silver pieces of eight weighing about 15 pounds and containing some 180 coins. The other one, smaller, weighing around 10 pounds, was also a conglomerate of coins. When Marx showed Edgell the clumps and pointed out the shapes of the coins in the encrustation, he saw the boy's eyes widen in recognition.

Later, the salvagers learned an interesting fact about the ballast. Not only did the vessel carry lots of river rock or Spanish egg ballast, but some of it was later identified as chunks of marble weighing 20 to 40 pounds apiece that had been quarried in the Tuscany region of Italy. Had the salvagers found only these rocks in the beginning, they may have thought they were working an Italian wreck and not pursued the search any further. Moreover, in port, some of the ballast was identified as pure silver ore. Marx later wondered how much of that had been thrown away as just another nondescript piece of ballast.

One of the excavation holes uncovered hundreds of Chinese porcelain fragments with pictures of people involved in domestic work on them.

The divers found a new excavation hole, about 20 feet across, littered with artifacts. Within minutes Edgell uncovered a complete sword, two silver pitchers, two silver plates, three silver spoons, and around two hundred silver coins. Next came two clumps of silver coins, a 5-pound silver bar, several iron pots, and hundreds of loose silver coins.

As the divers scurried to pick up the items, Edgell surprised everyone by showing them a gleaming two-escudo gold coin he had found. Then he popped it into his mouth for safe keeping. Marx hoped that in the excitement he wouldn't swallow it.

As the blaster widened the depression, Marx filmed the excavation with his underwater camera, recording finds as they were made. Even while he shot a sequence showing Edgell and his gold coin, the blower moved behind the diver and, through the viewer, Marx realized he was seeing the ends of five large silver bars being uncovered behind Edgell. Pointing them out, he filmed the divers scrambling to lift the 60- and 70-pound blackened chunks of solid silver, which resembled long loaves of bread left too long in the oven.

Finally, with all five bars safely aboard the *Grifon*, they checked the markings under the thin patina of black corrosion. From a copy of the original *Maravilla* manifest they learned which merchants had owned the bars. Two of them had belonged to a survivor, whose vivid account of the *Maravilla*'s final days had thrilled Marx when he read it in the archives. Now, here was the man's silver. It made the find all the more meaningful to the expedition leader.

Even Edgell's gold coin produced some hitherto unknown historical information. Until then, it was believed that the first gold coins struck in the new world originated in the Mexico City mint from 1679 on. This gold coin was struck in Bogotá, Colombia, in 1654. It was the first of many gold coins they were to find on the *Maravilla*. Years later, while researching in the archives at Seville, Marx learned that gold coins were minted in Bogotá as early as 1635 and in another mint in Cartagena, Colombia in 1615. Edgell's gold coin was the first evidence anyone had found to date of these early minted coins.

The businessmen who had financially backed Marx and his partners in their search for the *Maravilla* had contracted with the Bahamian government to share in whatever was found. According to this contract, the Bahamians were to receive 25 percent of the treasure. Whatever was recovered, according to the agreement, was to be deposited in a Bahamian bank in Nassau. Now, that the weather had worsened, the salvagers were interested in getting their booty under lock and key as quickly as possible, and Nassau was about five times farther away from them there on the Little Bahama Bank than was Fort Pierce, Florida.

"Trying to make such a long voyage in those rough seas just doesn't make sense," said Marx. So instead, they hoisted the *Grifon*'s anchor and pointed her into the storm seas for Fort Pierce.

The *Grifon* reached port safely at 2 A.M. the next morning. Leaving the sacks of coins piled on the galley table, Marx went ashore to phone customs. Upon returning, he found one of the crew members missing, along with two large bags of silver coins estimated to be worth at least thirty thousand dollars.

Though the crew member was later apprehended by the police, he denied the theft. "And that was the last of the matter," said Marx.

After that, Marx locked the remaining sacks of treasure in the trunk of his car and headed north to his home in Satellite Beach.

"The employees of my local bank were amazed when I pulled up and deposited over 500 pounds in silver bullion and specie," he said. One can well imagine that they were.

Marx later learned that, as soon as the *Grifon* left the wreck site, modern day pirates—rival treasure hunters—moved in and began their excavations. Two days later, the U.S. Customs reported to Marx that they had cleared a vessel through West Palm Beach bearing five large silver bars and several hundred silver coins, which were suspected as having come from the *Maravilla*. Classified as antiques over a century old, it was all duty free. Marx later learned the identity of the pirate divers and found they had sold each silver bar for fifteen thousand dollars.

Realizing what was happening, Marx did not tarry in port. Within 48 hours, the *Grifon* was revictualed, additional crew members were found, and she was on her way back to the wreck site.

Using two teams of divers, working six hours each, the salvors set about salvaging the *Maravilla* treasure with a vengeance.

This time, as finds were made, Marx tried to record the archaeological data as best he could, tagging recoveries, making measurements, and photographing mosaics on the bottom. Laying a grid of marker buoys, they started excavating with the blaster along the grid, uncovering hundreds of silver coins, musket balls, a scattering of gold coins, a 5-foot-long elephant tusk, silver forks and spoons, and many hundred pounds of lead shot.

One day, the blaster uncovered the top of an enormous ceramic jar. Beneath it were broken pieces of it intermingled with several human bones. Marx began working the site with a small water jet that gently removed the overburden of sand to reveal more ceramic fragments that made up a jar about 5 feet high and 3 feet in diameter. It had contained the remains of two complete human skeletons.

From the old Spanish documents that detailed the *Maravilla*'s cargo, Marx learned that it included the remains of two wealthy merchants who had died in Lima, Peru. Both had been preserved, placed in the jar, and were being shipped back to Spain for burial, when the gentlemen were prematurely buried at sea with the remains of the ill-fated *Maravilla*.

Months after they were found, Marx sent the bones to the American Embassy, so that they eventually could be laid to rest in the cemetery of their parish in Valladolid, 316 years later than anticipated.

As the excavation continued, so did the remarkable finds. One hole that produced broken Chinese porcelain and clay smoking pipes also yielded an uncut emerald. When Marx surfaced to show the others his find, he was shocked to hear several say, "Are you sure that's an emerald? We saw stuff like that before, but thought they were just pieces of broken wine bottles."

Marx quickly established a new rule: If in doubt bring it up anyway.

There was never a dull moment. Once the divers recognized the uncut stones as emeralds, they searched avidly for them. One of the divers had trouble keeping track of the uncut stones, which were about the size of half a Ping-Pong ball. The first time he found an emerald, he lost it. The second time he found one he put it in his mouth and accidentally swallowed it. Marx said it took 2 quarts of prune juice to get it back. After that, the diver put the stones in his face mask and came up that way.

Topside, the *Grifon*'s captain collected the emeralds in a jellybean candy jar and called the glistening green gems his jellybeans.

Periodically, silver bars appeared. Some were small, weighing only a few pounds, while others might weigh almost 100 pounds. Most averaged around 60 pounds, and in the early stage of their recovery, novice divers often dumped three or four bars into a lifting basket to be hauled up aboard the *Grifon*. The first couple of times this occurred, the lifting line broke and rained 60-pound silver bars down on the divers. After that, they hoisted the big ones one at a time.

Even then, minor accidents sometimes almost got the better of them. Marx and three other divers were working in the bottom of a sandpit beside the active blower, when all three of his companions ran out of air and had to surface for fresh tanks. Watching the blower excavating, Marx began to see the ends of silver bars appearing. At first, there were six of them weighing around 5 pounds each. He piled them in the center of the hole. Four more appeared. He stacked them atop the others. Looking up he signaled for someone to hurry down with his lift basket, while he continued searching.

As the blower widened the excavation, three more bars, weighing around 30 pounds apiece, appeared. Then another one, weighing around 80 pounds, was uncovered. Growing even more anxious that someone come down and help him with his finds, Marx looked up and saw the men strapping on their tanks. Even as he watched, however, sand suddenly started showering down on him and his finds.

The *Grifon* had shifted slightly and the blaster was devouring another crater in the sea floor, dumping its fallout on Marx, who was suddenly concerned about the bars being reburied.

By the time his companions were back on the bottom again, Marx was already buried neck deep in sand, one foot still on top of the 80-pound bar and the other on the 30-pounders. A quick shout to the surface crew stopped the blower and halted Marx being interred with his buried treasure. Quickly, his cohorts dug him and his silver bars out of the sand.

Not long after that, major problems developed for the treasure hunters. They began to hear alarming rumors that all was not well behind the scenes in Nassau. There had been some political changes in the government. People with whom they had made their original arrangements regarding the treasure's division and the handling of the finds were no longer in office.

They had been replaced by newcomers. Moreover, rival treasure hunters were pressuring these new authorities to give them possession of the wreck. Someone started the tale that Marx's group had spirited away tons of treasure and, instead of depositing them in Nassau, they had been smuggled into the United States.

Guessing that maybe it was all just about ready to hit the fan, Marx tried to speed up his operation. He wanted badly to find the main body of the wreck. With that in mind, one day he left the excavation in the *Grifon*'s small skiff with the magnetometer, and began searching on his own.

Three hours later, about 2 miles from where they were working the site, he registered a strong anomaly on the mag. Diving down, he found the tip of a large anchor fluke. Fanning sand from it, he recognized it as a large galleon anchor. Beneath it were ballast rocks.

Surfacing for a metal detector and a scuba tank, Marx continued surveying the bottom. Fanning near the anchor he uncovered seven pieces of eight. Excitedly he knocked the corrosion off one of them and found it dated 1655. Incredibly, he had found the main section of the *Maravilla*.

Hurrying back to the *Grifon* with the intention of moving the vessel over this new site, Marx was dismayed to hear some news. A radio report had announced that a Bahamian police boat was on its way to arrest the crew of the *Grifon* and take the vessel to Nassau.

Aware that they now stood to lose everything they had worked for, Marx was determined that no one else would benefit from his latest find.

Jumping back into the skiff, he headed quickly back to the site where he had found the old anchor. Diving down, he tied a line to it. Then, using the small boat's outboard engine, he laboriously spent an hour dragging the anchor across the sand bottom to finally drop it off the edge of the bank.

Returning with the magnetometer, he was happy to see that the spot no longer created a magnetic anomaly. Back he went to the *Grifon*, which was now making way for Fort Pierce.

They made good their escape, before the authorities could arrest them.

That night, as they entered Fort Pierce harbor, everyone breathed a sigh of relief. Their problems were over. At least so it seemed.

Their peaceful security suddenly ended in the abrupt glare of powerful searchlights from two U.S. Coast Guard cutters that drew alongside the *Grifon*. A dozen armed men leaped aboard even before she docked.

Ordered to raise their hands overhead, the crew was searched and ordered to sit in a group on deck, while the vessel was searched. No explanations were made as the boarders searched, even to the extent of tearing paneling off the cabin bulkheads and chopping up frozen food to see if anything was hidden inside.

Only hours later did one of the leaders apologize for their actions. Then he learned they had been boarded by five different United States agencies: customs, immigration, narcotics, FBI, and the coast guard—all due to a tip they had received from the Bahamian government that the *Grifon* was smuggling in over 20 tons of marijuana from Jamaica.

Such was the reprisal for their successful getaway from the Bahamian patrol boat.

From that point on, relations between the treasure hunters and the Bahamian government skidded rapidly downhill. The Bahamians demanded that all the treasure be returned to Nassau. Marx, his partner, and their backers questioned what was the wisest thing to do. Some felt that once the treasure was out of Florida, the Bahamians would seize it, and that would be the end of it. Others, however, felt that it would be unwise of the Bahamians to take the treasure when more remained to be recovered.

Marx and his partner hurried to Nassau to cinch an agreement that, if they brought the treasure back, they would be permitted to continue salvage work, while a definite date for a division was decided upon.

The Bahamians agreed to this.

All the recovered treasure was to be transferred to Nassau, but only half of it actually got moved there. Some of the treasure hunters were still reluctant to part with the whole pie.

Almost overnight, the situation blossomed into an international incident. Threatening to revoke their salvage license and claim everything as property of the Bahamian government, Darrell Rolle, the new prime minister, ordered the treasure hunters to return all items to Nassau within a week.

By the time the letter caught up to Bob Marx, he had less than twenty-four hours to get it all together and back to the Bahamas.

This he did, and afterward was told by the minister to either leave the country within four hours or be thrown into jail.

Infuriated, Marx hurried to the American Consulate, where he explained what had taken place. According to Marx, the consul said he had made a drastic mistake in bringing the treasure back to Nassau, because the *Maravilla* was in international waters and the Bahamian government had no legal claim on it. The consul telephoned our State Department in Washington about it.

In the following week Marx was contacted by different officials from our State Department, who guaranteed him that the salvors would get all the treasure and artifacts back and when they returned to the wreck site it would be with an armed U.S. Coast Guard escort.

After that, the whole affair bogged down in political threats and posturings. Suddenly, Marx stopped hearing from the State Department. Later, although the U.S. government sided with the salvors, apparently the Bahamian government suggested that they keep their nose out of the *Maravilla* affair or the Bahamians would have to reconsider whether or not they really benefitted from the twenty-odd U.S. missile tracking, Air Force, Navy, and Coast Guard bases in the Bahamas. It was the old squeeze play. When it came right down to it, the Bahamians had their way.

After almost eighteen months of delicate negotiations, the Bahamians agreed to allow Marx's salvage company back onto the site, provided that Marx and his partner were not involved in any way. On April Fool's Day, 1974, the treasure and artifacts that had been found up to then were divided.

During the following year the *Grifon* worked the site, close friends of Marx were put in charge of the salvage efforts. Again, large treasure finds were made. But once more, relationships between the salvors and the Bahamians broke down.

First, the Spanish government laid claim to ownership of the *Maravilla*. Then the Bahamians said they could no longer provide police protection of the site. Whenever the group left the area to unload her finds and restock the *Grifon*, rival treasure hunters jumped in to grab what they could. Eventually, with all the digging that had been going on around the bow area of the wreck, little remained to make it profitable for any one of the salvage groups.

Although the *Grifon*'s skipper knew the general area where Marx had found what he felt was the main body of the wreck, and had made many test holes searching for the site, it was never found again. As the *Grifon* sailed away from the site for the last time, others moved in to see what might have been overlooked.

Ten years after these events, I was sailing across the Little Bahama Bank with a group of divers when, in the distance, we saw a single small vessel, the only one we had sighted in days. Pulling near to see why she was dead in the water, we found a small salvage operation in progress. The salvors told me they thought they were working the bow section of the *Maravilla*, but were unsure. So far, they had found a few pieces of wood and a couple of silver coins so badly corroded, no dates were visible. It was not too enthusiastic a group.

For the moment it appears that the *Maravilla* has had her day—at least, until someone finds the after section of the wreck, the portion believed to hold the main bulk of the *Maravilla*'s treasure. If and when this occurs, then the merry-go-round will begin again.

# PART IV

## Burt D. Webber, Jr.: High-Tech Treasure Hunter

# Chapter 21

# The Secret of Silver Shoals

Over 70 years before the ill-fated Spanish treasure fleet of 1715 was scattered across the Florida reefs by a hurricane, the misfortunes of a similar armada occurred. These events were to be responsible for making an American sea captain an English knight and eventually the governor of Massachusetts.

On September 13, 1641, an armada of thirty treasure-ladened ships set sail for Spain from Havana. One of the flagships of the fleet was the *Nuestra Señora de la Concepción*, whose admiral was forced to sail against his better judgement. Before leaving Havana, he had complained that his galleon was not only unseaworthy, but that it was heavily overloaded with treasure. The ship's hull was rotten and had not been repaired since the admiral had set sail from Spain the year before. But it was the hurricane season, and the treasure fleet could delay no longer.

The galleons had been at sea for only a day and a half when the *Concepción* began leaking so badly that the commander ordered the vessels back to Havana for repairs. Divers immediately patched the *Concepción*'s rotten timbers, and twenty-four hours later, the silver fleet again put to sea.

This time it got as far as the narrowest part of the straits between Florida and the Bahama Islands. There it was struck by a severe hurricane. The *Concepción*'s ancient timbers were wrenched apart by the violent seas, and she began to take water. Her sails were shredded by the howling winds, and the crew was forced to chop down her masts to prevent the ship from foundering.

By morning, as the storm's fury abated, the galleon— miraculously still afloat—had become separated from the other ships in the fleet. With her pumps working day and night, temporary sails were rigged, and she tried to limp toward Puerto Rico for repairs. But the storm had blown the galleon far off course. A week later, the crew awakened in the middle of the night to find that they were surrounded by foam-flecked reefs.

When the anchors were dropped, the hawsers were snapped one by one, as the seas drove the disabled vessel closer to the rocks. Longboats were launched in an attempt to pull the galleon through a narrow channel between the shoals. All day the crew rowed, but the tide swept the galleon against first one coral head, then another.

By nightfall she had gained only a few hundred yards. Several of the galleon's twenty bronze cannon, tied to heavy hawsers, were shoved overboard to hold the ship fast until daylight. But during the night a wind sprang up, causing the vessel to strain against her moorings, until the lines parted.

The wind caught the galleon's high-pitched stern and drove her swiftly toward the treacherous reefs. With a grinding crash, she ripped open her hull on one reef and swung over to ground on another. And there she stayed, caught in the valley between two reefs, her prow sinking into 8 fathoms of water, while her stern rose into the air at a crazy angle.

The survivors huddled on the exposed portion of the wreck until morning, when they fashioned rafts from whatever was salvageable. These they dangerously overloaded with chests of silver and plate that had been stored in the admiral's quarters.

Then the castaways headed south in a direction they hoped would bring them to land.

Unfortunately, no one knew exactly where they were. The ship's pilot insisted that they had been on the Anegada reefs between Puerto Rico and Hispaniola when they had foundered. The admiral disagreed. He felt sure that they were still north of Hispaniola on the Ambrosian Banks.

As it turned out, he was correct. The few rafts that made shore landed at various points along the north coast of Hispaniola (the West Indies island that today is divided between Haiti and the Dominican Republic). Of the 514 people aboard the *Concepción* when she struck the reef, only 190 survived.

Strangely enough, Spain did not undertake salvage operations. This was perhaps because Spanish shipping at that time was under continual harassment by pirates and privateers, many of whom were sent out from France and England specifically for that purpose. In such cases, it was not uncommon for the admirals of stranded galleons to burn the ships to their waterline, so there would be less chance of their valuable cargos being discovered and salvaged by ships of other nations.

In the years that followed the sinking of the treasure galleon, however, many attempts were made by others to find it. Yet the exact location of the shipwreck remained a mystery. There was uncertainty even among the old sailors of the West Indies who claimed to have firsthand information about the wreck. To the southwest of the Turks Islands lay what the English called Handkerchief Shoal and the Abroxes. Was this where the galleon sank? To the southeast of the Abroxes lay the Ambrosian Banks and the "North Riff." Perhaps that was the place. Directly south of the Ambrosian Banks, about midway to Hispaniola, lay an oval reef known as the South Riff. That, too, was a possibility.

Ships of all nations searched these waters for the valuable wreck, but despite all efforts, *Nuestra Señora de la Concepción* might as well have vanished from the face of the earth.

On April 13, 1683, twenty-four years after the galleon had

disappeared, King Charles II of England commissioned two vessels, the frigate *Faulcon,* under Captain George Churchill, and the sloop, *Bonetta,* under Captain Edward Stanley, to find and salvage the *Concepción*'s treasure.

For three years they searched unsuccessfully before returning to England. Their only clue was the tale of one Thomas Smith, a seaman who claimed to have seen the Spanish wreck on the Ambrosian Bank. According to Smith, the galleon was located near a rock that rose nearly 50 feet from the ocean. The hull lay about 40 feet away, wedged between reefs that were "heaped high with sows and pigs [large and small molded blocks of silver]. Smith explained that his captain had not tried to salvage the treasure because a storm had come up, and the ship had to leave before it was washed into the reef.

Meanwhile, the man who was to solve the riddle of the lost galleon was sailing in another part of the world. He was William Phips, an American farm boy, born in Maine in 1650. He was a big, strong, fearless, kindhearted man, until he was upset. Then, it was said, he was a holy terror with boots, fists, sword, or pistol.

Phips had always been especially fascinated by the tales about pirates' treasure he heard along the American coast. He went to sea, first as a ship's carpenter, and later as the master of his own ship. Wherever he sailed, he collected all the information he could about rich shipwrecks and buried treasure.

Gradually, he accumulated maps and charts supposedly giving the locations of these lost riches. From sailors he met in his travels, Phips acquired a small treasure of his own—several coral-encrusted pieces of eight, some silver and gold trinkets, and a few bejeweled weapons. Armed with these modest riches, this American sea captain sailed to England, where he requested an audience with King Charles II. The good sea captain apparently convinced the king that he alone knew the whereabouts of the Hispaniola treasure, for King Charles lent him a small naval ship, the *Rose Algier,* and commissioned him to salvage the treasure.

The *Rose Algier* carried a crew of ninety seamen who were, as the salty phrase of the day went, "the rakings and scrapings of hell." But troublemakers soon learned that, despite their captain's outward good nature, he knew how to use his maullike fists and big seaboots. On one occasion, when the crew threatened mutiny in the waist of the ship, Captain Phips coolly surveyed the situation from behind the muzzle of a swivel gun mounted on the poop deck, and told the mutineers that it was loaded with pistol balls—"one for each of you." The mutinous crew retired to reconsider.

For almost two years Phips scoured the Ambrosian Banks and the waters north of Hispaniola in vain. His crew threatened to mutiny a second time and tried to persuade him to turn pirate with the *Rose Algier*. But once again Phips outwitted them. After that, he sailed for Jamaica and hired new hands to continue his search.

This time he sailed to Puerto Plata, a port on the northern coast of Hispaniola nearest the banks where the wreck was said to be. There he met a survivor of the shipwrecked galleon who gave him information that Phips was certain would lead him to the wreck. He searched the Ambrosian Banks again without success.

Finally, when his supplies ran low, he was forced to return to England empty-handed.

While he had been away, his benefactor, King Charles II, had died. He'd been replaced by King James II, who promptly had Captain Phips thrown into jail for obtaining a naval ship, as he said, "under false pretenses."

When Phips was released three months later, he went to see the Duke of Albermarle and once again demonstrated his remarkable persuasive ability. Not only did the bluff captain succeed in capturing the interest and financial support of the duke and several of his wealthy friends, but he obtained two ships from them—the *James and Mary* and the *Henry of London*—with which to carry on his search for treasure. His backers secured a royal patent granting them exclusive rights to the wreck, provided the king recieved a tenth of whatever was found.

Phips returned to the West Indies as commander of the *James and Mary*, a 200-ton ship carrying twenty-two cannon. Accompanying him was the 10-ton frigate, the *Henry of London*, with fifty guns, commanded by Francis Rogers, who had been Phips's trusted second mate aboard the *Rose Algier*. The two ships were equipped with the latest salvage equipment of the day. One account says they even possessed a "diving engine." If true, this probably consisted of a large lead bell-shaped device which, when lowered to the sea bottom, trapped air inside it, thus providing divers with a source of air, so they would not have to surface—all of which was the last word in the high-tech salvage gear of the day. Understandably, the optimistic Captain Phips felt sure he was on the verge of solving the secret of Silver Shoals by finding the long lost treasure of the century.

# Chapter 22

# Found Again, Lost Again

At Puerto Plata, Phips spent nearly a month taking on supplies, preparing his equipment, and trading with the inhabitants. Finally, on January 13, 1687, he sent the *Henry* to search for the wreck some 20 leagues to the north. Almost a month later, the frigate returned, and Rogers told Phips a long, sorrowful tale of failure. But even as he spoke, Rogers slipped a large oblong bar of silver from under the table where he sat.

Astonished, Phips stared at the treasure, then unlimbered a barrage of excited questions. Rogers hastened to explain what had happened.

"After fruitlessly searching the north side of the Ambrosian Banks, we sailed the *Henry* to the south side and, for safety's sake, anchored about a mile and a half from the reef in the latitude 23° 37′ north," said Rogers. "From that point, small boats were dispatched to search the intricate maze of reefs."

In one boat had been Rogers, accompanied by a diver and oarsmen; another crew with two divers had used a *periagua*—a cottonwood canoe capable of carrying eight to ten oarsmen for working close to the reefs.

For days they searched the surf breaking on the far-

179

ranging complex of coral heads, each night returning to the ship, which was moored safely in deeper water.

In late afternoon, on the last day of this discouraging search, one of the divers spotted an unusually beautiful "sea feather" growing on the bottom. Thinking that it would make an interesting curio, he plunged overboard to retrieve it.

Seconds later, he surfaced and shouted excitedly to the others, "There's a big cannon on the bottom here!"

Hardly daring to believe that they had at last stumbled onto the wreck, the diver went down again. This time he returned with a "sow"—one of the long bread-loaf-sized bars of silver with which Rogers had surprised Phips. Before marking the spot with a buoy and returning to the ship for the night, Rogers's divers recovered "two sows, fifty-one pieces of eight, a bar and a champeen, and some broken plate." They worked the wreck for the next three days finding more "sows and dowboys [bisquit-shaped mass] of silver" and nearly three thousand pieces of eight. Then the weather turned bad, the seas became treacherous, and the *Henry* returned to Puerto Plata with its good news.

Apparently, the reason the wreck had not been discovered earlier by searchers was because it had become completely overgrown with coral. Thomas Smith, the seaman who claimed to have seen it, said that the wreck rested between two rocks in 6 to 8 fathoms (36 to 48 feet) of water. Other searchers had possibly passed within an oar's length of it without realizing how close they were to making their fortune. Once shipworms disfigure a ship's recognizable features, and the sea layers the remains with a patina of coral, little is left to identify its original form. In this case, however, Rogers's diver recognized the ship's cannon, although they, too, were partially hidden by the bushlike soft corals growing around them.

Captain Phips stocked the *Henry* and the *James and Mary* with enough supplies for an extended stay at sea; then both ships sailed to the wreck site.

Again, the vessels anchored a mile from the reef and

longboats took the salvors to the shipwreck. There, sailors with long-handled rakes began fishing up bars and plate of silver bullion, while four divers descended 6 to 8 fathoms into the heart of the galleon to recover bags and chests of coins. To Phips's disappointment, his diving machine, the lead bell with its imprisoned chamber of air for the divers, proved useless; the wreck lay at such a sharp angle among the coral heads, that there was no practical way to deploy it.

Every day except Sunday for nearly two months Phips's men salvaged the treasure, which was carefully recorded and stored aboard the *James and Mary*. Hardly a week after they started, the ships were joined by two smaller vessels from Bermuda and Jamaica. Phips knew both of the captains from his earlier treasure-hunting ventures, so he agreed to let them join the salvage operations on shares in exchange for the use of their boats and divers.

A few weeks later, one of the visiting boats damaged a rudder on the reef and was forced to sail to Jamaica for repairs. Before leaving, the captain promised to tell no one about the treasure and to return to the site as quickly as possible.

When the sloop did not appear at the expected time, Phips began to worry. He was afraid the damaged vesel might have been captured by French pirates who freely roamed the West Indies. If this had happened, he reasoned, the pirates would soon descend on him like vultures, taking everything they had found.

To make matters worse, the daily routine of handling a fortune of gold and silver was beginning to tell on Phips's men. They knew that enough treasure was stowed in the hold of the *James and Mary* to make each of them wealthy for life. Openly they talked of taking over the ships and forcing the captains to sail for a port offering refuge to pirates.

Phips bided his time, waiting until he thought their threats were growing serious. Then he mustered the mutinous men on deck and told them:

"Hark to this men. At this very moment an officer is below

with a lighted fuse, ready to touch off a powder train to the magazine, upon my signal. Believe me, I have nothing to lose. If I return to England without the treasure, they will surely hang me. You men have absolutely nothing to gain, and everything to lose. If you mutiny, they will hunt you down and hang you, too. But if you behave yourselves and continue your work, I will see to it that everyone here receives a fair share of the treasure once it arrives safely in England. So, choose your fate!"

The would-be mutineers did not take long to decide which was the better course to follow. Grumbling, they went back to work.

Although he had handled this dangerous situation tactfully, Phips knew it was just a matter of time before his own men either turned against him or they were all attacked by pirates.

Finally, he decided he could delay no longer. He would sail his two ships to the Turks Islands, leaving the Bahamian vessel behind to work the wreck for an additional week. If the Jamaican sloop had not returned by then, the Bahamian boat was to join Phips at the Turks Islands.

A little over a week later, the Bahamian vessel arrived with no news of the missing sloop, but with more than a ton of silver that had been recovered from the wreck in those few days.

Phips paid the captain and crew of the Bahamian vessel, and then the two British ships set sail for England, where Phips received a hero's welcome.

According to admiralty records, the treasure he had recovered consisted of 37,538 pounds of pieces of eight; 27,556 pounds, 4 ounces of silver bars and cakes; 374 pounds of silver plate; 25 pounds, 7 ounces of gold, and a miscellaneous collection of less valuable jewels and trinkets.

True to his word, Phips set aside 3,070 pounds, 3 ounces of the treasure as his crew's share. The total value of the treasure he recovered is generally believed to have amounted to between one and two million dollars. The Crown received its one-tenth and the remainder was distributed according to the agreement Phips had reached with the Duke of Albermarle and the other backers. As an additional reward, Phips was knighted and given a royal commission to return to America as High Sheriff of Massachusetts colony. Later he became its governor. But before assuming this post, Phips had yet another task to perform for his backers.

Once the clamor over his astonishing feat subsided, Phips's backers wanted to know why he had stopped salvage operations, when there was obviously considerably more treasure to be recovered. He explained the circumstances surrounding his hasty departure. Now that word of the discovery was out, he urged that a full-scale salvage fleet be dispatched at once, before the rest of the treasure was scavenged by others.

His financial backers immediately agreed. This time Phips had no trouble enlisting support. Five months later, three ships were outfitted with trustworthy crews and divers. Two were heavily armed for protection of the third, which carried the chains, grapnels, powder, nets, baskets, dredges, and diving tubs—bell-like weighted tubs for use by divers in less coral-congested areas. Never before had England seen such a well-equipped treasure-hunting expedition.

When Phips reached the Ambrosian Banks, he was appalled to see a score of vessels already working the wreck. Seeing the British, many of the others hastily departed, apparently fearing confiscation of their valuable cargoes. Those that remained agreed to work with Phips in return for shares in whatever was found.

This time the operation was a disappointment. Phips had salvaged most of the easily accessible treasure on his last trip. Since then, hundreds of other treasure hunters raised as much or more bullion as Phips had. Now, the pickings were so sparse that, after a few days, even the vessels that had chosen to stay and work on shares quietly left.

Undaunted, Phips felt sure that all previous salvage efforts had merely skimmed the surface of the greater treasure that lay concealed in the heavily coral-encrusted forward section of the shipwreck.

The divers, working with pikes, could break off only small fragments of coral. Grapnel hooks dragged from above were equally ineffectual against the thick limestone shield. Phips attached an iron bar to the end of a 40-foot spar, fitted it to the prow of a longboat, and repeatedly rammed it into the unyielding barrier. For a month, he hammered in vain at the coral, by one means or another. Finally, he had his divers place a waterproofed keg of powder in the coral, directly over the treasure room. Next, he inserted a fuse into a long bamboo cane and had his divers attach it to the keg of explosive. Then Phips ignited the fuse on the surface and waited.

The experiment failed. The burning fuse had split the cane, letting in water, which dampened the powder.

A second experiment with underwater explosives was no more successful. Finally, the expedition returned to England with only a few pieces of broken silver bars.

Sir William Phips never again revisited the site of his greatest triumph. Instead, he returned to his wife in Massachusetts, went on to become a respected governor of that growing colony, and eventually returned to London, where he died on February 18, 1695.

Phips's feat in recovering part of the Hispaniola treasure became one of the milestones of treasure hunting. Yet, as time passed, the location of the site either died with the salvors or was forgotten by those who knew it. Any record of the location was buried in dusty archives by those who recorded it.

Ever since, treasure hunters throughout the world have searched the intricate maze of the remote 40-mile stretch of reefs north of the Dominican Republic, which came to be known as the Silver Shoals. Each hoped to find the treasure that Phips had missed.

In modern times, one of the better equipped and most publicized ventures was the team of scientists, archaeologists, and underwater specialists of Jacques Eves Cousteau's French oceanographic research ship, the *Calypso*. Although they found and excavated a coral-encrusted shipwreck, it proved to be of much more modern origin than *Nuestra Señora de la Concepción*.

Over the years, much has been written about the futile efforts to find this legendary galleon. It became almost mandatory for any treasure hunter worth his salt to make a pilgrimage to Silver Shoals to search for the legendary lost galleon. Not only did some of the more serious treasure hunters go once, but they went again and again. Everyone knew that, somewhere in that confusion of reefs, lay a fortune of undiscovered treasure just waiting for the man smart enough to find it.

Half a century ago, I too was one of the many who dreamed of finding the legendary lost loot of Silver Shoals. Moreover, after reading Colonel John D. Craig's enthralling 1938 book, *Danger Is My Business* at age eleven, I not only learned where the treasure was, but how to get it.

Deep-sea diver Craig revealed that he had found mysterious purple-black stains on the coral at Silver Shoals, which were, he suspected, caused by the deeply embedded bars of lost silver. To get it, one would have to dynamite the reef and blast it out. I filed that fact away for future use.

Unfortunately, I never got to Silver Shoals. It's a good thing, too, because both Colonel Craig and I would have had quite a head start on finding that treasure. The fellow who was destined to solve the secret of Silver Shoals and finally wrest the long lost treasure from its stony embrace, had not yet been born. In fact, he wasn't to put in an appearance for the next five years.

His name would be Burt D. Webber, Jr.

# Chapter 23

# The Making of a Treasure Hunter

Some 80 miles north of the large Caribbean island comprised of Haiti and the Dominican Republic, the sea suddenly changes. Its normally clear blue-green waters abruptly turn amber-brown, the color of old gold. For centuries this deeply hued 40-mile-long blemish has been as lethal to unwary seamen as a wartime mine field. This is the dreaded North Riff of Silver Shoals, a stony barrier of rocks and reefs reaching up through 50 feet of water to lie in wait for the unwary. Around these barely submerged sea mounts, the water surges, swirls, and boils like a witch's caldron. Most seamen go far out of their way to avoid the area.

Not so, however, for the small group of darkly sun-bronzed men moving gingerly through the surging waters of the hidden coral heads in three inflatable boats the *Good Guys*, the *Bad Guys*, and the *Uglies*. The men were seeking the treasure of Silver Shoals. They had found the key to unlocking the mystery. It had narrowed their search down from the thousands of reefs in that 40-mile swatch to no more than 400 yards—to a place at which, according to one seventeenth-century searcher, the coral heads formed what resembled a half-moon.

From dawn until dusk, for nine long days, the divers had worked their way slowly through the underwater rocky maze, looking for that particular configuration, while their hand-held high-tech detectors probed into the dark recesses of the inner reef itself. Their unique instruments electronically sniffed for clues to the prize they sought.

In the preceding days, the clues had ranged from non-existant to scant. All they had found was an occasional smooth oval ballast rock. But it was egg ballast, the kind carried by the old Spanish galleons. Almost all of the divers had found at least one such rock—everyone, that is except Jim Nace, a college senior and aspiring doctor from Lebanon, Pennsylvania. Though Nace, twenty-five, was relatively new to the hardships of treasure hunting, this was not the case with one of his companions swimming a few feet away. Thirty-six-year-old Burt Webber was a pro, an unsuccessful treasure hunter, but nonetheless a seasoned professional. So far, he had gotten that way by devoting much of his life to the hunt.

Now, shortly after 1 P.M., on November 30, 1978, as they slowly swam through the tepid water 45 feet below the seething surface, Nace, Webber, and their companion, Don Summer of Missouri, surely must have been reflecting on the apparent hopelessness of their efforts. Here they were, many hundreds of miles from home, poking under a dangerous and extremely remote chunk of rocky underwater real estate, looking for a shipwreck that no longer existed. It was one whose members had long ago been digested by centuries-old sea worms, the termites of the deep. "How crazy can you get?" they must have wondered.

Nace, just a few feet from Webber, was letting his eyes roam over the broken bottom rubble, when suddenly he spied his first ballast stone. His garbled exclamation lost in a burst of exhaust bubbles, he darted down and grabbed it. Triumphantly picking it up to show the others, Nace spotted something under the stone that forevermore would earn him the nickname "Lucky."

It was an encrusted silver coin!

Clutching it, Nace swam over and tapped Webber on the shoulder.

Webber turned. Nace held up the coin. Behind his mask Webber's eyes widened. Grabbing Nace, he hugged him, then snatched the coin away from him and whooshed to the surface.

As his head cleared the water, Webber saw his companions staring at him from the *Good Guys*'s inflatable. He held high the coin and shouted, "Praise God!" echoing the words Captain Phips reportedly cried upon seeing the first treasure from the *Concepción*. "Praise God! We are made!"

Now, 291 years later, so were the Good Guys, the Bad Guys, and the Uglies. Everyone shouted and laughed.

How this all came about creates a fairly accurate blueprint for the making of a typical modern-day treasure hunter—one who never pioneered it, never inherited it, nor even had the good fortune of having been born beside the sea. Already with three strikes against him, Burt Webber, Jr. was born in land-locked central Pennsylvania in 1942. His ancestry is Pennsylvania "Dutch," but right from the beginning, his interests were atypical of most German-American youths growing up in middle America with single-minded practical purposefulness. He differed from his neighbors in the small highly respected community that represented not only his hometown, but his whole world.

Then, at the tender age of six, this young rebel found a way to put windows in his world, to look beyond the physical confines of his hometown to a way of life that was totally different. For years, all he could do was fantasize about it.

"It began," said Webber, "when I was about six years old and developed a fascination with water. We had a mountain stream running into a mill and I would swim in it, fantasizing about being on the bottom instead of the top. About the same time, I began reading books on shipwrecks, and I knew I wanted to dive."

As a youngster, the closest hobby Webber could conceive of that was anything like treasure hunting was coin collecting. At sixteen he sold his coin collection to buy a scuba tank, then learned to dive with it in local stone quarries. These experiences helped satisfy some of his budding treasure hunting fever. There, in the depths of the deep dark cold-water stone quarry, he found his first treasure—a beat-up slot machine. Had it been a corroded iron chest full of Spanish doubloons, young Burt Webber would not have been happier.

As one chronicler explained, "Webber always wanted to be a treasure hunter—an obsession fed early by children's books and sustained ever since. A boy with his head full of nonsense, who liked to dive in local stone quarries, might be forgiven by his family and friends, even in a small Pennsylvania town. But it was a different matter when he left school at eighteen and refused to do the conventional thing and go to college."

Instead, Webber decided the best way for him to see the world, especially the watered down part of it, was to join the U.S. Navy. He tried to enlist, but failed the physical, because of his recurring bouts with asthma.

Dejected, but not enough to make him tuck his tail and trot home to try and fit himself into the conventional mold, Webber enrolled instead in the Divers Training Academy in Miami.

"That was in 1960," he recalled, "and people were coming to the academy trying to hire mercenaries for the Cuba situation. I thought about it, until someone told me, 'The money is big, but you don't come back to spend it.' "

With Webber's interest and living in south Florida, it was not long before he met pioneer treasure hunter, Art McKee, at his Museum of Sunken Treasure in the Keys.

McKee's museum was a fascinating storehouse of deep-sea diving and treasure-hunting memorabilia collected after a lifetime of seafaring adventures both above and below the sea. Gazing at the array of old hard-hat diving helmets, coral-encrusted anchors, pistols and swords, bits and pieces of shipwrecks, accompanied by a scattering of pieces of eight and big bars of solid silver bearing cryptic markings, here, at last, Webber found the realities of his fantasies. His own youthful fires fanned by the flames of McKee's enthusiasm for treasure-hunting adventures under the sea, Webber was solidly hooked. The following year, he joined McKee and others in one of their efforts to salvage an eighteenth-century shipwreck off Jamaica. As usual, the group found lots of artifacts, but no treasure.

From then on, Burt Webber began paying his dues to his chosen profession.

It was the endless hunt. One expedition after another, each searching for the same elusive goal—a Spanish shipwreck with some exotic name, which hopefully contained treasure. Neither their names nor where they were made much difference to Webber. What counted was their reputation for having hauled treasure in their creaking holds.

After a dozen such expeditions to far-flung areas of the Caribbean, always looking for that pot of treasure at the end of the rainbow, Webber too often had to summarize ventures with the terse comment that, "Some met expenses."

Between expeditions, while learning what it is like to become a full-time treasure hunter with no treasure, Webber returned home frequently enough to acquire a wife and four children. Between serious bouts of treasure-hunting fever, he supported his family the best way he could by working a variety of jobs, which included brickmaker, welder, and encyclopedia salesman. One can well imagine that to his staid Pennsylvania Dutch neighbors in his hometown of Annville, Pennsylvania, he was truly an enigma, a ne'r-do-well, a man whom the intensely proper bourgeois community looked down upon as both a folly and a failure.

But Webber was a man with talents far removed from the one-dimensional life in this starched-collar insular American community. Even within its conventional confinements, Webber sharpened his abilities, which would pay dividends later when he used them.

There was selling encyclopedias, for example. Not just

anyone is a crackerjack encyclopedia salesman. It takes a special talent to be able to sell both yourself and your product. Webber learned to do this so well that he won an award as an encyclopedia salesman. Though he had no way of knowing it then, his next award for salesmanship would win him the biggest prize of all—the *Concepción* treasure.

Long before this was to occur, however, Webber still had to fulfill his apprenticeship. One of the more famous shipwrecks on which he practiced was the now eminently famous *Nuestra Señora de Atocha*.

Intermittently for nearly ten years, Webber searched for this fabled Spanish shipwreck, following the same false trails that led many another treasure hunter astray. As it had for so many before him, the prize of Spain's 1622 fleet was elusive. He failed to find it.

Meanwhile, Mel Fisher, an already successful treasure hunter after his finds from the 1715 fleet, found the *Atocha*'s first scattering of treasure—enough to indicate that he was at least within reach of her final resting place.

More than ever, Webber tasted the bitterness of failure. Losing out on the *Atocha*, after looking for so long, was an intense disappointment to him.

"It was like a courtship with a beautiful woman, then someone else gets her," he reflected, his deep voice suddenly somber. "It had a heavy effect on me. I was almost to the breaking point. I asked myself, how much could I learn about another ship?"

Webber's disappointment over losing the *Atocha* was compounded by the fact that he was now also broke. He returned to his wife, Sandy, and their children in Annville, and on the surface he seemed to be fitting himself back into the conventional mold. For the next two years, he made bricks in a factory and sold encyclopedias.

Despite these seemingly conventional activities, Webber never ceased trying to make inroads into the profession that held his greatest interest. He made up his mind, "to shoot for a big one. I couldn't see being a scavenger anymore. I didn't want to sail in someone else's wake."

A decade earlier, Webber had joined forces with another Florida treasure hunter—Jack Goin Haskins, a forty-four-year-old independent treasure hunter, who was a rarity among the average run of treasure hunters. A former commercial airline pilot, Haskins early on realized that the key to successful treasure hunting had to begin with good archival research. The Archives of the Indies in Seville was a treasure house of this information, if one knew how to get it. All the early records were there, painstakingly written in an archaic Spanish, in which all the words were linked together in longhand on friable paper. The paper was so badly worm-eaten that there was often more air than paper to a page. The centuries-old, barely legible brown ink scrawls, bleeding through from one side to the other, defied the best of eyesight, even if one did learn to read the text.

Few people in the world were proficient at reading these ancient records. Yet, with stubborn Irish persistence, Haskins taught himself how to read them. Eventually, he became Webber's researcher, making annual trips to Spain to study the archives, in search of "the big one" that would make them all rich.

Webber sought to get leases from Spain that would allow him to search for galleons in Spanish waters. Spain failed to cooperate and Webber abandoned this idea.

Meanwhile, Haskins began turning up more information in the archives about the loss of *Nuestra Señora de la Concepción*. Naturally, everyone in treasure-hunting circles knew of the legendary lost galleon that Captain Phips had found and salvaged. When Haskins mentioned the possibility that they might make the *Concepción* their target, Webber was dubious. He had read Phips's story and found it boring. His initial attitude was, "Who cares?"

Webber really suspected that little treasure was left. Phips and a host of others had picked its bones for too long a time to make it a worthy prize, despite the prestige that would go with finally finding and solving the mystery of its whereabouts.

Haskins's research, however, seemed to indicate otherwise. He felt that there was treasure aplenty still left, because it had been too difficult for early salvagers to find and recover. Moreover, Haskins had been so fascinated by the story of the *Concepción* and Captain Phips since childhood, that he had already collected quite a file of material on the subject. He offered Webber use of this material and continued research on the subject in the archives in return for a share in any profits from the eventual recovery, when and if the site was found.

Persuaded that maybe Haskins knew what he was talking about, Webber agreed that the *Concepción* was to be their next best prospect. But Webber had no intention of making his treasure hunt in the same pattern of the hundreds of such hunts that had gone on before. Each of them had proved to be ill-fated, ill-planned, ill-researched, and technologically ill-equipped. After all, this was the "space age" and enormous advances had been made in the development of marvelous electronic detection equipment in recent years. Not to tap these resources was unthinkable to Webber, and this attitude set him head and shoulders above all treasure hunters before him, who had challenged Silver Shoals and failed.

But how would he do it? How would he pull the rabbit out of the hat?

Haskins's research narrowed the hunt to a 46-mile-long section of Silver Shoals. Somewhere in those convoluted reefs the treasure ought to lie. What hope was there of pinpointing the wreck?

By now, Webber was an old hand at technological innovations. Often not satisfied with the available equipment, he modified it to his own requirements. Thus, he had already invented special housings for underwater gear that were being used by the oil industry and other treasure hunters. Now he had an idea that perhaps by using scientifically enhanced aerial photographs some clue might be revealed about the reefs that would help narrow their search.

Though others said it was highly unlikely to succeed and that it was a wasted effort, Webber hired an airplane and photographer to produce a mosaic of aerial photographs showing the thousands of reefs in the 46-mile section of reefs believed to contain the wreck.

Webber proposed surveying the most likely-looking reefs with a magnetometer, trailing the sensor underwater from a shallow draft surface vessel, the supersensitive detector seeking metal anomalies that might pinpoint the *Concepción*'s remains. After that, divers with hand-held metal detectors would zero in on the goodies.

Such was the original plan. All it required now was lots of big money. The question was how could this part-time bookseller, brickmaker, and welder raise it?

How indeed. When Webber asked himself the same question, he already hoped he knew the answer. He hadn't won a prize for selling encyclopedias for nothing!

# Chapter 24

# Operation Phips

Webber had been in the treasure-hunting business long enough to know the kind of costs that would be involved in setting up the proper kind of expedition he needed to search for and salvage the *Concepción*. Most such ventures failed because they were poorly financed. Not only did the salvors have to sustain themselves throughout a long search of reefs located 80 miles from their closest supply base, but, even if the wreck were found, what usually followed entailed a series of unending, extremely costly delays. From the time any treasure was salvaged to the time the treasure hunters would realize any monetary rewards for their work might actually run into years of frustration. Meanwhile, there were the daily salaries and bills to be paid, not to mention possibly lengthy legal squabbles with contending claimants to the ownership of the treasure. After these problems were solved, the treasure would then have to be first shared with the country claiming ownership of it. Then a large part of the remainder would go to the tax people. After all this, somewhere far down the line after more frustrating delays, what was left would be divided among the expedition's investors.

Webber envisioned a treasure-hunting company so massively financed that it would run similar to a petroleum-prospecting operation—one so well funded that it could hire the best of everything—boats, planes, crews, high-tech exploration equipment, lawyers, accountants, and tax experts.

Though Webber had never been a successful treasure hunter, he believed steadfastly in what he was about to undertake. On his side was the archival evidence that the treasure existed on the shipwreck that just waited to be found, that the high-tech equipment available would make it possible for them to find it, and that his companions could provide sufficient skills, expertise, and sheer determination to make it all happen. All would be possible, providing they could find the proper funding.

In 1976 Webber walked into the office of Warren Stearns, a prematurely white-bearded investment banker who headed an investment organization called the December Group.

"Here's my plan," he said, as he laid out on the table the research, the charts, and the technology that he would use.

Stearns, an expert on bonds, oil leases, and dollars and cents, knew little about coral, the *Concepción*, or magnetometers, but he did know a lot about men, risks, and financial ventures.

Webber impressed him. So did the obviously well-done research and the technological knowledge Webber claimed to possess. But the Harvard educated, hardheaded chairman of the Chicago firm of investment bankers wanted someone else's more expert opinion on these matters.

He asked Dr. Richard M. Foose, a former Lancaster, Pennsylvania resident, who taught geology at Franklin and Marshall College and whose specialty was underwater geology, to check Webber's plans.

Stearns told Webber, "Sell Foose and you've got it."

Foose called Stearns back within a few days.

"He said he had three things to tell me," recalled Stearns later. "One was that Burt was the world's expert on magnetometers. That's an incredible statement. That meant that he knew more than Foose. The second thing was that the plan would work. And the third was that Foose wanted to be the expedition's scientific advisor."

After that, there was no question but that Webber had found his Duke of Albemarle. Stearns, backed by a consortium of thirty investors, raised four-hundred-and-fifty-thousand dollars and formed a corporation known as Seaquest International.

Stearns had convinced his investors that treasure hunting could be run like any other big business. Its success was based on the risking of capital supplied by extremely wealthy men, who were well aware that the existing tax laws would allow them to write off these investments. At the most, it offered them a chance of increasing their investments; at the very least, to be able to share vicariously in the excitement of the treasure hunt, with its added inducement of expense-paid vacations to the West Indies.

Everyone was happy. Webber got his funding; Foose got his position on the team as scientific advisor; and the expedition, code-named Operation Phips, got underway.

It was important to establish who owned the treasure once it was found. Webber knew that it was best to settle this on paper, fully documented and legalized before anything else was done. It made no sense to find a treasure, only to lose it to the competition claiming ownership.

Quite clearly, Silver Shoals, some 80 miles north of the Dominican Republic, was in international waters. Normally, such an area would be defined as the "high seas." But this was not the case when the matter came up before the three countries lying closest to the bank—the Dominican Republic, Haiti, and the Turks and Caicos Islands. All claimed the area. Since the closest by some 30 miles was the Dominican Republic, which also had sufficient naval strength to support this sovereignty claim, Webber, his lawyer, and a Spanish-speaking assistant headed to Santo Domingo to see what kind of deal might be arranged.

The Dominican government drove a harder bargain than

they had anticipated. It wanted half of everything found. Realizing the value of a good relationship with the powers that be, there was no doubt that the partners would have to accept their offer. At least, when they found the treasure, it would be good to know that the Dominican naval vessels could share in fending off any modern-day pirates who might be tempted to sample the goodies.

The task now was to try and pinpoint the most likely area to search in the 40-mile stretch of the North Riff. From the aerial mosaic Webber now had a chart made. It was to be the most accurate bird's-eye view of the Bank that anyone had ever seen. It revealed the exact layout of the North Riff, and from it, they now saw that it was comprised of three main portions of coral heads separated by deep-water channels.

The Spanish documents had indicated that the wreck site was in an area where the reef heads were exposed, so much so, that the survivors climbed up on them and stacked silver bars there for later salvage. But that was about all the information the salvors could glean from these early Spanish accounts—nothing that proved too helpful.

The English accounts that Haskins had found proved more informative. In them Phips had said that the "reef was like unto a half-moon and that the wreck lay toward the eastern end of the North Riff."

On the aerial mosaic chart the hunters located this curious formation. While it narrowed the search considerably, it was a long way from a pinpoint location, for Half Moon Reef was made up of over a thousand separate coral heads covering an area 6 miles long and ½ to ¾ mile wide.

Diligently Webber numbered each of these coral heads and was determined to search them one by one if necessary, until they found the wreck. Even then, the searchers were concerned about how responsive a magnetic target it would be. After all, Haskins's research indicated the ship had lost her anchors before foundering on the reef. Since she carried bronze cannon, which were nonmagnetic, any such armament remaining with her would not trigger a hit on the magnetometer. Making a mag survey in that treacherous maze of reefs, which could easily rip open the hulls of any vessels contacting the razor-edged coral, required using some kind of tough, lightweight shallow draft magging boats. Webber believed tough-hided inflatables were the answer, the kind once used by British commando assault teams during World War II.

After chartering a Florida fishing boat named the *Big G*, the expedition members boarded her and lay a course for the Dominican Republic. The men accompanying Webber came with an assortment of impressive qualifications. There was Jack Haskins, the ex-airline pilot, expert diver, and researcher, whose self-taught knowledge of seventeenth-century Spanish script had provided the catalyst that had fired up everyone into going all out for the *Concepción;* also accompanying them was Henry Taylor, whom Webber had known since 1971. Taylor, a wealthy man, had been involved in treasure hunting for years, both as a diver and as an expert on Spanish colonial coins. Others included Webber's old dive buddy from Pennsylvania, Duke Long, a cartographer and expert artist, who would do detailed drawings of artifacts; U.S. Navy veteran of twenty-seven years service, Johnnie Berrier, a skilled underwater photographer and ham radio operator; divers Don Summer of Missouri and John Harrier of Florida; and expedition dive master, Bob Coffey, one of Webber's old school chums from Pennsylvania, who had given up a successful career in textile management to go treasure hunting with Webber. All of the men knew how to handle boats and motors, how to use and interpret magnetometers and metal detectors, and came with years of experience as expert divers.

The expedition arrived at Puerto Plata in late January, 1977. Despite bad weather, the searchers spent several days comparing the numbered aerial mosaic to the reefs on the North Riff. Quite quickly, they identified all of those comprising Phips's Half Moon Reef, a prominent 6-mile crescent of coral heads, vividly marked like a white scar from the open seas breaking against them.

On the chart these were gridded into numbered squares,

each containing a group of coral heads. Webber assigned different squares to be investigated daily. The team set about doing this in two inflatables from which they would deploy their electronic snooping device. One boat placed buoys marking each coral head, followed by the second boat towing the mag around each head, then removing the buoy. When all buoys were gone, they completed the survey of that square and moved on to the next.

It was an extremely difficult and complicated procedure. It might not have been so tricky had the coral been nice tall giant columns, instead of 40- and 50-foot-tall coral trees with widespread sharp branches on the surface. The corals, named staghorn and elkhorn because of their shapes, often spread giant-pronged rust-colored antlers that looked more like enormous moose antlers. Imagine the difficulty, bobbing around on the surface in heavy sea swells while dragging a supersensitive magnetometer on a cable and trying to let that extremely valuable package of electronic components down under those branches to reach the sandy floor over 40 feet beneath them. Since they soon found there were different levels of coral to contend with, the mag seldom got deeper than 10 or 15 feet. It was constantly in danger of being snagged, and the boats were always threatened by the outstretched coral claws that could rip the bottom from beneath them in a moment's carelessness.

To make matters worse, the divers found the whole reef was a veritable graveyard of shipwrecks. In those 6 miles comprising Half Moon Reef, they found thirteen wrecks dating from the late seventeenth to the nineteenth century. So much shipwreck material was scattered through the reefs that their expectations were constantly being raised on high and then dropped to an extreme low.

Day after day they went through the same grueling procedure. Slowly but surely, they gradually exhausted all the squares on the Half Moon Reef grid. Surely, the wreck they sought was there somewhere. Why couldn't they find it? Why was it so constantly elusive? Not only were they on a psychological roller coaster that was draining all their enthusiasm but, without realizing it, each member of the expedition was slowly being poisoned from the food they were eating. It is called ciguatera, and it is caused by eating the flesh of fish that have become toxic from feeding on other toxic species inhabiting coral reefs. The symptoms include tingling of the lips, tongue, and throat and numbness in these areas, dizziness, headaches, muscle pains, and insomnia.

After three months of demoralizing search and the debilitating effect of the entire agonizing experience, morale was at its ebb. The men could hardly communicate with each other without arguing. Some even took to sleeping with a handgun under their pillows.

Still, Webber went on, staunchly believing that the *Concepción* was right there within his grasp on Half Moon Reef. They just had not found it yet. He maintained this optimistic outlook right up until the time they checked their 1,891st coral head at a total expenditure by then of a quarter million dollars. It was the last coral head on Half Moon Reef. When it too proved incapable of revealing the whereabouts of the wreck, then and only then, did Webber admit defeat and give up. It was a totally demoralizing defeat, especially with the realization that, until then, no treasure hunting expedition had ever been so well equipped to pinpoint the wreck.

Yet, once again, as it had for centuries, the well-guarded whereabouts of *Nuestra Señora de la Concepción* and its remaining treasure had eluded the best of the best. All the effort left in its wake was the continuing mystical legend.

The group went home and disbanded. Operation Phips was a failure. The partners formed another company, one that would seek permits to search for shipwrecks in other parts of the world. Then, even as the idea of their ever finding the lost galleon was being shelved, there occurred one incredibly lucky incident that would abruptly tip the scales in the opposite direction.

# Chapter 25

# Key to the Missing Galleon

One member of the group still refused to give up on the *Concepción*. It was the company's researcher, Jack Haskins. Staunchly believing that the answer to the riddle had somehow been overlooked in the archives, he was back in Spain searching for that key clue, when it came from a totally unexpected quarter.

In the archives of Seville, Haskins encountered a researcher for English economics professor, Peter Earle, who was then writing a book about Spain's 1641 fleet—the fleet with which the *Concepción* had been sailing. Hoping to learn more specific information about the galleon they were hunting, Haskins began corresponding with Earle. In one of Earle's letters, the professor mentioned, almost as an afterthought, that he had the log of William Phips's successful 1687 search for the *Concepción*.

The log was the long lost key. Haskins and Webber rushed to England in April, 1978, to see this vital piece of the puzzle. Earle quickly directed them to the original log, then in the Kent Archives at Maidstone. It was the logbook of the *Henry*, which had been captained by Francis Rogers when the *Concepción* was first found in 1687. The reason no one had discovered the logbook prior to that time was because it had remained in a family archive. In recent years, it was finally transferred to its present repository, an archive far from the beaten track of treasure hunters.

As Webber and Haskins breathlessly pored over the manuscript, they learned that it contained vital data on the wreck site never before recorded in such detail. For example, it provided them with several important elements of information—that the *Henry* approached the North Riff from the east and found the wreck in the first exposed portion of coral heads, thus confirming that the *Concepción* did indeed lay on Half Moon Reef. Then were logged the vital specifics in the old ledger. Scrawled in Captain Rogers's old English script was the revelation that the wreck could be found in the middle of the reef between three large coral heads, whose tops were dry at low water. Then, the most important data of all: "Shee bares from our ship E by S ½ S about 3 miles off, ye westmost end of reife in sight baring west of us & ye eastmost end SE by E ½ S."

With this information, Webber and Haskins's spirits soared. The log not only verified that the wreck was on Half Moon Reef, but it almost pinpointed it. The salvors felt sure that, taking these calculations into consideration, they could probably locate the very reef heads on the aerial mosaic chart that concealed the wreck. Indeed, Webber had studied the charts of this area so often, he had them memorized. In his mind's eye he could almost see the site.

By placing a two-armed pointer on the chart in such a way that it would take in Rogers's bearing on the east end of the reef and the wreck site, then moving it to account for magnetic variations and several sites that might have been the *Henry*'s anchorage, the salvors would then be able to bring their total search area down to a mere one-eighth of a square mile containing about one-hundred-fifty reef heads. Compared to the size of their first search area, this was tiny.

Still, one more major problem remained. It stemmed from the fact that they had already searched this area with the magnetometer. Indeed they were able to determine exactly which day they had done so and there had been no trace of the wreck. This indicated that their methods were not good enough. Somehow they needed to get their super-snooper beneath all those obstructing coral branches, close to the bottom, where it would then be able to detect even the smallest ferrous evidence remaining on the site. Since this might consist of nothing more than a few ship's spikes, it was vital that they now come up with some kind of high-tech device that would overcome the problem.

This was not too far out of the realm of possibilities, considering Burt Webber's knowledge of magnetometers, and their uniquely designed housings. Webber quickly saw that they needed a hand-held mag, one which a diver could take down beneath the coral reefs to poke around for some of those vital metallic readings that they were unable to get on the surface.

In the next twelve months, working with a Canadian magnetometer manufacturer, he developed the much-needed piece of equipment. It was a diver-operated, completely submersible, hand-held cesium magnetometer, with a long pointed sensor head that could be used to reach into the nooks and crannies of an underwater reef. These one-of-a-kind detectors were extremely delicate and had to be handled with utmost care in the vigorous currents around the coral heads. It called for considerable skill and caution, because each of the new hand-held mags would cost seventeen-thousand dollars apiece. Expensive though they were, they were ten times more sensitive than the towed magnetometers.

With this sophisticated new equipment and their new knowledge about the *Concepción*'s location, there was no doubt which way they had to go now. Operation Phips II went into the planning stage.

Once again, Stearns was called upon to raise the money from among his millionaire investors. Meanwhile, Webber began putting together the second expedition.

The *Samala*, a 102-foot converted minesweeper was leased with her crew at Antigua and fitted out in Miami. Despite the poisoned fish and hard times of the early voyage, most of the original expedition members were on hand for a second go at Silver Shoals. In addition, three newcomers joined the team— Jim Nace, Harry Weinman, and Billy Fothergill—all friends of

Webber, anxious to become part of the treasure-hunting legend that was about to become reality. Spirits were high. The new detectors and the new information added to the feeling of success.

Stearns's investors felt the same way about it. He had little trouble raising the four-hundred-fifty-thousand dollars for this second venture. Considering their first heavy financial losses, one might think it unusual that anyone would be willing to put any more money into this potential boondoggle. When Stearns was asked why it was they did, he replied: "The investors are savvy business people . . . they'd rather lose their money than not invest and have us find it. That's why I'm in it." And in it he was, as vice-president of Webber's treasure-hunting company, Seaquest International.

After endless delays, in early November the expedition finally sailed out of Miami for Puerto Plata. By the 24th they had reached the North Riff, anchoring a half-mile from the Half Moon Reef, where Webber tested the new magnetometers on a known wreck site. He proclaimed them "excellent beyond belief."

Two days later, diving off the *Good Guys*, the *Bad Guys*, and the *Uglies*'s inflatable boats, the divers began finding a long trail of shipwreck debris—pottery shards, metal fittings, Spanish ballast rock. Then, on November 30th, five days after they had reached the reef, Jim Nace found the coin that was to set them all shouting for joy.

It was the first of many such coins to be found on that memorable day. Before it ended, they had found 128 pieces of eight and a number of other coins of smaller denominations. None were dated later than 1639. Along with the coins came blue and white decorated pieces of Chinese porcelain (some of it unbroken) from the late Ming period, which ended in 1644. These pieces were probably products that crossed the Pacific from the Philippines aboard the Manila Galleon and were purchased at a trade fair in Acapulco for later shipment to Europe with the ill-fated fleet.

This was just the beginning of the remarkable treasure harvest that followed.

# Chapter 26

# Hard-Won Harvest

What began with a single coin soon became a steady flow of coins. The divers called their source the "Money Hole." It was silver coins coming up by the bucketsful, then by the clumps, and finally one massive conglomerate weighing nearly 200 pounds. It took three men and an air bag to hoist this mass into their reef boat, and only later, when the blackened lump lay on the deck of the *Samala*, was it realized that this one chunk of highly unglamorous-looking metal probably represented a worth of over six figures.

Using an airlift, the divers burrowed into a cavern of silver coins, plucking them from the rotted coral of the walls, the floor, and the ceiling of this seventeenth-century Ali Baba's cave. Sometimes after hammer and chisel loosened the surrounding coral, a silver cascade followed. It was reminiscent of a sudden slot-machine jackpot, and sometimes it was not all silver. On one occasion diver Jim Nace reached up to pluck a coin from the ceiling. It was quickly followed by a sudden cloud of glittering gold particles that vanished almost as quickly into the maw of the voracious airlift vacuuming up loose debris. In an instant Nace realized he had glimpsed the contents of a leather pouch of gold dust that had tumbled out of the ceiling and been whisked before his eyes into oblivion.

The money hole they were working seemed comprised of nothing but silver coins, which perplexed Webber. The site was only about 20 feet long and 12 feet wide, between 20-foot-high reef walls. The lack of ballast rock suggested that they had not yet found the main body of the wreck. But it was time to head back to Puerto Plata and to make arrangements for some kind of military support to protect what they already had.

The celebration that followed their arrival with the news of their discovery started with a bang and had worldwide repercussions of publicity about a month later.

After the initial whooping and hollering, it was back to work as usual, for the harvesting of treasure was just beginning—now with military protection.

As soon as he learned of the discovery, Jack Haskins flew to Santo Domingo to make contact with Webber's group and to see the site for himself. With the research historian's wealth of information about the *Concepción*, from its lack of anchors, cannon, and ballast, Haskins too felt there might be another part of the wreck yet to be found. But the steady returns from the Money Hole were far too rewarding to warrant stopping work to look for another site. Besides coins, the slot between the coral wall, which they were now calling the "Silver Trench," was surprising them with such goodies as a silver candle snuffer, a candle holder, silver dinner plates, some wooden cocoa stirrers, and contraband silver that had been cast into the form of plugs, cupcakes, and wedges.

Reasoning that it might be well worth their while to at least do some visual searching to the windward of their present site, Haskins and Duke Long, accompanied by author John Grissim, who would later document the entire story in his fine book *The Lost Treasure of the Concepción* (William Morrow and Company, Inc., New York, 1980), donned diving gear and started looking.

Fifteen feet below the surface they headed northeast, the direction of the prevailing winds. Swimming against the tidal surge, they swam slowly, but purposefully, along this course, remaining high enough in the water to give them a wide view of the bottom.

The divers' eyes missed nothing, especially the occasional ballast rock appearing amongst the bottom rubble. They passed a coral head, where Nace had found a complete ceramic olive jar, one of the large vase-shaped containers used by early Spanish mariners to carry foodstuffs. It took them some twenty minutes to move 130 yards from the salvage boat. Suddenly, as they made their way around a water-washed coral head, they saw something that sent shivers of excitement through them.

Below them stood a statuesque coral head growing upward to within 20 feet of the surface. On its summit, clearly visible to any surface swimmer in mask and snorkel, was a pile of ballast rock, some of the stones weighing over 100 pounds.

His heart pounding, Haskins swam down to look more closely at the area. Mentally he ran through the historical description of the wreck that he had long ago memorized from the documents. It all began to fit—the layout of the surrounding reefs matched exactly the way they had been described by Captain Rogers of the *Henry*. Naturally, there were no visible signs of the wood wreck, though later, excavating 8 feet below the bottom, the divers would find remnants of the galleon's planking.

As Haskins visualized the position of the wreck on its east/west orientation and the cavelike configuration of the coral wall that Phips thought concealed the stern portion, the self-taught marine historian privately exalted in the realization that after all his years of trying to interpret the clues long forgotten in the archives, here, at last, was the final resting place of the fabled galleon that so many had searched for over the centuries. Now fate had allowed him of all people the privilege of being the first human being to see it since its disappearance over three hundred years ago! It was a moment Haskins will remember for the rest of his life.

A couple of days later, using an Aquapulse metal detector

and a small airlift to suction off sand and debris, Haskins and his companions sampled just below the surface of the bottom and found pieces of eight in large numbers. With them was the sole of a leather shoe, still flexible, the stitching holes still showing. A foot below the bottom revealed fragments of ceramics.

As tempting as this new site was, so much treasure poured out of their first excavation that they decided to wait until after a Christmas holiday break before continuing further. It was during this period that the world learned more complete details of the historic find.

Though they were back at their original hole by early January, the site still continued to produce so well that it was March before Webber decided to tackle the main wreck area itself.

Interestingly, the exposed ballast rock sitting atop their coral pedestal were the tip-off to the *Concepción*'s final resting place. Had any earlier searchers been in the water in this area and spotted this clue, they would have had the key to the *Concepción*'s whereabouts.

Instead, Webber, as had virtually all the modern-day searchers before him, had relied not so much on a visual search—such as a towed diver on an underwater sled—but rather on a towed electronic instrument that had passed close to the clue without being capable of interpreting it. Indeed, Webber's logbook reference for 1977, during Operation Phips, showed that they had searched this very area on February 28th and that the magnetometer had failed to indicate the presence of the wreck.

In all those centuries of searching, had anyone spotted these telltale ballast rock and taken the time to look around the bottom beneath them, they would probably have found what Webber's divers did—the *Concepción*'s crumbling grave site now well picked over by early salvors.

What then was left?

After salvaging what he could from the bow section, Captain Phips and his men had been stopped by the coral, which they assumed had completely encased the galleon's stern section. Unable to penetrate this barrier with explosives, Phips finally gave up trying. Ever since, generations of treasure hunters believed that the bulk of the *Concepción*'s treasure was still there just waiting for them, encased in coral. All one had to do was break through the coral, and Eureka! The *Concepción*'s sternful of treasure would finally be theirs. It was this belief that kept the legend alive and brought droves of treasure hunters to Silver Shoals.

Now Webber's men were in position to open this coral-entombed after portion of the galleon that was believed to contain its main treasure load—open it, that is, if they found it where Phips thought it was.

Diligently, they searched for the hidden coral-encapsulated stern, but found only walls of living coral beside the fragments of wreckage. Apparently, after having cleared the forward portion of the wreck and finally reaching the coral impasse just aft of the ship's mast foot, Phips's divers believed this was where the coral had engulfed the galleon. Now, however, as Webber and his divers were able to view the site more closely, it seemed far more probable that the stern of the ship had broken away from the galleon before she sank and had somehow managed to drift downwind, caroming through the coral heads like the ball of a pinball machine and coming to rest some distance from the main site.

Having considered all other possibilities, Webber and his men concluded that probably the area they had first found, which produced the early outpouring of silver, was actually where the broken stern section had finally come to rest. The two areas 130 yards apart were linked by a scattering of ballast stone that marked its serpentine trail.

Since Phips never mentioned this site, incredible as it seemed, he and his salvors were apparently unaware of it. Also, it was from their initial Money Hole that Jim Nace—Mr. Lucky—who had found the first coin and the first intact olive jar, finally discovered what would be one of their most valuable finds. What he thought was a pulley wheel was in fact a bronze astrolabe, an early seventeenth-century navigational instrument, which is one of the rarest of period shipwreck finds. More than likely, this instrument would have been in the captain's or pilot's after quarters, rather than in the ship's forward compartments, which consisted largely of the crew and quartermaster areas.

Digging on the main wreck site, Webber and his men soon found that Captain Phips and his divers, along with all the other chance salvors who had sampled the site, had not entirely cleaned it out. But the going was rough. The treasure was not that bountiful. By the middle of May, they had recovered several thousand silver coins, scattered crude kitchenware, clay pipes, musket parts, and, from a seemingly innocuous sand pocket, Jim Nace found the first gold chain necklace. Shortly afterward, Bob Coffey discovered a second ornate gold chain weighing over 10 ounces. This elegant piece of jewelry was to be the most valuable artifact recovered from the *Concepción*.

During this period, historian Dr. Peter Earle picked up another piece of revealing information from the Spanish archives and shared it with Webber. From the document he read the testimony of an Englishman captured aboard an English ship shortly after the *Concepción* had foundered. The captive revealed that his vessel had encountered two large rafts containing 120 of the *Concepción*'s survivors, along with half a million pesos of gold and silver. The English vessel promptly relieved the survivors of their heavy burden. From this fact, it seemed apparent that the *Concepción* had remained afloat at least long enough for the survivors to avail themselves of the most easily reached treasure. Webber and Earle suspected that they most likely had helped themselves to the most ornate pieces of worked gold, precious stones, and jewelry. This then would account for the lack of these items in their finds.

After recovering what was more or less easily reached, now came the problem of how to get coins that had fallen into the cracks and crevices of the reef. Webber's Aquapulse indicated that it was there, but how could they extract it?

Again specialized tools were required. An underwater jack hammer and a chain saw with carbide cutting tips were used to shatter the coral to reach the coins. But this proved slow going. By far the most practical of these high-tech underwater tools was a hydraulic fragmentation tool called a Porta-Power. The device resembled a caulking gun linked by a hose to an expandable flat pad or a rodlike nozzle. When either the pad or the nozzle was inserted into a crevice, hydraulic fluid could be pumped into the expandable probe, until the coral was shattered.

With this underwater fragmentation gun the divers were able to break off 1800-pound coral boulders and air-bag them to a dump area. Numerous coins and artifacts were found is these crevices.

When it was learned that sand pockets deep beneath the coral often contained pockets of treasure, Webber began using fragmentation explosives to crack the larger bed of coral, so that it could be air-bagged away in smaller pieces.

After removing nearly 15 tons of such coral from over a sand pocket too deep for the Aquapulse detector to pinpoint, but targeted by the cessium magnetometer, the divers penetrated 8 feet of solid coral to reach the sand and the remains of a wooden chest. It measured 2 by 4 feet. Stacked four high in orderly rows, where they had sat in the chest's false bottom, were pieces of eight hidden there centuries ago as contraband silver, whose owner hoped to avoid paying the royal tax. The main body of the chest itself contained ornate silver plates and twenty exquisite Chinese teacups, with only three broken!

After that, there began a concerted effort to use the explosives to penetrate the mass of coral overlaying the area where Webber believed treasure had spilled from the broken ship. In just one session of working the site in this manner, the salvors lifted 45 tons of coral. Beneath it, they found a bed of silver coins and artifacts similar to those recovered from their original Money Hole site.

Quite obviously, Webber planned to literally leave not a "stone" unturned in his search for the scattered treasure. He did not want some competitor to later search the site and find something he had overlooked. One of the last things he did in order to learn whether or not it was true (as the documents and the legend said) that the survivors of the *Concepción* had had enough time to stack treasure on a nearby reef top (with the idea of returning and collecting it later), was to scrutinize the towering coral head islands themselves.

Selecting what they suspected was the largest and most obvious reef head beside the wreck site that might have been used for this purpose, Webber and his crew checked it out carefully. The Aquapulse metal detector gave them no reading of any buried metal. Did this mean that none existed, or that it was simply overgrown too deeply with coral?

Webber checked the coral head with the hand-held cessium magnetometer. This time he got readings of buried metal in the coral. There was only one way to tackle the job.

Webber and his divers placed explosives along the top and sides of the reef. After the explosion, beneath the rubble, the divers found deep fissures 5 feet below the surface that contained thousands of silver coins and another astrolabe.

After that, every day for a week, they systematically detonated carefully placed charges in the remaining coral mount, gradually slicing away the head, until it was cut down to 15 feet below the waterline. Each time they did it they found more silver coins, then candlestick holders, a Greek-style statuette carved in an elephant's tusk, a gold perfume container, and finally even a third astrolabe recovered by Duke Long and dated 1632. Webber's men had found the treasure left stacked on the reef and overgrown by centuries of living coral, until it had been solidly encased in the limestone.

Eventually, Webber called a halt to operations and returned to the Dominican Republic with the remainder of the treasure. It had taken him a total of eleven months to complete the salvage. In that time his divers removed over 250 tons of coral, from which they extracted sixty-thousand pieces of eight and an assortment of other valuable artifacts.

Even after everything was divided equally with the Dominican government, its share of the treasure was large enough to occupy the entire second floor of the Dominican Republic's National Museum.

Eventually, a selection of this treasure toured a dozen U.S. cities, where over 1.5 million people saw it. A CBS documentary film, "The Lost Treasure of the *Concepción*," thrilled television audiences everywhere.

Through a combination of research, luck, good old Pennsylvania Dutch stubborn stick-to-itiveness, and a dash of high-tech instrumentation, Burt Webber and his associates succeeded where all others had failed.

It was a fitting end to a legend.

# PART V

## Barry Clifford: Pirate Hunter

# Chapter 27

# The Making of a Pirate

Wednesday, July 24, 1715 was warm and muggy, despite the gentle sea breeze rippling the cobalt waters of Havana harbor. Aboard his flagship, General Juan Esteban Ubilla, commander of the flota, surveyed the armada that awaited only his signal to sail for Spain. The fleet consisted of twelve vessels, including the French frigate *Grifon*, which was sailing with the armada for her own safety. Five of the galleons, under the command of General Antonio de Echeverz, were laden with the wealth of South America—gold, emeralds, and pearls from Cartagena, Colombia, and Peruvian silver loaded at Portobelo, Panama. Ubilla's five galleons contained the wealth of Mexico—2,290 chests of newly minted silver and gold coins from Veracruz, as well as delicate porcelains and silks from China and an assortment of exquisite gem-studded jewelry crafted in the distant Orient and destined for Spanish royalty. The total treasure amounted to more than 14 million pesos. Since Spain's annual treasure shipments from the New World were curtailed for years by the War of Spanish Succession, this especially large accumulation of gold and silver was badly needed by the war-impoverished Spanish monarchy.

As the heavily ladened armada sailed out of Havana harbor

on a course taking it northward up the straits between Florida and the Bahama Bank, not a single soul aboard the ships could have guessed that they were on a collision course with catastrophe and that the cargo they carried would change other people's lives for centuries to come.

Six days out of Havana, the fleet realized it was in trouble. By midnight, the ships had been pounded by five vicious squalls, each worse than the one before. At 2 A.M., Wednesday, July 31st, the hurricane struck the vessels with winds of up to 100 miles an hour.

Caught in the mountainous waves, the ships were helplessly driven ashore, mortally wounded by the Florida barrier reef paralleling the coast. As the individual ships foundered, their fates were a litany of death and destruction: disemboweled from stem to stern on the first reef it struck, General Ubilla's *Capitana* disgourged ballast, cargo, cannon, and treasure from the gaping wound in its hull, as the ship smashed into a second reef that totally demolished it. The general and 225 of his passengers perished. Caught broadside by the storm, General de Echeverz's *Capitana* sank a short distance from a point of land. Although the beach is little more than a stone's throw away, the general and 113 others perished in the turbulent seas. De Echeverz's *Almiranta* broke up under the weight of the waves. His merchant ship and sloop were swallowed by the sea, never to be found. Two of the patrol vessels were literally torn apart in the rampaging surf. On one, 135 persons perished; on the other the crew was more fortunate. Although two dozen drowned as the deck lifted off the hull, some 100 survivors rode the wreckage ashore like a raft. Ubilla's *Almiranta* sank in shallow water within wading distance of the beach, but the pounding waves rapidly demolished it and 125 persons were battered to death before they reached shore. A Dutch merchantman was cast high and dry by the hurricane, but the crew miraculously escaped without a fatality. Ubilla's sloop ran aground at the mouth of a river and 35 crew men survived.

In those horrifying moments the hurricane of 1715 took its

terrible toll on the fleet. Of twelve ships only one survived, the French vessel *Grifon*, which was sailing so far to the north that her captain, Don Antonio Darié, was unaware that the other vessels were in trouble. In that ensuing storm, 14 million pesos of registered treasure and one thousand lives were lost along the Florida east coast. It was one of the worst maritime disasters of all time.

For those who survived—and old records report that some one thousand made it ashore along the over 20 miles of desolate beach south of Cape Canaveral—the nightmare was far from over. During the early morning hours, as the hurricane moved inland, dawn broke to reveal wreckage and bodies tumbling in the surf and littering the shoreline. Survivors clustered in isolated groups, tending to the more seriously injured. There were no nearby towns; no medicine, food, or tools had been salvaged. Many who survived the ordeal of the night died from their injuries the next morning. Gradually, as the gales subsided, the officers restored order.

The closest settlement was St. Augustine—150 miles to the north. No one wanted to strike inland, because the wilderness was inhabited by fierce tribes of Indians. Most decided to establish a camp on the beach from salvaged wreckage, while a small party attempted to reach St. Augustine in two longboats that had washed ashore virtually undamaged. Still others found an opportunity to prosper by robbing the dead. With their pockets loaded with loot, this group started up the beach toward St. Augustine.

A week later, the first of the survivors struggled into that Spanish settlement. The looters who had walked the beach were apprehended and, six weeks later, in September, seven rescue ships arrived at Sebastian Inlet to end the last survivors' long ordeal.

Due to the difficulty of obtaining seaworthy ships and crews for a long stay abroad, it was March, 1716, six months later, that Spain began trying to recover some of the treasure from the shipwrecked fleet. Over the next few months, with 280 Indian divers at their disposal, the Spanish salvaged four million pesos of silver, which were placed in a guarded storehouse, then loaded aboard a ship for Havana.

Surprisingly, the shipment got through without being intercepted by any of the pirates and privateers who then prowled the Florida Straits southward into the Caribbean. These rascals considered unescorted treasure galleons the plumpest of game, and when word swept through the Caribbean that an entire fleet of treasure ships was foundered along the Florida east coast, it was as tantalizing to these scalawags as a whiff of carrion to a population of buzzards.

When news of the lost treasure and the Spaniards' frantic salvage efforts reached the infamous pirate stronghold at Port Royal, Jamaica, an army of rogues began planning some salvage operations of their own. Unluckily for them, however, a respected Virginia gentleman, named Captain Henry Jennings, was one jump ahead of them.

Jennings was an English privateer commissioned, as were others of his day, to use privately owned war vessels to prey upon enemy shipping. Between wars, privateers were supposed to suppress piracy. The Treaty of Utrecht, signed two years earlier, had established peace between England and Spain, but Jennings was not a man to let such a trivial matter as a peace treaty stand in his way. When he sailed from Williamsburg, Virginia, with five ships, three hundred men, and a directive from Virginia's Governor Spotswood to "see what was about," the suppression of piracy was not exactly what the daring privateer had in mind.

Jennings sailed his fleet directly to the Spanish salvage site in Florida, landed his three hundred well-armed men, and attacked the Spanish camp. After a brief skirmish, he overran sixty guards at the storehouse and made off with three hundred fifty thousand pesos of silver. With this much booty aboard, there was no longer any question of returning to the comparatively respectful life of a privateer. Jennings sailed to Port Royal and took up the career of a pirate.

The successful raid on the Spanish salvage site was encouraging news to every cutthroat on the Spanish Main. Pirates far and wide were attracted to the site. Although the Spanish reinforced their operation with more armed ships and men, the area would be a favorite "fishing" ground for freebooters using rakes, grappling hooks, and divers for the next few years to come.

As modern historians suspect, it was this tremendous Spanish treasure loss that lured and changed the lives of two nearly middle-aged adventurers from the New England area. One was an Englishman named Samuel Bellamy, who is believed to have left his family in County Dorset, England, and sailed to the New England area. The other was a Rhode Island man named Palgrave ("Paul") Williams, a forty-year-old family man, who also left his wife and children to seek his fortune. Exactly where along the road to adventure these two met, is unknown. Legend has it that Bellamy—possibly because of family relations in Eastham on Cape Cod—stayed with the Hallett Family there in 1715. Perhaps it was there that he befriended fellow fortune hunter Paul Williams. Legend would also like us to believe that one of the men—either Bellamy or Williams—had had an affair with Bellamy's young cousin, Maria Hallett, and that the following year, when the pair of fortune hunters sailed off into the sunset to see what they could fish from the Florida wrecks, young Maria was pregnant by one of the two men.

Supposedly, the adventuresome pair, with their ragtag crew and a leaking excuse for a sloop, found wreck fishing less profitable than they had thought. Possibly the imposing array of armed Spanish vessels now guarding the site made the venture unwise, or perhaps trying to wrest treasure from treacherous seas in their leaky old vessel seemed equally unwise. Apparently, what offered more appeal was the idea of joining forces with the kind of fellows they saw sailing in from Jamaica and the Bahamas—free-spirited scoundrels who banded together in efforts to get rich at the expense of others. More often than not, the "others" were the wealthy Spanish, who were trying to conduct business as usual, despite these roving gangs of sea leeches.

By the spring of 1916, both men were living the lives of

pirates aboard ships skippered by the infamous Frenchman Louis Lebous and Englishman Captain Benjamin Hornigold. Apparently, it was a good year for apprentice pirates. At about the same time Bellamy and Williams were establishing their reputations with the Brethren of the Coast, old Captain Hornigold was grooming another English seaman for a similar infamous role in history. His name was Edward Teach, but before long this scourge of the seven seas, dressed all in black, carrying three brace of cocked pistols, 10-pound cutlasses in his sash, daggers in his belt, and smoldering matches in his waist-long greased beard, would be feared far and wide as the infamous "Blackbeard."

Captain Lebous, with his crew of mostly Frenchmen, set off on his sloop *Postillion,* plundering any ship they could outsail and force into submission. Captain Hornigold of the *Mary Ann,* with his mostly English crew, which included Bellamy and Williams, did likewise. What they did exactly and where they did it is a matter of record that has come down to us through the documented reports left by their victims. Surprisingly, contrary to the kind of image created by the more bloodthirsty of pirates, most pirates were not nearly the murderous psychopaths some popular fiction would have us believe. Thieves, rogues, and ruffians they were to be sure; but apparently, there was a sense of fair play among even the most rascally of them.

The pair of pirate ships sailed down through the Caribbean searching for ships to plunder. Making their way to Portobelo, they caught a Dutch ship recently from that Panamanian port, and practiced their trade upon her, relieving the vessel of both valuables and men, including a Swedish seaman named Peter Cornelius Hoof. Threatened with death unless he joined the pirate crew, Hoof allowed himself to be "forced," rather than to have his career end on the spot. Only later, before his short, but prosperous, life of crime was terminated by authorities on a seashore gibbet, did he shed some light on their nefarious activities during this period.

One suspects that there were many such ships and encounters in which Hornigold and Lebous made themselves richer in whatever manner took their fancy. There was seldom any bloodshed, such was the fear caused on sight by these swift predators of the Spanish Main. Their small, sleek sailing vessels easily outmaneuvered the larger, lumbering merchantmen. Once these ships came under the guns of the pirate vessels and the black banner (its white skull and crossbones, unfurled over the cursing crew, brandishing axes, cutlasses, and muskets), the sight alone was all that was needed to make prey vessels swing up into the wind and heave to.

In this manner they sailed from Panama back toward Cuba. Off Havana they caught a heavy log-carrying Dutch vessel that they kept for several days. They took what they wanted, then returned the ship to her crew and let them sail on. Off the southwestern tip of Cuba they overtook two Spanish brigantines "laden with cocoa from Maraca." They were somewhat disappointed about finding more cocoa than coins aboard the ship. When the pirates demanded ransom, the Spanish simply shrugged and were unable to come up with the asking price. Such an affront might have drawn swift retaliation in the form of flashing cutlasses or a plank-walking party from other piratical factions. Instead, Lebous and Hornigold ferried their prisoners ashore, then burned their ships.

Off the Isle of Pines on Cuba's southwestern coast, they attacked and cowed three English sloops. That proved a mistake. The sloops were empty. Again, rather than pitch a tantrum over wasted efforts, the pirates used the captured vessels and crews to help them careen and scrape the barnacles off their pirate ships. Then they returned the sloops and sent the Englishmen on their way. After that, the swashbucklers sailed for the balmy shores of Hispaniola "to tarry in the tropics for about three months."

That June they spent anchored in a palm-sheltered bay, enjoying the fruits of their plunders, while sampling the delights of this balmy island paradise. The inactivity, coupled with a certain discontent among the men, brought about some changes.

Most pirate crews were made up of random nationalities. When there were ships to be plundered, nobody played favorites; none was spared. This was the accepted code of their kind. Therefore, trouble began when the venerable old pirate chieftan, Captain Benjamin Hornigold, decreed that they would no longer plunder English ships. He and some of the English pirates were adamant about this.

The others disagreed. They argued that the fat English merchant ships were just as wealthy as those of other nationalities. Moreover, if they were caught by the English, their fate would be just as swift swinging from an English yardarm as from any other. So plunder them all!

As most such issues were decided aboard pirate ships, this one was put to a show of hands. The majority opted for attacking any ship, no matter what its nationality. Apparently, since he felt so strongly about the issue, Captain Hornigold and his followers were "drummed out of the corps," so to speak.

Since his loyalty to the English was unswerving in this matter, Hornigold had to go. The pirates decided he was unfit to serve any longer as their captain. He and his men moved aboard a captured sloop and sailed off to practice piracy as they saw fit. The man who succeeded him was chosen by a large majority. He was a relative newcomer to their ranks—Samuel Bellamy.

Captain Bellamy took command as master of the *Mary Anne* and her remaining crew of about ninety men. His friend, Paul Williams, became his second in command aboard the ship, and now it was the twin pirate ships of Bellamy and Lebous that left Hispaniola in search of more rich prizes.

This swift escalation from common seaman to commander in the pirate ranks, after only a few months with them, speaks volumes for the kind of character comprising Samuel Bellamy. His status among pirates could only be acquired by someone possessing all the qualities admired by pirates—good seamanship, courage, bravery, coolness under fire, cunning, skill, and the ability to handle men. Bellamy apparently had all these things—plus the desire to better himself in his chosen profession: to become a bigger and better thief than anyone else.

Captains Lebous and Bellamy, aboard their pirate ships, prowling the trade lanes of the Virgin Islands, capturing ship after ship, gradually made their coffers richer with plunder. Bellamy was looking for a larger ship to call his own, a "ship of force" that would make him even more of a threat to the seaways than he already was. In historical retrospect, it is noteworthy that Bellamy's obsessive belief that "bigger is better" was probably the single factor that would lead to his violent downfall faster than any probably expected.

Possibly it was due to his sudden rise and short apprenticeship as a pirate, but he somehow failed to heed what he should have learned. It was the single most important secret to successful pirating. Even as a beginner, he should have realized that where sudden storms, hidden shoals, and the threat of pursuit were common hazards to pirates from the Atlantic seaboard to the Caribbean, what counted most in the pirate profession was not a big ship, but a fast, highly maneuverable vessel that a crew could handle well through stormy seas or calm—a vessel that could overtake larger, more cumbersome ships with ease; a sloop swift enough to outdistance heavily armed pursuers; and one shoal draft enough to sail across shoal water escape routes that would stop deeper draft men-of-war.

Still, Bellamy yearned for a larger, more luxurious vessel that would carry him and his crewmen on more distant voyages of piracy. But, for the moment, what he had was the *Mary Anne*, a swift sloop crewed by mostly British and Irish seamen, along with a couple dozen blacks the pirates had "liberated" from a prize ship that may have been a slaver.

For weeks and months the sea wolves prowled the sea lanes, swooping down upon the lumbering merchant ships, plying the distant waterways of the West Indies. Near Saba in the Virgin Islands, they caught and kept the ship *Sultana*, a large vessel that seemed to have more the lines of a man-of-war that Captain Bellamy wanted as his new flagship.

Retreating with their prize to the Bay of Honduras, Bellamy and his men moved aboard the *Sultana*, and Paul Williams was made captain of the *Mary Anne*.

Twenty leagues off Saba, another ship was captured, and her crew held on a small nearby island, while the vessel was plundered and then returned to her master. Fourteen new recruits were persuaded to join the pirates; the rest were allowed to go their way.

Now, with the *Sultana* outfitted as his pirate flagship, Bellamy soon parted company with Captain Lebous. Feeling perhaps that now he had his "ship of force," he could plunder the Spanish Main by himself. Escorted by his fighting sloop under Captain Paul Williams, the pair set off for the Windward Passage, seeking more rich prey.

The rogues now numbered about 180 men. Always on the lookout for a way to better himself in this business of pirating, in February, 1717, Captain Bellamy spotted the ship of his dreams—an eighteen-gun, 300-ton, sleekly designed sailing galley, a slave ship from the Gold Coast of West Africa. Named the *Whydah* (pronounced "widdah") for the bustling slave port of her origin, she looked every inch the kind of prize flagship that Bellamy now itched to own. Carrying a crew of fifty and a cargo of sugar, raisins, varnish, indigo, and some silver and gold, she was homeward bound from Jamaica to London.

Anthropologist and author, Dr. Edwin Dethlefsen, in delving into the history of the *Whydah*, believes that the ship probably transported a load of slaves and gold from West Africa to Jamaica in exchange for silver and other cargo. As others have pointed out, in the early eighteenth century, this popular slave port on the Gold Coast was shipping out a thousand slaves a month to fill the need of the New World slave market.

Captain Bellamy and his pirates homed in on this handsome prize, but the trim African lady had no intentions of surrendering her virtues easily to the rambunctious rogues. Spreading all sail her three masts could carry, she fled down the Windward Passage, the pirates in hot pursuit.

For over two days and nights they pursued and she

outsailed them. How frustrating it must have been to Bellamy. Apparently, it was no longer a contest of swift sloops against a larger, more lethargic prey. Williams in the single-masted sloop *Mary Anne* may have been no match for the *Whydah* in open ocean, under full press of sail; while Bellamy must have seen that his recently acquired *Sultana* also fell far short of his expectations. We can only surmise that he probably had mixed emotions about the swiftness of the *Whydah*—frustrated in his inability to overcome her, but thrilled by her performance.

In any event, history only records that on the third day the pirates eventually caught up to the fleeing ship in the vicinity of the Bahama Islands, and she finally hove to under their guns without a threatening shot being fired.

Obviously pleased with his conquest, as tediously difficult as it had been, Bellamy at once showed his pleasure with courtly behavior to the English captain and crew of the vessel.

The three vessels sailed together to Long Island in the Bahamas, where they dropped anchors, and the pirates got on with the business of ravishing and robbing their victim. In short order the rogues transferred all of their captured booty from the *Sultana* to the *Whydah*, transferred unwanted cargo from the *Whydah* to the *Sultana*, then gave the former pirate flagship to *Whydah*'s former captain and crew, along with their freedom. Moreover, the gentlemanly Captain Bellamy threw in 20 pounds of gold and silver to help the captain defray some of his charges that would result once he sailed back to England to explain to her owners and an official board of inquiry just how he happened to lose his ship.

The historical record suggests that seven or eight of *Whydah*'s original crew voluntarily joined the pirates and that three others with needed specialties were forced to join. Also, from the testimony of pirates later captured, we learn that the newly outfitted *Whydah* now carried between 20,000 and 30,000 pounds of gold and silver in her hold, 50 pounds for each of her 180-man crew, all stowed in bags packed in wooden chests between decks. As she sailed from the Bahamas, pointing her rakish bows southward toward the well-traveled sea lanes of

Hispaniola, she was a sight to gladden any rogue's heart. Her 100-foot length carried an astonishingly large number of cannon—twenty-eight guns thrust their black maws out unused galley ports. Though the lead sheathing to protect her from sea worms had been ripped from her oak hull in an effort to increase the ship's speed, her 300 tons were further burdened by additional tons of shot for her cannon, rocks for her ballast, and several water casks weighing a ton apiece. All this had come to Samuel Bellamy in less than a year of pirating.

So imposing a sight did the *Whydah* make for vessels she swooped down upon off Hispaniola, that again the plundering was easy. No ships ever resisted. No bloodshed was ever necessary. The pirates' coffers were made richer by several more thousand pounds of gold and silver from the *Whydah*'s conquests. Finally, toward the year's end, Bellamy began dreaming of distant seas and even more grandiose treasures to be taken from such wealthy sources as the Indian Ocean and the Red Sea. He dreamed of adding diamonds, silks, spices, and unlimited chests filled with rubies, emeralds, and gold to his collection.

With these distant conquests in mind, Bellamy sailed northward up the coast, following the route of the treasure fleets back to the Old World. But instead of veering eastward off the Carolina Capes, the *Whydah* thundered toward the New England coast. Samuel Bellamy and his friend Paul Williams wanted one last time to go home, to perhaps revisit the people and places they knew as relatively impoverished adventurers only a couple years earlier. Perhaps they intended to flaunt their good fortune—their new wealth and position—before their friends. Perhaps they intended to do some pirating along this thriving coast, before leaving it for a long time. Perhaps, too, Bellamy or Williams wanted to see the attractive Maria Hallett again, the girl he had left behind.

No matter the reasons, as *Whydah*'s sharp bows knifed northward through the Atlantic swells, she and her crew were soon about to fulfill their destinies.

# Chapter 28

---

# To their Just Rewards

Somewhere off the Virginia Capes, the *Whydah* and the sloop *Mary Anne* parted company. Captain Paul Williams, anxious to get back to see his family living on Block Island, agreed to rendezvous there later with the *Whydah*. Bellamy, however, was in no hurry. He decided to tarry a while off the Virginia Capes and see what he could catch.

On April 7, 1717 his catch was pretty good. Three vessels were captured. The crews were released, but one ship was sent to the bottom. Four days later, another vessel fell prey to the pirates. All the plunder was transferred aboard the prize snow *Ann*.

On April 26th, the pirate ship and her prize overtook a wine-laden cargo vessel out of Nantasket bound for New York and added her to their convoy. She was the fat-hulled pink *Mary Anne*. The three vessels—*Whydah*, *Ann*, and *Mary Anne*—then sailed north toward Cape Cod. By four o'clock that afternoon they encountered thick fog. Later, as dusk came on, the fog was blown away. But Bellamy grew concerned about sailing through the treacherous shoals off the Cape, especially now that he saw the seas beginning to build as the wind freshened.

Before dark, his convoy hailed a small Boston-bound sloop, the *Fisher*, and asked if the crewmen knew the local waters. Learning that they did, Bellamy ordered the captain and mate aboard his flagship to guide them. As full dark descended, each ship, with stern lanterns lighted, followed one another, as they beat into the wind that was now sweeping like an invisible scythe over the black seas, slicing the heads off waves and leaving them to roll onward as foaming whitecaps. In the darkness the seething and crashing waves reflected an eerie, ghostly pallor. Whether or not all the pirates were concerned over the worsening conditions is not known, but at least some of them lost no time sampling some of the Madeira wine from their recent victim's cargo.

By ten o'clock that night, the weather had worsened. One heavy rain squall after another swept over the struggling vessels. The wind's howl was matched only by the groaning ship timbers and the wail of strumming rigging. In the rapid flashes of lightning the pirates saw the mountainous seas working chaotically around them at all points of the compass. The shallow waters beneath their keels created a wild caldron that had long been a death trap for legions of lost ships. Few sailing vessels ever survived this graveyard of the Atlantic under such conditions. From Barnstable out the full length of Cape Cod this clawlike land mandible reached far out into the Atlantic, as if to grasp any unwary mariner within reach. The danger was not so much this claw as it was the hidden shoals that preceded it for miles. With this combination, when the seas went wild, neither man nor their vessels were a match for it.

Shortly after 10 P.M. those unfortunates aboard the pink *Mary Anne* learned about the Cape's wrath. Over the roar of the storm her helmsman heard the thunder of breakers. He strained to swing the ship around, to tack and try to beat out to the seaward, but the vessel failed to respond to her helm. Suddenly, with a lurch and a grinding crunch, she ran aground.

As the seas shoved the vessel over on her lee rail, the crew scrambled to release the straining canvas sails. One seaman grabbed an ax and chopped away the foremast and mizzen to release the pressure. Then the crew crabbed aft and sought shelter in the vessel's hold. In this hellishly black pit the booming of the seas against the bulwarks was as deafening as cannon fire. If the hull held, they had five or six hours of this torment to endure before dawn. Praying for devine deliverance, they spent the night reading Scripture loudly by flickering candlelight, while alternately swigging deeply of the Madeira wine to keep up their courage.

Between the two something must have worked, because at daybreak, amazingly enough, they realized that their flat-bottom shoal draft pink had saved their lives by skidding over the worst of the shoals and delivering them right up to dry land. In fact, despite their hangovers, the jublilant survivors jumped out onto a sand island, one of the many shifting sandbars that frequently appear and disappear off Cape Cod. Though marooned there, at least they were still alive. All they had to do was await rescue, which arrived shortly in the form of two men in a sailing canoe.

Quickly the castaways were carried ashore, and when it was soon learned that they were pirates, the local people cast them into jail. During the storm, *Mary Anne*'s survivors had lost sight of the *Whydah* and the others. When dawn came and the seas abated, no signs of the ships were seen on the horizon. Nor was there any wreckage from them in the surf. Where then, they wondered, was Captain Bellamy and the *Whydah*?

As the ships struggled through the storm, the pink *Mary Anne* had fallen far behind. In fact, the *Whydah* and the other two vessels in the convoy were miles to the north when the pink had run aground. Having lost each other in the storm, the two captive vessels and their crews were never heard from again. Meanwhile, *Whydah* was staggering through storm seas off the forearm of the Cape near Wellfleet, with nothing but miles of cliff-backed harborless shoreline to the lee of the ship. The high winds and violent seas kept the ship deep-heeled to the extent that her lee rail was often deeply buried in the torrent of black water rushing by her hull.

By midnight, Bellamy realized that the ship was being

driven too close to the lee shore. There was no room to bring her around and try to sail her back into deeper water. The only other alternative he had was to try to anchor and ride the storm out where he was.

Shouting above the roar of the storm, he ordered the bow anchors released. As the crew members crawled forward, the helmsman swung the heavy ship bows on into the gale. The bower anchors went down; the ship settled back on her cables.

As they strummed taut, *Whydah*'s fine bows knifed into the onrushing seas, which now threatened to swamp her. As the seas rolled over her bows, Bellamy ordered the anchors cut free.

*Whydah* fell back and was immediately engulfed in the tumultuous waves that rolled her over on her beam ends. Frantically, the pirates tried to cut free the cumbersome rigging to loose her sails. But before they could, the ship broached severely, washing away her masts, rigging, and most of her crew. Instead of surfing shoreward, as a smaller shoal draft vessel might have, the deep-hulled, heavily laden *Whydah* crunched against the bottom and rolled bottom up in the mountainous waves that were pounding her unmercifully. No boiling shallow water surf pounded her as it had the *Mary Anne*. The *Whydah* was being savaged by tons of water that ground her hull against the shoals, until by morning, Samuel Bellamy's big, heavily laden dream ship was smashed to pieces. As she passed into oblivion, she took with her the lives of Samuel Bellamy and most of his men.

In the days that followed, 102 battered corpses washed up on the beach. Forty-two other crewmen known to have been aboard were never seen again. All together, 144 of the pirates were presumed dead. Only two of *Whydah*'s crew miraculously made it ashore to tell their tale of disaster.

One was twenty-two-year-old shipwright, Thomas Davis, who had been "forced" into joining the pirates after being captured aboard an English vessel the year before. The other was John Julian, an Indian pilot whom Bellamy had hired to guide them through the treacherous Cape Cod shoals. Both men were promptly jailed with the *Mary Anne* survivors and held for their trial as pirates.

When word reached Massachusetts' Governor Shute that a pirate ship had foundered upon the shoals, he quickly dispatched special investigator, Captain Cyprian Southack, to secure whatever riches he could from the wreck.

Thanks to the travel difficulties of the day, it took Southack a week to reach the site. Meanwhile, local Cape Cod wreckers had already helped themselves to anything of value washing ashore. When he finally arrived, Southack had a frustrating time trying to scavenge anything of value for the governor. Visiting the wreck site, where she had first struck the shoals, he saw the *Whydah*'s bower anchor in the water. But the special investigator worried that others had beat him to the treasure itself. In his report to the governor, Southack said that on April 29th he had sighted a "great sloop" up against the wreck, apparently trying to fish for treasure. Historians have since wondered if this might have been Captain Paul Williams and his sloop the *Mary Anne* from Block Island, for Williams in his smaller, fleeter vessel would have been able to avoid running aground at the wreck site. He and his men were no doubt devastated to learn of the terrible disaster that had taken Bellamy, their companions, and the treasure that had been stored for them aboard the now capsized and demolished *Whydah*. No one knows for sure whether Williams and his men ever recovered any of their lost treasure. History does record, however, that his band of pirates, later joined by Captain Louis Lebous and other infamous sea rogues, kept Cape Codders fearful of their presence along the coast for the rest of that summer.

Williams and the others probably hated to leave all their booty behind. Maybe, too, they hoped to exact some retribution for the fate awaiting their comrades who had survived the shipwrecks.

Details of the pirates' trial are well described in Arthur T. Vanderbilt's book *Treasure Wreck, The Fortunes and Fate of the*

*Pirate Ship Whydah* (Houghton Mifflin Company, Boston, 1986). In the trial's aftermath, two of the accused were released, because it was believed that they had truly been "forced" into becoming pirates. The remaining six were declared "pyrats." They were taken to Boston Harbor, rowed out to a strip of shoreline between the high and low tides, and, before a large crowd of spectators, all were hanged simultaneously from a scaffold that was cut from under them. There, the six bodies twisted in the wind over the water, clearly visible to all sailors leaving or arriving at the port. They served as a grim warning to all sailors, who saw the corpses swinging there for years, until they finally decayed and disappeared.

The *Whydah* and her ghostly crew led by Samuel Bellamy sailed off into the realm of legend. It was said that, when severe gales raked the outer banks of Cape Cod, the ghost of the drowned pirates hurled old Spanish coins through the breakers onto the beach. Whether or not it was piratical ghosts that did this, it is a fact that, for over two and a half centuries, beachcombers strolling the coast opposite the site where the *Whydah* was lost, periodically find sand-worn, blackened silver coins believed to have once belonged to *Whydah*'s treasure store.

It is reported that one individual, who searched this beach for several years after each severe nor'easter, collected a cigar-box full of 578 Spanish pieces of eight. Through the years, others, including Henry David Thoreau, claimed that, when the tides were at their extreme ebbs, they had seen the ship's iron caboose or galley chimney which, in the old wooden sailing ships, was located on deck, thrusting up out of the breakers off Wellfleet Beach. Occasionally, an old anchor thought to have belonged to the *Whydah* was salvaged. One after another modern-day salvagers tried to wrest a fortune of pirate treasure from the *Whydah*'s grasp, but were usually defeated by the condition of the seas over the shoals in the supposed wreck area. Apparently, none of them ever made enough to repay the expense of their effort.

At most, all that was reported recovered were a few cannon

balls, some old chunks of wood, and a few corroded coins. As one salvor in the late 1940s concluded, "It will be a very lucky treasure hunter who ever does more than pay expenses, while attempting to find the elusive gold and silver still aboard the *Whydah* . . . the great billows, which constantly break at this part of the coast, will cause all but the most determined treasure hunters to give up in despair, after a few hours of being battered and tossed by the combers of Wellfleet."

# Chapter 29

# Chasing Bellamy's Ghost

A winding, weed-choked road wanders up to an old, worn gray Cape Cod shack not far from the ocean's edge, known as Robbin's Hill Fish House. The wind and sea-weathered shack crouches low in the sand and weeds as if to avoid the often cold offshore wind. Its brittle, paint-chipped boards are entangled in honeysuckle, long-forgotten bleached nets, and sun-cracked fishermen's floats. Beside this shack, when he was about eight years old, Barry Clifford's favorite uncle, Bill Carr, first told him about the big, mysterious graveyard sprawled before them.

Out beyond where the sand meets the surf and sometimes loses it in slinking mists and wool gray fogs, "way out there, as far as the eye can see," said the boy's uncle pointing, "is what they call 'the graveyard of the Atlantic.' "

"Why is that?" asked the boy. "Are people buried there?"

"Yes, indeed. Lots of people," said his uncle. "That's because, ever since the 1700s, it has spelled shipwreck to over three thousand vessels, big and small alike. Not many get spared when the Cape gets mean . . . but let me tell you about one of them . . ."

It was then that young Barry Clifford learned about the

Cape's oldest and most tantalizing shipwreck—a pirate ship full
of treasure in the hands of pirate chieftan Black Sam Bellamy
that sailed along the coast one stormy night in 1717. He ran his
ship *Whydah* onto the shoals, spilling a fortune of plundered
gold, silver, ivory, and gems all over the bottom, and nobody to
this day had ever found that long lost treasure.

Young Clifford's eyes surely were a lot wider by the time
his Uncle Carr finished elaborating on his most cherished subject, the one that many a Cape Codder like himself always
hoped to find some day. Uncle Carr, something of an adventur-
ous fellow himself, never tired of telling young Clifford about
the times when, out fishing along the coast after a storm, upon
looking down, he had glimpsed sparkling objects on the swiftly
shifting sand bottom. He knew at once that these were pieces of
the pirate's loot being shuffled around on the bottom of Davy
Jones's locker. More than once, he told Barry, he had dived in
after those phantom coins and jewels, but they always somehow
were snatched from his grasp. The long gone Black Sam
Bellamy had a way of doing that to people who got too curious
about his booty.

"But mind you, Barry," his Uncle Carr promised. "One
day I'm going to dive down and catch those sparkles in my fist
so tight that even Black Sam won't get 'em away from me!"

The boy never forgot the tale. Everyone knew the story. It
was a legend along the coast. But Barry planned to do something
about it.

As a teenager, he spent more time than most of his friends
wearing a dive mask and swim fins, drifting and swimming along
the ocean beyond the breakers. Always, when he watched the
sand bottom below, he looked for glittering things, hoping to
spot some of the sparkles that his uncle had seen—maybe a gold
doubloon or a silver piece of eight that had somehow become
uncovered from the treasure lost there.

All he saw was an occasional sea shell or metal can tab, but
they never failed to start his heart beating double-time, until he
could dive down and identify the object. In those long summer
days beyond the rollers off Marconi Beach, eager and anxious

Barry Clifford dived up many a glittering can tab "coin" in his early pursuit of the pirate treasure.

In the 1960s he took a job as lifeguard on Cape Cod and learned how to scuba dive. Occasionally, he would spear a small shark while diving and would tie it off to a buoy. Later in the day, before a beachful of wide-eyed spectators, Barry would swim out with a large knife clenched in his teeth and thrash around with the shark. His audience never failed to be awed by this spectacle.

"When I was seventeen, after our last high school football game," Barry later told a newspaper reporter, "a half-dozen of my buddies and I went exploring along the beaches near Wellfleet, too excited to go home. We were standing beside a little hollow, when the largest, most perfectly formed moon I've ever seen rose, creating a path of light out to a point in the ocean. I remember saying, 'There's a shipwreck out there, along that path, and I'm the one who's going to find it.' I'll never know what prompted this feeling of certainty, but it has remained with me ever since."

He spent as much time as he could in local seamen's hangouts, listening to the legends told about the *Whydah*. As best he could judge from what they said, the treasure was lost within swimming distance of the shore. Many believed the wreck occurred because the whole crew was drunk on a cargo of Madeira wine they had taken from an Irish trade ship. According to local legend, Bellamy had been coming back to the Cape to find his lover, young Maria Hallett, the black-haired, ravishing beauty, said to be seen still wandering the dunes above Wellfleet on stormy nights searching for her lost lover.

A sports enthusiast and an outstanding athlete, Barry went on to Western State College in Colorado, where he took on every sport the school had to offer, from football, marathon running, to rodeo riding, power lifting, and speed skiing. He excelled in all of them.

"I graduated a terrific skier with a degree in sociology. I had no idea what I was going to do with my life. All I knew was I was having a lot of fun and I didn't want it to stop."

After college, Clifford married, and had two children. He worked for a while as a Boy Scout administrator and then as a high school physical education teacher. Then, realizing that money was to be made in the building business, he became a building contractor. Between 1971 and 1978 he bought land on Martha's Vineyard and built what he estimated to have been around a million dollars worth of property. "Making money," he said, "was never that difficult for me."

Weekends and vacations he continued diving the waters off Cape Cod and Martha's Vineyard in search of shipwrecks. The more he researched the old ships, the more interested he became in them. It was not just their maritime history that attracted him, but also the possibility of finding artifacts. Clifford was a collector, carrying on more or less an old family tradition. Both his grandfather and his father were antique dealers, and, for as long as Barry could remember, he had been collecting every antiquity that came his way, ranging from old stamps and Indian head pennies to seashore artifacts.

Soon, his part-time interests grew to the point where he was spending all his time either researching shipwrecks or trying to salvage them as a professional diver. In 1976 Clifford salvaged his first historic wreck—the *General Benedict Arnold*, an American Revolutionary privateer that sank off the coast of Plymouth, Massachusetts, in 1778. Next, he discovered the remains of the four-masted schooner, *Agnes Manning*, lost in the late 1800s off Pasque in the Elizabeth Islands.

Always, however, he tried to learn as much as he could about the whereabouts of Samuel Bellamy's *Whydah*. There were stories aplenty, but the trick was to separate the fact from the folklore.

In the course of his research, Clifford kept encountering references to Cyprian Southack, the captain and cartographer who had been sent by Massachusetts's Governor Shute to investigate the loss of the pirate ship in April, 1717. The more Clifford dug for information, the more intriguing the story became. In his mind's eye, he could well imagine the kind of storm that had claimed the *Whydah* and her crew that night off

Cape Cod's treacherous shoals. He could also sympathize with the frustration Southack felt upon finding stormy seas too rough to venture into before the shifting sand bottom buried the heavier part of the wreckage, washing ashore anything that would float, distributing the debris for miles along the coast. Southack had clearly and painstakingly documented his efforts in reports to the governor, which Clifford found in his search of historical archives.

Was it possible, he wondered, that the treasure had already been found by local wreckers who had ample time to scavenge along the coast and possibly even reach the site of the shipwreck many days before Southack actually arrived on the scene?

Clifford read this same unspoken question in Southack's report. Others had often quoted this sentence from Southack's writings that especially bothered Clifford: "There have been two hundred men from 20-miles distance plundering the wreck."

If true, Barry believed the treasure might be long gone, and the only thing left in its wake was the legend. Yet, he well knew how impossible it would have been back then or, for that matter, even now, for salvors or wreckers to work a shipwreck in the surf after a major storm, especially since it had occurred in April off the Cape Cod coast, when the water is still freezing. Clifford could not help but believe that once the wreck went down, the heavy things such as cannon, ballast, and chests of treasure quickly settled down deeper into the layers of rocks and sand and remained buried right there.

Several years later, by chance, while researching another vessel at the Boston Public Library, Clifford stumbled onto Southack's original journal. Intensely and carefully, he read the document, taking his time over the archaic old English constructions and the severely misspelled words. Suddenly, he read the often quoted passage and spotted four key words that answered his question: ". . . there has been at least two hundred men from several places at 20-miles distance plundering the Pirate Wreck *of what came ashore* . . ."

Those four words in Southack's journal substantiated what

Clifford believed. No treasure washed ashore that soon after the wreck. Moreover, no one, at least to Southack's knowledge, had been able to dive in those savage seas and salvage what must still be there.

Even two weeks later, at the end of his investigation, Southack's report to Governor Shute was quite clear on that point: ". . . I find most of the wreck is come a shore in Pieces So I am afears that when weather Permitts to Goe Off the Riches with the guns would be Buried in the sand . . ."

Apparently, only floating debris came ashore. Southack believed the treasure was sinking into the sand offshore.

Further researching the subject, Clifford found an old map Southack had drawn of Cape Cod, which was published around 1730, thirteen years after the *Whydah* disaster. On the old chart, opposite a place now known as Orleans, Southack had noted:

"The Place where I came through with a Whale boat being ordered by ye government to look after ye Pirate Ship Whido Bellame Commander lost ye 26th of April 1717 where I buried One Hundred & Two Men Drowned."

According to Southack's directions, the wreck was located "2 miles from Samuel Harding's house, and 3½ miles south of Billingsgate." Billingsgate was now the center of Wellfleet, but Harding's house had long since disappeared. Clifford realized that, geographically, much may have changed since Southack's day. Still, since Southack was a cartographer and quite accurate in all of his other documentation, Clifford felt that he should believe his description of the wreck's location.

Barry began searching old deeds, wills, and property lines to locate Harding's house. After that, it was just a matter of positioning the geographical points. Finally, he narrowed the search area to a 2-mile section of ocean, just 1500 feet from Wellfleet's Marconi Beach.

After obtaining a permit from the Massachusetts Board of Underwater Archaeology in February, 1983, Clifford rounded up some long-time diving companions, outfitted a salvage boat with high-tech electronic sensing gear, Fisher-style mailbox blowers, and got serious about locating the *Whydah*.

# Chapter 30

## End of a Boyhood Quest: Pirate Booty

Despite the treasure hunters' high hopes that they would go out to the area Clifford had selected, tow their magnetometer around the site until they got a major hit, blow away a few feet of sand with their mailboxes, and find the lost treasure of the *Whydah*, the ensuing search proved to be anything but that easy. First, it took time to set up an accurate survey system. It was extremely important that they know precisely which parts of the ocean bottom they had searched. Otherwise they would be overlapping their efforts. Moreover, it was important that they hire people who knew how to handle and interpret the highly sophisticated electronic gear aboard their salvage vessel.

Mel Fisher of Treasure Salvors Company in Florida served as an expedition consultant. Interestingly, Fisher had found some of the 1715 Spanish treasure that had in the first place enticed Samuel Bellamy to Florida and eventually into the profession of piracy. Now, along with providing his top technician for magnetometer surveys, he was helping Clifford search for Bellamy's flagship.

Months of fruitless searching followed. The same kind of problems that would later add confusion to Fisher's magnetometer survey for the *Atocha* off Key West, also plagued Clifford's search for the *Whydah*—the area had been a test-firing range during World War II, and the magnetometer kept targeting old bomb fragments and dud ordnance. Since there was no way to determine in advance that a target was something more modern than a pirate ship's anchor or iron cannon, the divers had to dig each and every target with their mailbox blowers, excavating down through the sand and rock perhaps a dozen feet or more before learning what triggered their mag.

In the following year and a half of unsuccessful searching, rival *Whydah* hunters applied for search leases on both sides of Clifford's claim, hoping to make the strike first. Their searches were based on the same historical material Clifford had examined, only they interpreted it differently. Early on, Clifford's divers had found the merest trace of possible clues—a clay pipe, a handmade nail, and a rusty rudder strap—not too impressive an array of *Whydah* "treasure," but enough to make Clifford believe that his group was working the right location. It was just a matter of hitting the hot spot where the treasure lay.

In the beginning, Clifford and his diving buddies welcomed as much good press as they could get from the media. Certainly, the public responded by turning out in droves each day, lining the beaches with binoculars to watch their treasure-hunting heros in action not too far offshore. Eventually, however, after a year and a half of failure, Clifford's crew was not too anxious to publicize its continued failures. In fact, in July, 1984, when an NBC news crew arrived with television cameras intent on filming the treasure hunters' activities, Clifford tried his best to put them off by running the camera crew offshore to film a passing pod of whales. Finally, when he could avoid it no longer, Barry brought the news team aboard the *Vast Explorer* and they headed offshore to do their thing for the media.

As the heavy salvage vessel cut through the 2-foot seas, Clifford could not help feeling that all they would do on this run was document yet another failure—the extremely costly finding, excavating, and recovery of another bunch of old bomb fragments.

At least the media had plenty of exotic-looking state-of-the-art search and salvage equipment to ogle with their camera lenses. Barry showed them the magnetometer sensor and recorder, explaining how the towed head registered anomalies on a printout, so they could be plotted and checked later. He explained in layman's terms their sub-bottom profiler, or boomer, which, when towed behind the vessel, sent pulsed sound waves through the ocean bottom. If they came into contact with solid objects, they bounced back to create an echo picture that showed the object's shape, size, and depth. Then there were the mailboxes, the elbow-pipe blowers that fitted down over the vessel's screws to direct the prop wash to the bottom, digging the holes. Clifford made sure that everyone understood the destructive force of these mailboxes, explaining that they could be highly destructive if not used with care. "Otherwise they can be as destructive as driving a bulldozer through the Museum of Fine Arts. . . . We've got to be careful and proceed very slowly or we could make a hell of a mess."

At least in their year and a half of searching they had learned where the *Whydah* was not. Clifford still had faith in Southack's sightings, as far as they went, but now he had learned another significant piece of the puzzle—this storm-lashed coast had been suffering the onslaughts of strange currents and freak tides for centuries. Over time, they had taken their toll on the land—how great a toll, Barry was to learn. As he discovered, in 1870, the local lighthouse keeper had logged the fact that the 50-foot bank dropping to the ocean was then 228 feet from his two brick lighthouses. In less than ten years, storm seas had consumed 228 feet of land straight in through that 50-foot bluff and had toppled both lighthouses.

Clifford calculated that, since 1787, the seas had consumed over 7 acres of land. Considering an annual 3-foot beach erosion, this suggested that the site Southack had originally marked as the location of the *Whydah* was actually some 900 feet out to sea, instead of closer in, where they had been searching.

On this day, with the *Vast Explorer* loaded with media

people, the vessel's dual 250-horsepowered engines were throbbing on course over the new ground, when the mag reported a hit.

A marker buoy went over the side. The vessel moved into position, anchored, and the mailboxes dug their hole. Suiting up, the divers went down. With them was a cameraman linked to a TV monitor aboard the salvage boat. Watching this monitor, NBC reporter Nancy Fernandes saw the sand and mud pit with the shadowy forms of divers moving around it. Then, suddenly, "There was a big piece of something!" At her shoulder a diver gasped.

"Hey! That's a cannon!"

As more sand swirled out of the crater, other dark objects appeared. From far away, Barry heard a diver surface and shout that he had found some coins and a cannon and that there was more—much more—down there.

Clifford raced to the rail, reached down, and took the small, black disk from the diver's hand. As he looked at it, he saw the broad cross of Spain, and then he read the date: 1684. It was a silver two-real coin minted in Peru. Under 18 feet of sand in just 25 feet of water, they had found the *Whydah*, the only pirate wreck anyone had ever found anywhere in the world!

At that instant of realization, as if on cue, nature responded. "The sky had been pitch black from a summer storm hanging over the Cape," said Barry, "and when I saw that coin, there were terrific claps of thunder—the spirit of Sam Bellamy, perhaps? I'll never forget it: black sky, black ocean, and white cracks of lightning in the sky; the white cliffs of Wellfleet nearby."

As the crew excitedly passed around the Spanish coin, everything abruptly changed. "The whole project was instantly revitalized," said Barry. "We all went crazy. I felt like I was breathing pure oxygen. It was like being on the highest mountain, breathing the purest air!"

There, 1,500 feet off the beach, in their 20-foot-wide excavation, the divers found what everyone else had been talking about for two hundred sixty-seven years—Bellamy's treasure, the centuries-old accumulated plunder from over fifty victimized vessels, shared loot belonging to all of the long-dead pirates. What the divers found in that single excavation was not revealed publicly for the next six months, but it was a bonanza so staggering, that it both shocked and stunned Clifford and his crew. Cannon, coins, cutlasses, jewelry, plates, buckles, shot— it was all there in one confused pile. To dig right down through the loose sand into the *Whydah*'s Mother Lode so surprised the salvors that, "We finally just closed the pit back up," said Barry. "We left it filled with treasure. We found more than we ever expected. You could see all the stuff sticking out of the sides of the pit. The ship had never been touched. It scared the hell out of us."

After a public announcement that the pirate ship *Whydah* had been found, nothing more was reported for the next few months. During that time, Clifford's company, Maritime Explorations Incorporated, hired a number of underwater archaeologists and preservationists. He and his associates realized how important it was that this one-of-a-kind shipwreck, with all of its contents intact, be worked in the proper archaeological manner in order to preserve as much of the historical information as possible from the deposits. Once his company lined up the experts, proper storage facilities for the artifacts, and the best means to catalog and preserve their finds, work began at the site during the summer of 1984.

It was not until early that following December that the public learned something about the magnificence of their discovery. From their first excavation they had dug, divers recovered over 3,000 Spanish silver coins, four gold coins, various pieces of gold and silver jewelry, a candle snuffer, along with some of the ship's armament—a 3,000-pound cannon, cannonballs, and 580 musket balls. From another pit came three more fused-together cannon, an 8-foot anchor, silver coins, a silver ingot, gold bars cut into chunks (as if for division among the pirates), more gold and silver jewelry, and a mortar jar with the letter "W" scratched on its bottom.

"It amounts to several million dollars in treasure," Clifford said. "One of the coins is valued at forty thousand dollars." Clifford estimated that the ship had 10 tons of treasure aboard and that the surface had barely been scratched. The 1985 diving season was largely lost, while the salvors waited for the frustratingly slow wheels of the bureaucratic process to move. A permit from the Army Corp of Engineers was needed, which would allow Maritime Explorations to begin bringing up the pirate treasure.

When the permit was finally granted that fall, the divers hastily tried to make up for lost time and were able to recover a dozen navigational tools, pewter eating vessels that bore a Royal African seal, a gold ring, a casket of East Indian jewels, small gold bars that showed knife marks where the pirates had divided them, and gold dust, which Barry said, "ran through the wet sand like chocolate through ripple ice cream."

Despite the finds, academic archaeologists and historians not working with the salvors were still unconvinced that Clifford and his crew were actually working Bellamy's flagship, the *Whydah*.

"We reserve our opinions until we see more convincing evidence," they said.

That evidence came in 1985 in the form of a heavy, encrusted bronze ship's bell. Once this 18-inch prize was raised, it was just a matter of chipping away a thick coating of concretions. "Underneath, just as I had expected, was the inscription, 'WHYDAH GALLEY 1717,' " said Barry. The skeptics had their proof.

"It would seem to me that this is the type of identification that we have been waiting for—not waiting, but hoping for," said Joseph A. Sinnott, director of the Massachusetts Board of Underwater Archaeological Resources. "I don't think you could logically hope for more," he said. "Short of the quarterboard, I don't think you could get anything better than the bell. That should do it."

Sinnott's board licensed the *Whydah* salvage efforts and supervised the archaeological work.

By the fall of 1986, one of the specialists hired by Maritime Explorations to work with the artifacts, Kenneth Kinkor, was gradually piecing together some of the historical information resulting from their study. Kinkor had been researching the background of a pirate connected with the *Whydah* for his Illinois State University masters thesis, when Clifford suggested he join their operation.

"Kenneth seemed to be the only one who really knew something about pirates," explained Barry.

While Daniel Defoe's *A General History of the Robberies and Murders of the Most Notorious Pyrates*, written in 1724, is generally considered a fairly accurate account of their activities, Defoe quite skillfully blended fact with fiction to create his own material. He had done the same with the writing of *Robinson Crusoe*, in 1719, which was based on the factual, but far less exciting, adventures of marooned seaman, Alexander Selkirk. Most of the books that followed his lead romanticized "the golden age of piracy" in the first quarter of the eighteenth century, and most such books were written for children. Other than these books and Errol Flynn movies, the true-to-life history of pirates had gotten lost in the shuffle, just as badly as did the true-to-life history of the American Indian. Now, however, "piratologist" Kenneth Kinkor is shedding some new light on that long overlooked subject.

Kinkor is the kind of fellow who couldn't care less about how many or what kind of coins came up from the pirate ship *Whydah*. The sealed wooden barrel recovered recently from the *Whydah*, which had sat submerged in the laboratory tank of water beside loaded cannon, pewter plates, brass buttons, and a coin or two, would hold far more interest for him, if it proved to be filled with bones from the remains of the pirate's meat locker, rather than a barrelful of silver coins. After all, one silver coin is much like another; but the remnants of the pirates' food supply would tell us something about their diet, adding a far more important piece of information to our rather sketchy picture of pirate life 269 years ago.

Other authorities seem to feel the same way. Said Dr. Paul Johnston, curator of Maritime History at the Peabody Museum of Salem, "The *Whydah*'s potential as a source of information about pirates is tremendous." Historical archaeologist, James Bradley agreed. "This wreck is going to finally cut the fluff away from the *Whydah* and what fiction tells us about piracy. It is a major archaeological find."

With only one percent of the site excavated, the highlights of Kinkor's findings are intriguing. For example, pistols from the wreckage were found in pairs, connected by varying lengths of silken scarves tied to the pistol butts. Kinkor believes that, when the pirates attacked and boarded a vessel, they wore the weapons slung around their necks, not tucked into their belts, Errol Flynn style.

Any seagoing vessel of that day required only a single good set of finely calibrated navigational instruments, but to date the salvors have found nine such sets of dividers and compasses. They were probably taken as plunder by the freebooters who were well aware of the value of these instruments in other major seaports.

*Whydah*'s cannon were fully loaded and ready for action, just the way they were found when brought up. One, with its tampon still in its muzzle, was found to have a still dry barrel inside. What intrigued Kinkor were the kind of projectiles he found loaded in place, ready for firing. They were packages containing a 3-pound cannon ball and two bags filled with gumball-size shot. It was a scatter-gun load guaranteed to clear the deck of any opposition from another vessel. Actually, the load was intended to save the ship. "That combination," said Kinkor, "would cut a destructive swath through the crew and a ship's rigging, while leaving the hull largely intact. It seems to have been your basic, primitive neutron bomb. Knock out the crew and the rigging, but save the ship for your own future use."

Historians now believe that piracy flourished in the Spanish territories and in the English colonies of the New World, after the Spanish War of Succession in 1713 for this reason: widespread unemployment among seafarers who once served aboard French and British men-of-war. When they lost their legal wartime license to prey on Spanish ships, they became pirates. But rather than pursue the violent careers attributed to such infamous characters as Bart Roberts and Edward "Blackbeard" Teach, most were far from bloodthirsty.

Kinkor believes that, wherever possible, there was more of an economic incentive for the pirates to avoid fights, since it meant less injury all around and easier work for the ship's carpenter, who often doubled as the ship's surgeon. Furthermore, a reputation for mercy often encouraged a crew of an overtaken ship to surrender and perhaps even join up with the pirates. There is no record of Bellamy's crew ever killing or engaging in battle.

Kinkor has learned that newly recruited pirates were required to sign allegiance to several articles of conduct. They agreed among other things to swear fidelity to each other, and to an equal sharing of all loot among themselves. Violators of their sworn code of conduct were marooned. All they asked for was freedom, democracy, and the right to be rogues.

One of the more interesting discoveries from the *Whydah* is several small brass three-ringed pendants. It is believed that they were worn around the pirates' necks and used to sign the ship's articles, the brass seal was pressed into warm wax on the documents. The printing face of the seals contain crude carvings with individualized imagery, which probably enabled the illiterate pirates to place their "mark" on ship's papers detailing their fraternal agreement. Maritime historians say the discovery of such seals in connection with pirates is unprecedented.

So far, none of the treasure has been sold; the question of ownership is still being argued in the courts. For Barry Clifford's part, he feels that the real value of the treasure lies in the historical story and the unprecedented information that the pirate ship is passing on to us as its legacy. He would like to see all of it—the treasure and the artifacts—in a pirate museum he proposes to build.

"Right from the beginning," he says, "I promised myself that if I ever found the *Whydah*, I would keep her riches in a place for everyone to share. My dream was to find the treasure and build a pirate museum, a place where children of all ages could see and ponder relics from a long lost era—the Golden Age of Piracy."

Thirty years after Barry Clifford's Uncle Bill had told him about Black Sam Bellamy and the pirate ship *Whydah*, Clifford sat on the edge of Uncle Bill's bed. "This time," said Barry, "it was my turn to tell him a pirate story. He knew I'd found her. His eyes sparkled like a child's in anticipation. Uncle Bill died later that night. I'm sure he dreamed of treasure."

# PART VI

## Melvin Fisher: Today's the Day

# Chapter 31

# Day of Days

The year is 1985. It is the beginning of the end, the last chapter of the sixteen-year search for the final resting place of the *Atocha*, a Spanish galleon that disappeared over 360 years ago, with an estimated $400 million worth of treasure aboard. For sixteen hard years, one man—Melvin Fisher—and his small band of dedicated followers pursued a tantalizing trail of treasure clues as complex as any maze imaginable. All their hopes, destinies, and dreams hang on one fragile premise—if they can last long enough, if they can endure, one day the clues will lead them down a yellow brick road to their golden reward.

In all those years, it was largely an unrewarding, hopeless search. False clues always led to dead-end corridors in the maze. Yet they stubbornly kept searching the blue-green ocean's emptiness 40 miles west of Key West for the dream. Despite all their efforts in this watery ships' graveyard between the Atlantic and the Gulf of Mexico, the fates only reluctantly and begrudgingly revealed their clues along the underwater trail to this fabulous crypt. Though Fisher and his followers had no way of knowing in advance, the year of everyone's final reckoning with the long lost galleon would be 1985. Over the years, key clues seemed to be putting them in the right area. But always they were only fragmentary, terribly tantalizing pieces of the puzzle—an anchor here, a series of bronze cannon there, a pocket of treasure, a dribble of gold and silver riches often linked by beautifully sculptured golden-linked money chains. But always, these clues never quite added up to the one major target they were looking for—the *Atocha*'s Mother Lode.

Then suddenly out of the blue depths came a faint suggestion that the searchers might be beginning the last leg of their journey, gradually moving down a corridor that could be the exit of the maze.

The first of these final puzzle pieces to fall in place had occurred almost a year before. Before that, everything had been tried; even a psychic in white robes stood poised in a boat's bow trying to communicate with the hundreds of lost souls who had perished on the ill-fated galleon in the hope that they might offer some out-of-the-world insight as to where they might now reside. Supersophisticated scientific gear looked though the bottom of the ocean with sound waves and tried to "see" the galleon. Supersensitive metal detectors snooped every nook and cranny trying to sense the presence of the Money Pile. By psychic or scientific means, Fisher touched all bases in his obsessive search. Finally, as so often occurs, it was neither the psychics nor the mechanical gadgets that did the job. It was the good old Mark I Eyeball contact that made all the major finds. This time it was the accidental finding of a cannon.

The man who found it was Fay Feild, the electronics wizard, who had provided Fisher with an improved magneto-meter for detecting shipwrecks, during Fisher's search for the 1715 shipwrecks. Feild was also the man partially responsible for developing the innovative blower device all serious treasure hunters now use in their underwater excavations. It is appropriate that it was Feild who found what was perhaps the first of the key clues. While he was being towed behind one of Fisher's smaller search boats, helping Bob Moran establish a remote sensing survey, he spotted a large bronze cannon lying exposed on the sand bottom. The gun later proved to have belonged to the *Atocha*. Careful searching of the site revealed two large galleon anchors to the northeast of the gun. All considered, these final finds completed a string of armament and anchors that pointed straight as a compass arrow either into an area known as the "Quicksands," shallower shoals of shifting bars, or seaward into the murky mud-bottom depths of Hawk Channel.

It was in this latter direction, the deep-water area, that Fisher decided to concentrate his search—one leading off into the blue, where the water deepened, the visibility grew more limited, and the searchers probed the lengthening corridor of mud with every physical and mechanical means available to them. The recording of their finds in the ship's log, interspersed with the letter "N" for "nothing," sometimes read like a war surgeon's case book; at other times, they read like an inventory for a junkyard: "Bomb frags., Bomb frags., N., N., N., Bomb Frags., Ship spike, N., N., Barrel hoop., Nail, . . ."

The "junky" finds elicit a wild "Wahoooo!" from the searchers, because they mean the trail is heating up . . . maybe, at long last, for the big payoff! Wallowing its way into deepening Hawk's Channel is the rust-stained 165-foot former oil freighter, the *Saba Rock*, on loan from a Louisiana salvage firm. Its owner is furnishing Fisher the big boat, with its giant blowers for punching holes in the bottom 50 feet below them, in exchange for a percentage of the Pile when it is found. Skipper of the *Saba Rock* is twenty-five-year-old Ed Stevens of Fort Lauderdale. The small group of divers aboard are a mixed bag. They come from many different parts of the country. Their backgrounds are equally diverse. They have been so long at sea now that they make a game of guessing which day it is. Newspapers come once a week by boat with their food. Despite their differences, their goal is a common one: to follow the clues and find the Pile.

*"Look for ballast stone,"* was the message hammered into each of them by Fisher's underwater archaeologist R. Duncan Mathewson III. "Find the stones and you'll find the Pile." He believed this so firmly that he once had divers counting all the

ballast stones they found, so he could calculate how big of a Pile they could expect once they found it. Such was the meticulous manner of their search—carefully documenting each and every find, no matter how insignificant it might seem at the time.

That year the Memorial Day weekend was just another routine work day for the crew of the *Saba Rock*, at least that is the way it began. But for blue-eyed twenty-six-year-old Susan Nelson, who had once worked as a Fort Lauderdale recreation specialist, the day, Saturday, May 25th, quickly became anything but routine. On the bottom, in 50 feet of water, searching in one of the sand and mud craters dug by the mighty blowers, she saw something that changed their routine instantly.

"They said look for ballast stone, ballast stone," she later reported. "So I didn't recognize the gold. Suddenly, I kicked, and there was a gold bar. I kicked again, and there was another gold bar, and suddenly there I was holding four gold bars in my hands, and I was a little in awe. I was hyperventilating underwater. I said, 'Oh, my Lord!' "

The *Saba Rock*'s ship-to-shore radio crackled the good news to Fisher's Treasure Salvor's headquarters in Key West. Maybe the radio reply that came back was garbled, but to those aboard ship, it sounded like a lot of wild yelling amidst the popping of champagne corks.

It proved to be a stunning pocket of treasure that swiftly turned the monotonous notations in Captain Steven's ship's log to much livelier reading fare: It went from "Bomb frag., Barrel hoop, Nail," to "13 Gold bars, 7 feet of Gold chain, 414 Silver coins, 5 silver plates, A silver platter, 16 emeralds . . ."

Morale soared. Then the pocket ran dry. The divers stopped hyperventilating and the logbook of finds went back to its monotonous Bomb frag., and N. The treasure trail had run out.

Kane Fisher, Mel's son, who had long believed in the deep-water theory of the *Atocha*'s whereabouts, was ordered to take his vessel, the *Dauntless*, farther down the southeast corridor to investigate some mag hits believed to be part of the scatter pattern. Kane's crew promptly uncovered another treasure pocket containing ballast rock, copper ingots, and thousands of silver coins. It *had* to be the Mother Lode. Parts of the ship's rigging were entangled with the finds. What more of an indication was needed? Everyone was anxious to break the news to the world, that the *Atocha*'s Mother Lode had been found.

Everyone that is, but those who knew better. Chief among them was archaeologist Duncan Mathewson. Where were all the ballast stones he had calculated to be somewhere? Where were the chests of silver coins stacked one atop the other, and the hundreds of bars of silver that should constitute a sizable bottom configuration? The manifest said all these things were there. So now Mathewson asked, "If this is the Pile, where are they?"

Where indeed? The fates were not quite ready to reveal the whole secret. Not yet. After keeping the secret for 363 years, surely four more tantalizing days would not matter. Keep them dangling to the end.

Mel Fisher's almost daily intoned words of encouragement to his often discouraged crew of searchers, his "today's the day," after sixteen years of repeating, finally came true. That day was July 20, 1985.

Kane's divers aboard the *Dauntless* were bringing up a steady flow of coins, copper ingots, and ballast rocks. They had moved the *Dauntless* 10 feet to a hole producing a couple of dozen silver coins, another dozen copper ingots, and pieces of broken pottery. One more 10-foot move, another hole with the blower, and the third pair of divers; Greg Wareham and Andy Matrocci, dived down through the 54-foot depths to inspect the crater. It was the fifth hole of the day and, like the others, it proved richer than the one before it. Finding the bottom littered with coins, the divers busily filled their goodie bags. The two momentarily left the money pit to scout the area. Matrocci was the first back to the hole, adding more coins to his bag.

Suddenly, Wareham tapped him on the shoulder. Looking at him, Matrocci saw his wide-eyed buddy gurgling excitedly in his regulator and beckoning urgently for him to follow him out of the hole. At the crater's edge, Wareham stared into the distance to orient himself. Visibility was about 20 feet. Then he finned off. Dropping his bag of coins, Matrocci swiftly followed.

Forty feet from their hole, the divers saw a hard gray linear shape materialize from out of the low bottom growth. It was no more than 2 feet high and several yards long, resembling a stack of long gray loaves of bread.

The moment he recognized it as a reef of silver bars, Matrocci felt the hairs on the back of his neck bristle. Suddenly, he threw his arms around Wareham and the two rolled and tumbled about the bottom, shouting through their regulators, "Silver bars! Silver bars!"

Shooting to the surface in a welter of bubbles, Greg Wareham came flying out of the water with Matrocci right behind him, shouting and choking, "This is it! There's silver bars everywhere! We hit the Mother Lode!"

Everyone aboard the *Dauntless* started laughing, yelling, and embracing each other. It was pure bedlam. "*Atocha, Atocha*—we got it!" The whole crew was jumping up and down and shouting.

As some semblance of sanity returned, lanky Kane Fisher stalked into the wheelhouse and keyed the marine radio microphone.

"Home base, this is *Dauntless*, come in."

Forty miles away, at the Treasure Salvors headquarters in Key West, they responded. "Go ahead *Dauntless*."

With a remarkable attempt at composure, Mel Fisher's son, Kane, said, "You can put away the charts. We found the Pile!"

As the news flashed through Key West, its electrifying effect soon streaked across the country. Mel Fisher's sixteen-year search for a pot of gold under a rainbow named the *Atocha*, had finally ended. This was the long-awaited *Day*, the one this particular man had been shaping his life for from the first moment he had gotten hooked on the idea of diving for treasure.

# Chapter 32

## In the Beginning

As had so many others who devoted their lives to diving for sunken treasure, young Mel Fisher caught the fever by reading adventure books about sunken treasure and pirates at a very early, impressionable age. He was born in 1922 and, though living inland in the midwest town of Hobart, Indiana, by the time he was twelve years old, young Fisher decided he had better get started in this business of exploring the underwater world.

Since such essential items as scuba gear, face masks, swim fins, and snorkels were yet to be invented in those pre-Cousteau days, like all kids who had been nourished on such fare as Robert Louis Stevenson's *Treasure Island* and Jules Verne's *Twenty Thousand Leagues Under the Sea*, he tackled the problem. He and a friend decided to build a diving helmet.

It was a typical example of Yankee ingenuity, one that advanced by trial and error, improving along the way, provided it did not kill the do-it-yourselfers in the process. This one almost did. But then, most kids resourceful enough to build their own sport equipment during the Depression years were usually tough enough to survive it, mistakes and all.

Fisher and his friend's diving helmet started out disguised as a 5-gallon paint can. Turned upside down, it looked like the real McCoy. So they padded the lip of the "helmet" with a tire Fisher had cut off his bicycle and wired around the edge of the can. To give the helmet weight and make it less likely to float off his head underwater, Fisher melted all his toy lead soldiers and poured them into the tire.

Their first trial dive in a local gravel pit without a face plate or air hose worked well, until Fisher ran out of air. He corrected this problem by taking a valve out of his bicycle inner tube, bolting it to the top of the paint can, and connecting a length of garden hose from the helmet to a bicycle pump at the opposite end.

After that, Fisher's friend sat in an old Model A's inner tube and pumped air down to Fisher, while he towed him around the gravel pit by the air hose. This worked fine, though occasionally, Fisher's buddy would stick the air pump underwater and give him a shower.

The next improvement on the helmet was a window to see out of. First he taped it on, believing that the water pressure would help hold the glass in place. But when he tried it underwater, the window blew outward from the air pressure inside the helmet, and Fisher shot to the surface, sputtering and coughing before the thing did him in.

Finally, he made a good window for it and, from then on, the young adventurer began taking his first long look at the underwater world which would enthrall him from that day on. Later he built bigger and better helmets and even started constructing a submarine in his basement, but he never finished it. After working on the project for two years, when he got to a complicated part involving carbon dioxide cartridges and items that were just too difficult to come by in those years, he gave up.

Fisher grew up and finished high school in Gary, Indiana, then went on to major in mechanical engineering at Purdue University, joining the Army Reserve there. When Pearl Harbor occurred, he went on active duty. The Army placed him in its own engineering program at Purdue, then sent him off to France with the Army Engineers. Landing in France in the wake of the Normandy invasion, Fisher's job with the engineers was to pick up the pieces and repair what the army of invasion had just blown up.

After his stint in the service, Mel received his army discharge and began traveling around the United States—working here and there, first in Chicago, then in Denver, where he carpentered for the Bureau of Reclamation. "Fine country," thought Mel, but a bit far from places for good swimming or diving. He moved to Tampa, Florida, where he worked as a building contractor on small construction jobs.

During those four years in Tampa, he learned how to skin-dive and spearfish and found it all a highly exhilirating experience, so much so, that he quit his job and really got into it. As he recalled later, "I took about a six month vacation to do nothing but beach-bumming, diving, and spearfishing. I really enjoyed it. No responsibilities; nothing to do but just go off and dive."

That is when he acquired his first aqualung. This self-contained underwater diving apparatus was advertised in the *Tampa Tribune* by a Frenchman named Rene Bussoz, who lived in Westwood Village, California. He was visiting the United States with six brand-new French-made aqualungs to sell.

Fisher leaped into his car, drove 3,000 miles to California, and bought one from Bussoz, telling the Frenchman that he would like to have the Florida franchise to sell the diving unit that Jacques Cousteau and his companions were then popularizing in Europe.

Returning to Florida with his new purchase, Fisher suddenly realized he had a dud on his hands. No one knew anything about the equipment and no one was interested in knowing. No one had a way to refill the cylinder with high-pressure air, even if they were interested. In fact, the general public wondered why in the world anyone in his right mind wanted to go underwater in the first place. It was too dangerous.

Fisher used his newly acquired aqualung one time. He descended to the muddy bottom of a ship channel beside a bridge abutment, intending to spear a 300-pound jewfish. He found the water so murky and the ghostly shadows of sharks, rays, and giant fish so intimidating, that he spent most of his time hiding behind a bridge piling and staring wide-eyed at the huge shadows moving through the water around him. Out of air, he came up. With no way to refill his air tank, he tossed his equipment in the back of his car and forgot about it for the next six months.

After that, the Fisher family moved to California. Mel's father wanted to set up a chicken ranch near Torrance, so Mel helped him build it. They got in about five thousand laying hens and four thousand fryers and went into business. Mel used his G.I. Bill to take a night course in poultry husbandry and agriculture, and received a degree in that field.

Chicken ranching was fairly profitable for the Fishers over the next four years, but somehow, watching five thousand eggs being laid every day was not as exciting to Mel as diving underwater to spear fish.

Southern Californians at the time were leading the country in the new sport of skin-diving that was quickly becoming popular. For Mel, this was more like it. Building a machine shop in one of the feed sheds, he began designing and developing special kinds of spear guns for spearing fish. His friends liked his equipment so well, they started buying it from him. Mel expanded his machine shop and began manufacturing diving equipment on a larger scale. Joining a dive club, he once again started using his aqualung. As did everyone else, however, Mel had to drive to Rene Bussoz's place in Los Angeles to get it filled each time he used it. This was so impractical, Fisher saw the benefit of owning his own air compressor—one that would fill the tank to the extremely high air pressure required by the unit.

Once this piece of equipment was added to his machine shop, a veritable torrent of divers began wending their way to the Fisher's chicken ranch. Now Fisher not only filled these divers' aqualung tanks, but he started manufacturing dive equipment for jobbers and distributors in the Los Angeles area. Though his feed room dive shop was only open a couple of hours in the afternoon each day, he soon was making more money working those couple of hours building diving equipment than he was working the other twenty-two hours with the chickens. He made another feed shop into a retail outlet for his products and began what he said later was the first specialized skin-diving shop in the world. Mel found that the more people he taught how to dive, the more of them became his customers for diving equipment and air fills. It was a fast-growing business, right up to the time when Mel's father decided to sell the chicken ranch.

The ranch was bought by the Horton family from Montana. Mel agreed to stay a while and show them how to run the business. The Horton's daughter was a lovely, red-haired sixteen-year-old girl named Dolores, nicknamed Deo, and it was not long before Mel invited her and her younger sister to one of his dive club meetings. · That night he showed an underwater film about diving, which Mel had filmed in Florida. The girls were fascinated. Later he taught Deo how to snorkel and skin-dive; then how to use scuba equipment. Together they explored the depths around Catalina Island and Deo was enthralled by everything she saw. Mel was not only taken by her beauty, but saw that Deo was a natural diver, completely unafraid underwater, but fascinated by the beauty and excitement she found in this largely unexplored new world beneath the surface.

Mutual admiration soon turned to love, and Mel and Deo married in June, 1953. It was the kind of honeymoon that only divers can appreciate. The newlyweds headed for Florida, ended up in Key West, chartered a boat, and told the captain to take them to as many shipwrecks as he could find.

He did exactly that and the newlyweds spent a large part of their honeymoon in sunny Florida, swimming through the murky hulls of long-abandoned well-rusted and coral-encrusted sunken ships. But it was not all just for the fun of it. Mel made his honeymoon a working vacation by shooting underwater films of the wrecks and their spearfishing adventures, which he later sold to the Voit diving equipment manufacturing company. This was not the first, nor would it be the last time that Mel found a way to get others to pay him for doing the thing he enjoyed the most—diving.

Since the diving business was booming, Fisher decided to build a dive shop at Redondo Beach, California. To help finance the project, he and Deo started diving commercially for lobsters. Dressed in long underwear and dry suits, Deo would snorkel along the surface, while Fisher on the bottom caught a lobster. As soon as he got one, she swam down and brought it up to their skiff. By the time she checked him again, he would have another lobster. Every time a spiny lobster perforated their dry suit, they were quickly chilled by the cold water. Soon they learned to wear overalls and sweatshirts over their dry suits to protect them from snags.

Periodically, they dumped their collected lobsters into holding traps Fisher had spotted every quarter of a mile apart. By the day's end, they had an enormous number of lobsters ready to go to market. These they sold to restaurant chains at below fish market prices. From the profits, he paid for his ocean-front diving shop.

From the day Mel's Aqua Shop opened its doors business was so thriving, it was almost more than they could keep up with. Often they worked until midnight, introducing the uninitiated to diving and its equipment. Of course, the idea was to sell all his customers diving equipment. Deo worked with him as much as possible. Then she got started on the Fisher family. Son Dirk was born in 1954, and a second son, Kim, came in 1956.

With an expanding family, Mel had to find ways to expand his business and add to his profits.

"I got interested in underwater photography and did a lot

of that as a hobby," he said. "Then pretty soon they began asking me to show these films on TV, which I did. And as it happened, for four and a half years I had my own television show, showing these movies I'd made."

Always the promoter, Mel made every idea pay dividends. It was a shrewd business formula. To people interested in diving, he sold scuba lessons and diving gear. Then he set up diving trips to distant places along the coasts of southern California, Mexico, and exotic islands in the Caribbean, for which they paid. Meanwhile he filmed their activities for use on his television show and to sell to dive-equipment manufacturers.

When California divers learned that scuba gear enabled them to find nuggets and grains of gold scattered around the bottom of rivers throughout the old gold-bearing areas of the California mountains, Mel the promoter was there to fill their needs. He would take a group of customers up into the mountains to dive in the rivers for gold, then make a movie about it.

Next, he made a good gold-dredging machine for divers to use. His customers were impressed with his findings to such a degree that it proved another bonanza for him. Soon, their gold-rush fever started funneling their gold into Mel's bank account, while he manufactured and sold them gold-dredging units as fast as he could make them. He never had to go gold-diving again in the icy mountain streams. Instead, he mined gold in the comfort of his dive shop.

Since the idea of finding gold and finding treasure is practically synonymous, Fisher had little trouble expanding from one to the other. And once he got rolling in that direction, he went full speed ahead.

# Chapter 33

# Target: Treasure

Fisher and his friends were off on one of their dive trips when the treasure bug bit him and he caught the fever. They were in Mexico, where Mel was filming a feature about Acapulco diving. While he was sitting on the beach one day, watching the bikinis go by, his attention was diverted by a young Mexican boy with a tale to tell. It concerned big treasure aboard a fabled ship known as a Manila Galleon, which had sunk in Acapulco Bay . . . right out *there*. . . . Mel's eyes glittered in the afternoon sunlight, as his gaze reached out into that broad expanse of inviting water. He had the divers and the gear, so it was the most natural thing in the world that they go down and look for that galleon.

Mel rounded up his companions and began searching the bottom of the bay. Nothing was found resembling any galleon, but Mel enjoyed the thrill of the hunt. All the divers encountered were modern shipwrecks, but Mel learned that the boy's story was true. Acapulco had been where the fabulous one-ship-a-year arrived from the Philippines loaded with 600 tons of gold, silver, Chinese porcelain, silks, and other valuable items. At least one of these valuable vessels had sunk there. What quickly cooled Fisher's ardor for treasure wrecks in Mexican waters was

273

that the Mexican government had no intention of sharing such historical treasures with outsiders. The government simply took 100 percent of whatever was found.

Still, the idea stuck and, once treasure hunting was in his blood, Mel lost no time trying to figure a shortcut to locating it. He had heard about one piece of magical equipment that could be the answer—a magnetometer—a device capable of detecting iron objects at a great distance underwater. Mel saw it as a way to find iron cannon, cannonballs, ships' spikes, and other hard parts of an old wreck that would most likely mark its final resting place. Logically, if other divers had not picked it over first, that is where any treasure would be. But how to acquire a mag?

Mel wrote to all the detector companies in the country, and found no one manufactured equipment that had satisfactory sensitivity—the capability of detecting iron objects at a good distance.

The best available was the magnetometer used by the military to locate submarines. It was called an ASQ-1. The source was in Arizona. Mel drove a truck there and found a fieldful of surplus airplanes that were being scrapped. With them were tons of military equipment. The would-be treasure hunter searched through the junk until he found enough parts to make up what he hoped would be a magnetometer. For one thousand dollars he bought a truckload of the parts and headed home to California.

Once he got everything there, he started hunting for a good electronics man, someone who could help him put all the pieces together. The man he found was Lou Black. He knew his stuff. In short order, Mel had his military mag, an ASQ-1. And that was just the beginning.

"A little later on, I got an ASQ-3, which was a little more modern. Then an ASQ-5 and an ASQ-12. I believe they are still using the last one in the military today for locating submarines," he said. "But they also have newer types. It is very complicated equipment, very hard to maintain. They are large and cumbersome. It takes a talented man to keep them running."

Mel's Aqua Shop was soon the meeting place for would-be

treasure divers. The club quickly grew to one hundred and twelve members. They practiced with all their detection and salvage gear, each week working in a different offshore area, checking out shipwrecks. Mel had a kind of rotating crew that would take off from work about once a month. Everything they found, they sold and split the profit.

What they found was treasure of a more modern vintage—huge bronze ship propellers, monel shafts. One day they found a midchannel shipwreck, about 100 feet deep, loaded with hundreds of fishing anchors entangled in it. They recovered and sold anchors, until they were blue in the face. It all added up to cash in their pockets, money to spend on even more elaborate diving or treasure-hunting equipment.

Another profitable salvage operation occurred the day they found one of Al Capone's sunken gambling ships. It had been anchored just outside the 3-mile limit at Long Beach, California. Capone used shuttle boats to run customers out there to gamble. Another rival gang operated a similar vessel off Santa Monica. It was named the *Star of Scotland*. When a gang war started, thugs from the *Star of Scotland* blew up Capone's boat, while she was anchored offshore. A week later, Capone's people retaliated, sinking the *Star of Scotland*.

Fisher researched the story in old newspaper articles and was determined to locate Capone's old gambling ship. Without too much trouble, he and his divers found the bomb-shattered remains of the old vessel in 60 feet of water. Gaining entry through the vessel's open hatches, they swam into the shadowy interior of the hull. There, covered with a thick patina of silt, lying in disarray, they found what remained of the gambling king's casino—slot machines, cash register, broken roulette wheels.

The divers emptied the cash register of its soggy bills and rusty coins, then salvaged the machine. Sitting the antique in front of his dive shop, it attracted much attention—so much, that someone finally relieved him of it. For years, however, Fisher kept part of Capone's roulette wheel as a souvenir.

Once or twice a year, Mel organized serious expeditions to

find sunken treasure. These were no small undernourished ventures. They were the best he and his companions could put together, and they were learning experiences for all of them. One of their expeditions took them to Panama. It was scheduled to be a three-month operation, but Fisher was not that familiar with what expeditions cost at that time.

"I had a twenty-four thousand dollar budget for the trip and it cost fifty-four thousand dollars. So I went in the hole," he said. "It took me two years of hard work to pay off all the bills and debts I had on that expedition."

Apparently, even in those days, while raising a family, Mel managed to find ways to pay the bills. He was a sharp business promoter, always optimistically believing that where there was a will, there was a way. Somehow he always had both in abundance.

As it had for so many others, Fisher got caught by the lure of Silver Shoals and the legend of the lost galleon of *Nuestra Señora de la Concepción*, sunk somewhere on the reefs north of the Dominican Republic.

"I'll tell you how I picked that spot," Mel confided. "Me, a friend of mine, and our wives were lying on the floor in our living room one night, and we said, 'Let's go on a vacation together.' I said, 'Why don't we make it a treasure hunt? It'll be more fun.' They said, 'Great! Where are we going to go?' Well, I had a huge atlas about treasure hunting and treasure maps and I said, 'I'll just close my eyes, open the atlas and point, and we'll go there.' So that was the system. Very scientific. I opened the atlas and pointed my finger and it was Silver Shoals."

Mel collected and read all the material he could find on the subject, lined up the modern charts with the old charts, read several accounts of Sir William Phips's find, then started out. The only trouble was, on their first trip they never quite got there.

The two couples of expedition members drove across country from Los Angeles to Miami, where they chartered a 65-foot boat and sailed to Nassau. Then they went down through the Bahamas to Great Inagua, where they refueled by dugout canoe and continued on to Port de Paix, Haiti. Refueling and revictualing there, the expedition members decided they could not pass up some of the choice pirate hangouts in the Caribbean. So they went to Isle de la Tortue, where pirates had built a fort about two hundred years before.

Checking around the site and in the nearby caves, where legend had it that the pirates had hidden some of their loot, the experience was rich in adventure, but not too fruitful, when it came to finding treasure. Still, when they dived near the island, they found six shipwrecks with cannon. They tried their luck digging on these. Their captain refused to continue on to Silver Shoals. Fisher decided it was a wise decision, because none of them were too familiar with what it required to support an expedition that far from home base. At least, when they returned to Miami, they had a few things, such as cannonballs, swords, and rusted artifacts, to show for their efforts.

Eventually, Fisher and his divers organized two more expeditions to Silver Shoals, and this time they got there. On the second trip, he had with him a group of dedicated divers who would later form the nucleus of his Florida treasure-hunting team. For the moment, however, the treasure target was Silver Shoals, where they spent sixty days diving in the complex, treacherous reefs that had proved a death trap for so many ships. There they found several old shipwrecks, which they worked as best they could. In the process they also learned why finding the *Concepción* and its treasure would be far more difficult than most searchers might have believed. It was the same kind of problem that defeated many another treasure hunter, until Burt Webber came along years later and found a way to solve it.

Said Fisher, "It's a beautiful, fantastic reef . . . all kinds of tunnels and live coral. But most of the wrecks are covered with from 10 to 20 feet of live coral, completely encrusted over. So it is very difficult to get at them. That was one major problem."

The searchers never found any gold, but they did come up

with a few encrusted artifacts and some silver coins. With him on that trip was a diver named Fay Feild.

Feild had come to Fisher's dive shop one day, inquiring about shipwrecks. He was interested in knowing more about Mel's magnetometer for detecting the wrecks. Feild was no treasure hunter or salvor. His main interest in shipwrecks was due to the fact that they provided a hospitable environment for the spiny oyster, a sea creature with a beautiful shell, for which collectors paid premium prices. Feild wanted to find shipwrecks, so he could harvest more of the valuable shells.

Mel invited him to join some of their offshore expeditions to known shipwrecks, so Feild could see how they used their mag. The shell hunter was impressed. However he disliked the instrument's bulkiness. He knew enough about electronics and thought that he could build a lighter, more sensitive instrument that would work better. Fisher quickly offered to furnish all the material and pay for everything, if Feild would build the unit.

He agreed. His effort resulted in a magnetometer much easier to handle. It was small and portable. It even worked better than the ASQ-12 military mag, which Fisher was then using. Since it was better than what the military had, patents were applied for. Later manufacturing rights were sold on Feild's improved model.

A third trip was organized to the Silver Shoals. This time Mel took Deo along. They worked the magnetometer out of a small boat, locating new sites for the divers to investigate. They tried to continue where they had left off on their earlier trip, but found similar problems—lots of shipwrecks, lots of overlaying coral, and this time, they were also bothered by a lot of curious sharks.

Even then in those pre*Jaws* years, Mel recognized and quickly cashed in on the public's morbid fascination with sharks. Well aware of their entertainment value, he never missed a chance to film them on his trips.

"When I brought the films back to California, I could sell any footage with sharks in it for ten dollars a foot, and any footage with a shark and a man in it for twenty dollars a foot.

This paid for my vacation, more or less, and I had no fear of sharks. They all seemed to be afraid of me. But at Silver Shoals I changed my mind . . . there were so many of them."

Mel's method for dealing with curious sharks was to bop them on the snout with his heavy underwater camera housing. His companions usually kept them at bay with a shark pricker— a hand-spear with no prongs or barbs on the end, but just an inch of point backed with a flat washer welded around it, so that it cannot go into a shark. No need to wound an animal and make him mad enough to bite. Just prick him and hope that he takes the suggestion to leave.

After that, it was expeditions to Yucatán to make movies of their dives in sacrificial wells and cenotes, hoping to find Mayan artifacts. Things they found and brought up out of the wells and sat along the edge of the sinkholes often disappeared. The more superstitious might believe it was because they were making the Mayan gods mad. Instead, they later learned that local Indians were taking what they found for their own purposes. "Gringo" divers could always be counted on to supply them with goodies from the depths of their sacrificial wells. Maybe the local spirits were perturbed, but the local people were happy with the arrangement. "Gringos" were not supposed to keep things they found anyway.

One day a man named Lou Ullian stopped by Mel's Aqua Shop. Ullian was one of the divers working with Kip Wagner on the 1715 shipwrecks in Florida. He had heard about Fisher's vacuum dredges, which he used in the mountains for sucking up gold. Ullian wondered if a modification of the dredge might help in their excavations of the Florida shipwrecks.

On his next expedition to the Caribbean, Fisher stopped to talk with treasure hunter Kip Wagner. According to Fisher, Wagner took him out to the Cabin Wreck site near Sebastian Inlet and showed him the depth of water and the rise of land and the fall on the other side. Fisher designed a dredge system that could be operated on land to vacuum off the wreck and run everything over sluice boxes.

Fisher offered Wagner a proposition, which both parties

felt had merit. Fisher pointed out that Real Eight had more 1715 wrecks along the Florida coast which, if found and worked properly, would take more time and effort than Wagner's limited team could afford to give them. After all, Wagner's group of Real Eight divers all had full-time jobs and only got a chance to go out and work the sites on Sundays.

Fisher said, "You need someone there full time." He suggested, "I can bring a group of select divers from California, who would be willing to work a year without any reimbursement, to try and find some of the other wrecks and salvage them, splitting any new finds fifty-fifty with Real Eight."

Wagner liked the idea and brought it up before the Real Eight members at their next meeting.

Meanwhile, Fisher and his friends returned to California, where Mel immediately got busy putting together the people he wanted to take to Florida. Some measure of Mel's promotional talent and credibility among his diver friends can be judged by the events that swiftly followed, which would alter all their lives forever.

"From the 112 members I had in my club," said Mel, "I picked the 6 best men. We sold all our assets and moved from California to Florida. I sold my business, my yacht, my home, my extra car, and everything I had, paid off my mortgages and time payments, and just cashed out. The other guys did the same. We just came to Florida and said, 'Kip, here we are. We're ready to go.'

"He was kind of surprised that we actually did that. We made a pact between us that our group would chip in on expenses and would work for one year with no pay and see what we could do. Before this, our longest expedition was ninety days. So we figured if we had a year, we could succeed."

Three hundred and sixty days of trying to succeed passed them by without success. The divers had no idea water conditions were going to be so bad. The sites were so close ashore that the constantly rolling surf destroyed any hope of visibility. When Fisher's group tried to use the dredges he had designed and developed, they were unable to see what they were doing.

They had to feel everything to see if they could find a coin. It was like working in the dark all the time. How could anyone possibly find treasure if they couldn't see it?

It was these conditions that made Fisher wonder if there was some way to divert clear surface water to the bottom, so that his divers could see what they were doing.

The device they came up with was called a "mailbox," because its original shape resembled those the U.S. Post Office sat on street corners. Lowered over a vessel's propeller, it diverted the prop wash toward the bottom.

"The first time we tried that thing out, we were over a wreck in 50 feet of water near Fort Pierce," said Fisher. "The top layer of the water, the first 10 feet, was crystal clear, but the bottom 40 was very muddy. We knew that there was a wreck down there, but we didn't know what it was. So we turned this machine on and, as the prop wash went through the elbow and down, it drove a column of clear water down to the wreck. We drifted down the column and, much to our amazement, as we sat there, this bubble of clear water got larger and larger, and pretty soon, we could see the whole wreck from one end to the other and everything on it, all the fish and everything, when before we couldn't see a thing."

When they used the mailbox blower in shallow water, the divers were amazed to find that it excavated deep holes wherever they directed the down-wash. Fisher had found an ideal device for underwater excavating, one that proved to be the key to upgrading his present low rate of treasure-hunting success.

Five days before their year was up—a year in which they had earned no pay, because they found nothing significant to be paid for—the men with their new mailbox struck it rich south of Fort Pierce, on what was later to be called the Gold Wreck.

"Five days before our time was up," recalls Mel, "we tried out this mailbox dusting machine there. We turned it on for fifteen minutes and went down and the ocean was paved with gold . . . There was gold everywhere."

It was the first of many such big finds, which Fisher's men

made while working the 1715 shipwrecks as partners with Kip Wagner's Real Eight divers. After finding literally tons of coins and going to market with them, it would seem that Fisher's financial troubles were over.

However, despite news articles of the day, which had all the treasure hunters becoming extremely rich, Fisher's money problems were only just beginning.

# Chapter 34

# Troubles

By the late 1960s, most of the press hoopla about the "The Great Florida Treasure Find" was over. As things wound down during this period, Fisher's company of divers, now called Treasure Salvors, began having contractual difficulties with Wagner's Real Eight Company.

By the decade's end, the two companies had dissolved their partnership and Real Eight went out of business. Fisher was now anxious to get on with other enterprises, primarily the search for one of the world's richest treasure galleons—*Neustra Señora de Atocha*, which had disappeared somewhere off the Florida coast in 1622, with a reported cargo manifest of over one million pesos in treasure.

Fisher read about the loss in John S. Potter, Jr.'s *The Treasure Diver's Guide* (Doubleday, New York, 1960) possibly the best compendium of lost sunken treasure ever compiled, one that continually excites the imaginations of professional and armchair treasure hunters alike. It would seem that now he had struck it rich. Mel had the wherewithall to go after the *Atocha* in style, but it was not necessarily so.

It is one thing to find tons of corroded Spanish silver coins and a few shoeboxes of gold coins, but it quite another thing to get those coins converted into the kind of cash that will buy groceries and pay the bills.

In the first place, all the treasure that was recovered underwent a lengthy bureaucratic process, often taking many months before the State of Florida selected its 25 percent; the remaining 75 percent of the finds were returned to the salvors. After that, if the coins were not chemically cleaned, they then underwent that process. Eventually, they were put up for sale, usually in an auction at which interested parties from throughout the world would make their bids. The difficult thing about this procedure is the fear of the treasure hunters that too many coins on the market will dilute their value. Therefore, possibly a year or longer after the item has been found, it has not even come close to going to market and being sold. When this moment finally arrived for Real Eight and Treasure Salvors's recoveries, only a small part of the treasure was actually ever sold. Yet, the treasure hunters had enormous operational expenses, which had to be met if they hoped to stay in business.

Under the circumstances, to keep his Treasure Salvors Company from foundering in debt, Mel managed to get bank loans against the treasure they had that had not yet been sold. In Eugene Lyon's well-documented book, *The Search for the Atocha* (Florida Classics Library, Port Salerno, Florida, 1985) he quotes Fisher describing the method he used:

"I borrowed a hundred thousand dollars from a Vero Beach bank and another hundred thousand from a bank in Fort Pierce and then sixty thousand from a Fort Lauderdale bank. They took Spanish coins as collateral, and then they'd loan us about 60 percent of the retail value of those coins. Some of those coins were up as collateral for as long as ten years. I finally borrowed a larger amount—I think two hundred and seventy-five thousand—from a bank in Tampa. I paid off the other loans and moved the treasure over there as collateral for the new loan."

With this financial shot in the arm, Fisher hoped to hold off his debtors until he could make the big find, the "golden galleon" that would lift him and all the others out of debt for ever more. Whenever possible, he talked a good tale of treasure yet to be found convincingly enough to occasionally attract outside investors to his operation.

Moving to the Florida Keys and forming another company, Armada Research, to keep his various business deals from becoming entangled with one another, Fisher and his divers gave themselves one hundred days of intense effort, searching the coastal areas of certain keys with their magnetometer, running surveys up to twelve hours a day to try and find the fabled galleon.

Almost everyone in the treasure-hunting business knew the story of the *Atocha* and her sister ship the *Santa Margarita*. These two large galleons, bearing an incredible amount of treasure, had sailed out of Havana on September 4, 1622, along with twenty-six other ships comprising the homeward-bound fleet, which would work its way up through the Florida Straits on its return to Spain.

A week out of Havana, the fleet was caught by a hurricane, which scattered the vessels from the Florida Keys to the Dry Tortugas. Most made their way back to Havana. Others went down at sea. Among the missing were the *Margarita*, the *Rosario*, and the *Atocha*. The Rosario was stranded on the Dry Tortugas. The *Margarita* and the *Atocha* sank within sight of each other: "in the place of the *Cabeza de los Martires* in *Matecumbe*," according to the old records. The Spanish salvors recovered part of the *Margarita*'s treasure, but when they tried to do the same on the grounded galleon, *Atocha*, they were unable to gain entry. Returning to the site sometime later, they found that a subsequent storm had totally demolished the ship. Neither its remains, nor its treasure, were ever seen again.

Since the word *Martires* was an old Spanish name for the Florida Keys and the northern string of these islands contained Upper and Lower Matacumbe Keys, everyone believed that east of these keys was the most logical place to look for the lost galleons.

Mel and his men magged every mile of ocean up and down the Matacumbes all the way north almost to Miami and southward almost to Key West. Old shipwrecks aplenty were found, but none of them was the *Atocha*. Finally, they reached the only conclusion possible—the galleon simply wasn't there. Rival treasure hunters, such as Burt Webber and his company, were working just as hard to find the *Atocha* in adjacent contract areas. They, too, were coming to the same conclusions. What Fisher now needed was a new lead—something to put him ahead of his competition.

If there were new facts to be found, he knew where they would be—in the one and only source for such information, the Archives of the Indies at Seville—the source that had provided Kip Wagner with its detailed information on the 1715 plate fleet. But how to find such a miniscule scrap of information in a repository of worm-eaten incredibly difficult-to-read old Spanish documents that covered every detail imaginable over centuries of Spanish occupation in the New World?

As luck would have it, when Mel learned that a friend of his, Gene Lyon, was leaving for Spain to do graduate school research at the Archives of Seville for his dissertation on Florida's Spanish origins, the treasure hunter asked him to look for any reference to the 1622 shipwrecks—especially anything that might reveal the location of the *Atocha*.

In the course of his research, Lyon located the manifest lists for the two galleons and determined that they may have been lost somewhere near the Marquesas Keys, a group of small islands, about 60 miles west of Key West, between Key West and the Dry Tortugas. These uninhabited keys were named for the Marquis de Caldereita, who had been sent with his men to salvage the 1622 shipwrecks.

Realizing the value of Lyon's research, Mel and Deo flew to Spain and hired him as Treasure Salvors's research consultant.

Fisher quickly moved his company to Key West and began searching the wide open expanses of ocean around the Marquesas Keys. Hundreds of miles of magging provided plenty of hits, but they all proved to be modern-day wreckage or bomb fragments left behind from when the area was a World War II military practice bombing range.

Then, one day in 1971, the mag responded to a large sunken target. Diving on it, the divers found a huge galleon anchor, one large enough that a man could swim through its ring without touching! Checking out the area himself, Mel found a musket ball nearby. Excitedly, he announced that they were on the verge of finding the galleons themselves. "Today's the day!" he told the news reporters.

A far more valuable find was made a few days later, when professional underwater photographer, Don Kincaid, visited the site to photograph the anchor for a freelance feature assignment. As Kincaid finned down into the sand crater excavated around the anchor, a glint of gold caught his eye. Reaching out, he slowly pulled from the sand an 8½-foot-long gold chain, later valued at over a quarter of a million dollars.

It was the first of any valuable find in the area that could possibly be attributed to the treasure ships. Mel Fisher and Treasure Salvors were ecstatic. In appreciation for his find, Mel presented Kincaid with a valuable gold escudo coin from the 1715 treasure coin collection. The photographer promptly had it set in a gold mounting and, from then on, wore it on a thong around his neck. Hired as the company's official photographer, Kincaid went on to become Treasure Salvors's vice-president and a member of its board of directors.

Though a few pieces of encrusted armament turned up on the site, including a couple of 6-inch bars of gold, none of it was traceable to the two sought-after galleons.

Fisher contracted with the state of Florida for salvage rights to the area, but what followed was a long, dry period of no recoveries, until the spring of 1973. Then the divers uncovered a pocket of some four thousand Spanish silver coins, a scattering of shipwreck artifacts, and one of the rare bronze navigator's astrolabes.

Despite the finds, trouble was brewing for Treasure Salvors

from all quarters. Florida claimed they were breaking their contractual agreement and often working outside their salvage areas. Rival treasure hunters claimed Fisher was salting the claim with phoney finds in the hope of attracting new investors. Outside pressures were building from academic archaeologists across the country, who were quick to criticize treasure hunters such as Mel Fisher's organization for allegedly "raping historical shipwreck sites in their hell-bent drive to find treasure."

The summer of '72 was something of an ebb tide time for Treasure Salvors. The Fisher family—sons Dirk and Kim, now joined by another son, Kane, and a daughter, Taffi—all lived aboard a large houseboat in Key West. Of the original group that came east with Mel from California, only Deo and a Panamanian named Mo Molinar were still hanging on. The others had sold out their interests. Some idea of the kind of pressures that went with their undertaking may be garnered from the parting statements of original salvors, Rupert Gates and Fay Feild. Said Gates, "It isn't much fun anymore—the whole thing has become an ulcer factory." Apparently, electronics specialist Feild had similar sentiments when he admitted to friends that, "Treasure hunting is a disease; it wiped me out financially, destroyed my marriage, ruined me physically—I had to get away. I had to find a new life."

The only one who was not apparently depressed by their difficulties was Mel Fisher. His rudder was already firmly fixed in place. Nothing—not even the tragedies to come—would alter his course. He simply hunkered down and went at it all the harder, whether it was beating the bushes for more investors, or beating the ocean to a froth with his blowers, to find what he was looking for.

His efforts produced a few more investors, including a couple of *National Geographic* contracts for future features and films. Suddenly from under the mailbox blowers of Bob Holloway's *Holly's Folly*, while working in an area off the Marquesas called the New Ground, they uncovered the remains of a shipwreck containing encrusted anchors, cannon, buried timbers, and hundreds of artifacts including slave shackles, pewter plates, and a pair of ivory elephant tusks. Their guess was that they had uncovered an English privateer.

With both federal and state people beginning to take stands on the moral issue of treasure hunting, and with his own treasure-hunting brethren nipping at his heels, it was obvious to Fisher and some of the others that something had to be done to upgrade the company's public image, if it was to continue to attract good publicity and investors.

In particular this was the studied opinion of those around Mel, who knew something about the power of the press. Probably the three people who emphasized this the most were Don Kincaid, researcher Gene Lyon, and the company's publicist Bleth Mc-Haley. McHaley had met Mel in his Redondo Beach dive shop in the 1950s, when she was working for *Skin-Diver* Magazine. Later, she met him again in Key West, where she invested in the company and became its director of public affairs. These three felt that the best way they could develop any kind of credibility in what they were trying to do, not to mention give them some academic respectability, was to hire an accredited academic archaeologist. Maybe he could make some academic sense to all the chaos the company seemed to be generating.

The man they found was R. Duncan Mathewson III, a thirty-three-year-old, who had put in four years of graduate studies toward his Ph.D. at the University of Edinburgh and at the University of London, then he was overcome by the urge to go afield and work in his chosen profession. After working as an archaeologist in West Africa, he came to Jamaica, where he was hired by the government there to deal with artifacts recovered from the sunken city of old Port Royal. Mathewson, particularly knowledgeable about seventeenth-century ceramics, had met Gene Lyon at a Florida Historical Society conference in 1972. So it was logical that he was one to be considered. Mel lost no time sending an invitation.

His telegram reached Mathewson in Jamaica. It read: "June 15, 1973. I have discovered the remains of two seventeenth-century shipwrecks. One is English and one is Spanish, I need an archaeologist. Gene Lyon has told me of your interest in pottery. We have loads of it for you to study. I am sending you a round trip ticket. Call if you are interested in coming to Key West. (Signed) Mel Fisher, President, Treasure Salvors, Incorporated."

Mathewson accepted. When he jumped feet first into the foray of charges and countercharges, of back-biting rivals, bureaucratic nit-picking, and criticism from academic colleagues, Gene Lyon said of him, "He hit the ground running."

# Chapter 35

# It's a Powerful Ocean

On the morning of Mathewson's arrival in Key West, a major find in the search area had just occurred. Mel had made his two oldest sons, Dirk and Kim, captains each of their nearly identical salvage vessels. Dirk skippered the 54-foot *Northwind*, and Kim skippered the 59-foot *Southwind*. Both vessels were Mississippi tugboats converted for salvaging by the addition of large double stern-mounted blowers on each vessel.

Just hours earlier, *Southwind*'s blowers excavated a sand crater, from which one of the divers found a miniature coral and gold bead rosary. Mel Fisher's youngest son, Kane, donned diving gear and went down to look around. He found a long, loaf-shaped blackened silver bar, weighing some 60 pounds. Nearby was a second, and then a third bar.

Here, at last, was evidence of a major treasure find, the kind that might now be traced to the manifest and eventually the ship from which it came. Until then, with all their piecemeal finds, no one had known whether they were finding things from the *Margarita* or from the *Atocha*. It had all been fairly chaotic.

As the salvors handled the heavy silver ingots, some of the black silver sulphide encrustations flaked off the top of one of the bars. They saw deeply incised numbers there. *Southwind* quickly radioed the numbers to Key West, where Bleth McHaley contacted Gene Lyon, who set about trying to trace the numbers in his microfilmed copy of the galleons' manifest lists.

It was at this moment that archaeologist Duncan Mathewson walked aboard Treasure Salvors headquarters, which now shared space with Fisher's treasure museum aboard a life-sized galleon replica, the *Golden Doubloon*, moored at the wharf.

As usual, whenever anything good happened to Treasure Salvors, it was celebrated in the best Fisher fashion affordable. Mathewson found the place looking like a madhouse. Tourists, reporters, and sightseers crowded the decks. Buckets of beer were being passed around.

Writing about his first impression of the company that had hired him, Mathewson said, "As I looked at this wild scene unfolding around me, all of the uncertainties I'd had about coming to Key West welled up in my churning stomach. How had a serious archaeologist like me gotten into the middle of all this? Archaeology was supposed to be done patiently and quietly, in a remote location, holding a small whisk broom. Here I was on the deck of a floating tourist attraction with a virtual circus going on around me."

"It was unbelievable," said Bleth McHaley. "The boat radioed that they would be in by three o'clock that afternoon. The Miami *Herald* had called, and I was on the phone with them, when Gene Lyon walked in. We hadn't seen him for five days. He'd been at the library using their microfilm viewer every day, from the time they opened, until the time they closed, going through the entire *Maragarita* manifest, and there was nothing to match the numbers and information he got from us by radio when we examined the bars at the site. So he started in on the *Atocha* manifest.

"When he came in, I said, 'What are you doing here? Do you have one of the bars?' And he just broke into this big grin and he said, 'Yes, I got one of the bars on the *Atocha* manifest.' "

Lyon had found a listing for bar number 4584. What was

now important was that the found bar would actually tally with the same weight as that listed for the bar on the manifest. Lyon had already figured it out. The bar would have to weigh exactly 63 pounds.

They had found a heavy scale at the fish house and moved it over to be ready when the boat arrived. They had preset the scale to 63 pounds. The boat finally arrived, the bars came off, and then came the time to weigh bar number 4584.

"I couldn't look," said McHaley. "I don't think anyone was breathing on the *Galleon*. We were watching that bar being weighed and Preston shouted 'Put it down on the scales!' and I couldn't look. I had my back turned. It was just like this; I couldn't breathe.

"Then a shout went up. I turned around and the balance bar came up and didn't even waver. It just stopped at 63 pounds on the nose.

"That started it. There was absolute pandemonium on the deck—everyone jumping up and down, hugging and kissing each other, and Gene Lyon is walking around with this grin on his face . . . and typical of Treasure Salvors, it should have been a champagne party, but we couldn't afford champagne, so we had a plastic garbage can full of beer. That's what we were celebrating with."

Days later, Treasure Salvors's jubilation was soured by the barrage of suspicion and doubt cast upon their new find by some members of the press, competing treasure hunters, and even officials then in charge of Florida's treasure-salvage program. One well-known treasure hunter claimed that the bars were found originally on the site of his treasure wreck and had been placed where they were recovered, so that Treasure Salvors could claim they came from the *Atocha*. He announced to the media that Fisher had done it only to attract more investors.

Another rival treasure hunter claimed that the bar number was nonexistant on his copy of the *Atocha* manifest. Though both critics were later proved wrong, the seeds of suspicion had already been sewn. Mel Fisher was getting a bad-guy image.

Even reluctant Florida officials refused to accept the evidence as finds from the *Atocha*, as long as there was room for doubt, and, while the controversy raged, there was always room for that.

So this was the milieu that R. Duncan Mathewson III found awaiting him when he accepted the job as Treasure Salvors's archaeologist. His first act was to familiarize himself with all the known facts. Since Gene Lyon was privy to all the historical information they had accumulated so far, Mathewson worked closely with this scholar. He hoped to tie historical facts to the archaeological finds. To accomplish this, he began mapping the exact locations of all their finds made until then.

Despite Lyon and Mathewson's personal belief that they were indeed working the *Atocha* site, the archaeologist anxiously wanted to find more corroborating evidence. Two years of digging failed to produce it.

Understandably, Fisher's people were mainly interested in finding the Mother Lode, the main deposit of treasure. But Mathewson was more interested in the larger bulk of shipwreck indicators. For example, where were the *Atocha*'s twenty bronze cannon that she carried when she went down? Where were the remaining four main anchors weighing 2,200 pounds apiece, plus numerous smaller anchors? Where were the remains of over five hundred olive jar storage containers known to have been aboard the ship? Even more significantly, where was the *Atocha*'s ballast? Mathewson calculated that the 550-ton galleon would have carried an enormous volume of rocks deep within her hull to stabilize the sailing ship. A similar-sized vessel in 1733 had carried ballast that created a pile 90 feet long, 30 feet wide, and 3 feet high. Somewhere, such evidence existed to mark the *Atocha*'s grave. But where?

Mathewson tried to come up with a figure of how much ballast rock had been found by the divers up to that time. Based on what they could remember, he arrived at an estimated figure of from 70 to 80 tons that had been found in the Galleon Anchor area. If this was anywhere near correct, then he estimated there should be another 70 or 80 tons remaining to be found.

The Spanish salvage officer, who had tried to breach the *Atocha*'s hull and recover the treasure when the vessel had first been found, reported that the ship sank in 55 feet of water. This fact should have been of paramount importance to the searchers, if they were to put any faith in the accuracy of historical facts. But as Mathewson was to realize later, it was not easy persuading divers to look deeper into the murky 55-foot depths, when they were already finding traces of treasure in the easier-dived 20- to 30-foot depths of the so-called Quicksands area.

In the next few years, Treasure Salvors searched the site with magnetometer, side-scan sonar, and sub-bottom profilers that sought unseen targets with sound waves, in conjunction with their ever active mailbox blowers. So many holes had been excavated with these that, from the air, the area resembled craters of the moon.

Special offshore towers were constructed by Fisher's people to enable them to run boat surveys accurately to within a few feet of each other. They gridded the ocean in all directions, until Mathewson's map began developing an interesting pattern of deposits.

As finds fell off in the northwest direction from the Galleon Anchor find, it began confirming Mathewson's early theory that the main deposit would be found in water about 50 feet deep in the southwest corridor.

The Fishers' oldest son, Dirk, perhaps believed in the deep-water theory more than anyone else in the company. He had even taken a course in a southern Florida school that trained deep-water divers. It was this belief that led him and the *Northwind* crew into this area to check it out.

Anchoring over a mag hit, Dirk was digging down to it with a water jet, when the *Northwind* dragged anchor, moving slightly to the east. Dirk swam out to reset the anchor, when he suddenly came upon five bronze cannon. All lay in a close group, fully exposed on the bottom in 39 feet of water.

The find galvanized the Fisher team into action. Mathewson, Kincaid, and all the others quickly zeroed in on the site, for the archaeologist felt that the positioning of these bronze cannon would provide a key clue to the whereabouts of the primary cultural deposit—what the treasure hunters called, the Mother Lode.

A short distance from the first group, divers found a second group of cannon, totalling nine in all. Since they were all bronze, none had registered as a target for the magnetometer, which responds only to ferrous targets. Had the mag been a man on a sea sled, he would have sighted them easily. But these modern-day treasure hunters were too committed to relying on electronic search systems. This was but another instance, however, when the old unsophisticated Mark I Eyeball would have done the job better. The find was a good example of how much a part luck plays in such matters.

Interestingly, one of the bronze cannon muzzles had been worn away at such an acute angle that its profile resembled a sharp-nosed shark. Divers called this one the "shark cannon." The guns had been a turtle roost, so loggerheads commonly stayed around them. The eroded muzzle of the cannon was believed to have been caused by the turtles repeatedly rubbing their shells against this nicely positioned propped-up barrel "scratching post." After carefully mapping the site, then lifting the bronze cannon, the divers brought up one of the turtles that was still there.

"This has probably been a turtle roost for quite some time," said Mathewson. "Perhaps as long as the cannon have been there." From the amount of bronze worn off the muzzle, at roughly a 45-degree angle, 353 years of rasping turtle shells might not be far from wrong!

So anxious had Fisher been to find cannon relating to the galleons, that he had made a standing offer to pay the finder of the first bronze cannon a prize of ten thousand dollars. Now, nothing pleased him more than to be able to present his son Dirk and his attractive wife, Angel, this reward. The happy couple quickly headed for Miami to buy themselves a Peugeot sports car.

A week later, however, the happy event had a tragic ending. In the middle of the night, at her anchorage, 7 miles to the leeward of the Marquesas, the salvage vessel *Northwind* took on water through a faulty hull fitting. It was severe enough for the already top heavy tugboat to capsize.

Twenty-one-year-old diver Rick Gage and Dirk and Angel Fisher lost their lives when the vessel sank. The other survivors, in life jackets and on rafts, including photographer Don Kincaid, were rescued shortly after 8 A.M. the next morning by another Treasure Salvors boat that had anchored nearby. It was a terrible tragedy.

"It's a powerful ocean. It takes men and ships," said a distraught Mel Fisher. Even as the funeral took place, another vessel with fresh divers was sent back to the *Atocha* site. "Dirk would have wanted us to go on," said Mel.

Somehow they managed to do exactly that. The *Northwind* was never salvaged by Treasure Salvors, but was sold as she was on the site. The *Southwind* too was sold. The vessel's captain, Kim Fisher, left the sea, married, and decided to continue with his college education.

Such a terrible tragedy as this would easily have been capable of tearing the company apart. It was not the first tragedy that had occurred either. Two years earlier, the twelve-year-old son of *National Geographic* photographer, Bates Littlehales, had been sucked into the salvage boat's propellers that were powering a mailbox blower. He died of severe lacerations. After that, all blowers were fitted with safety grills.

Instead of destroying the company and its quest, however, these tragic events somehow only seemed to strengthen it. Perhaps it was primarily because the group was already under seige from all quarters and now, even as these terrible things added to their woes, instead of destroying them, it made the faithful draw in tighter together and resolve all the more staunchly to keep on searching for their dream.

R. Duncan Mathewson III later expressed it eloquently in his book detailing the difficulties of their search, *Treasure of the*

*Atocha* (Pisces Books, New York, 1986): "The loss of human lives made my commitments to the *Atocha* all the more important. I couldn't abandon it now. I became obsessed with my professional responsibilities on the site . . . I was driven by the desire to do good archaeology . . . I no longer cared what my academic colleagues and the government bureaucrats thought. I was committed to the end, whatever that might bring."

Few may have believed it then, perhaps, but the end of the treasure trail was still a long way off. To be more precise, it would be exactly 111 more court battles and ten years from the day of Dirk's death, before it would end.

# Chapter 36

# Riddle's End

From the placement of the cannon Dirk had found, Mathewson plotted the finds and theoretically determined what the vessel's course had been when the big guns slid off the *Atocha*'s careening decks.

Pursuing this lead into deeper water, they found that their blowers now were not nearly as effective at depth. Mel came up with an idea for a Hydra-Flow, a blower that divers could carry down to the bottom with them to excavate. Mel had it built and leased the device, which worked fine, digging deep holes almost effortlessly. But the unit was expensive to rent and failed to produce anything more than a lot of bottom craters.

Over the next half-dozen years, every conceivable idea any of them could think of was tried, including a psychic. Experts everywhere were invited in, usually with their sophisticated equipment, to try and sniff out the *Atocha*'s whereabouts. Fay Feild came back to see if he could sharpen their efforts with his magnetometer. Kincaid tried aerial photography with a newly developed Kodak blue sensitive film, to see if they could look photographically through the water and spot anything in the depths of Hawk Channel that looked like the Mother Lode. But the depths of the channel proved too murky to fathom even with the new film.

Over and over, the salvage vessels dug in the cannon corridor, trying to pick up the ballast rock trail that would lead to the main deposit. But nothing was found. Meanwhile, other company members wanted to continue their search in the opposite direction, where a few finds from the wreck's scatter pattern were at least better than no finds at all.

In the course of this search a subcontractor first found an anchor, then pottery fragments and clumps of silver coins. Plotting these finds on the chart soon prompted the company cartographers to suggest that the searchers try looking farther to the north. Then they found a number of gold bars. The excitement mounted. Were they from the *Atocha* or the *Margarita*? Moreover, now that very valuable treasure was appearing, legal questions arose as to who indeed owned it at all. The state of Florida, the federal government, or Mel Fisher's Treasure Salvors Company?

The attorney Fisher hired to confront the issue in the courts was Key West lawyer David Paul Horan. No novice to the troubles of treasure hunters, Horan had represented others in their battles with the bureaucrats, and he had a reputation for winning.

Over the next seven years, Horan would fight for the company's rights in over one hundred court proceedings. In the end he would defeat the state, the federal government, contesting rival treasure hunters trying to sneak some of the action, and finally, he would win the salvage rights to it all for Fisher and his Treasure Salvors company. This one man probably did more toward getting the *Atocha* and the *Margarita* for Fisher than any other single individual in the company. It is possible to find a treasure ship through good historical research and supersophisticated sensory equipment, but, if you lose possession legally, it is irrevocably lost forever.

The new finds proved to be rich and wonderful, and they led the searchers directly to the final resting place of the *Atocha*'s sister ship, the *Margarita*.

A 23-foot-long chunk of the wooden hull still remained buried beneath the artifacts and ballast. Though the Spanish had heavily salvaged treasure from the site, much still remained in the form of silver bars, conglomerates containing thousands of silver coins, copper ingots, plates and cups of gold, more finger-sized bars of the precious metal, and the kind of archaeological shipwreck material that delighted Mathewson. He and his divers immediately set up grids on the site and began working it in textbook fashion, detailing it all to the finest degree, before removing it.

The treasure was spectacular. Over forty-three finely wrought solid gold chains totaling 180 feet in length were brought up over the next eighteen months. With them were found Colombian emeralds, a gold boatswain's whistle, a solid gold poison cup nicely engraved and studded with gems, and a beautifully designed solid gold 8-inch plate—all of which were estimated to be worth over $40 million. Here at last was what Mel Fisher needed to repay some of the debt he had built up with his big money investors.

One circumstance bothered Mathewson. Not only had Treasure Salvors magged the area and gotten no indication of its presence there before, but so had rival treasure hunters. In fact, one claimed his group habitually anchored the vessel for the night where the site was found. Then why had no one found it before Kane came along and discovered the Pile sitting right out in the open?

The searchers could only conclude that, maybe it was not always so nicely exposed. Don Kincaid pointed out that the ballast rock were whiter than most and remarkably free of encrustations. It suggested that perhaps the site was hidden deep beneath the sand, until recent storm seas had shifted the sand and uncovered it. Whatever the reason, the needle in the haystack had miraculously been found—not from expertise, but by pure luck. Everyone hoped it would hold long enough for them to find the *Atocha*'s Pile.

While work continued on the *Margarita*, the push was on to find the *Atocha*. In the next four years, the final clues came slowly, but significantly, each one another important piece of the puzzle to be precisely located, then plotted on the chart that showed the locations of all their finds.

It began in the summer of 1981, when Bob Moran and the crew of the *Plus Ultra* discovered three large anchors, dated 1618, hooked onto the outer reef. It was the kind of evidence often associated with large ungainly ships that are being storm-driven toward a leeward shore. In an attempt to avoid the ultimate doom, anchors are swiftly shoved overboard with the prayer that they hook bottom securely and all cables hold, saving the ship from being torn apart on the reefs.

This mute evidence indicated where the attempts had been made to save the *Atocha*. Then came the discovery of an old iron wrecking bar, the kind used by early salvors to pry their way into old shipwrecks. Its presence seemed to signify that they were at least close to the end of the trail. When Kane Fisher and his crew of the *Dauntless* found the first silver bars and pursued the meandering, curving trail of treasure through the southeastern corridor that leads into the depths of Hawk Channel, it was the beginning of the end.

At last, the momentous day!

When word of the fabulous find reached Key West, the news they had been awaiting every day for sixteen years brought pandemonium to Treasure Salvors headquarters. Incredibly, one of the last company members to hear about it was the man who started it all in the first place—Mel Fisher.

Nobody could find him. They checked all of his local haunts, every place that Mel Fisher was known to be. But they absolutely could not find him. They put it out over the local radio station: "Mel Fisher, go to your office. You've just found the Mother Lode!"

"Where *is* he?" everyone asked as champagne corks popped like the Fourth of July.

Where indeed! Mel was in a local dive shop buying mask and fins so he could go diving! When the news caught up to him, he headed back to the office with his bagsful of purchases. A light rain began falling. Someone encountered him and held an umbrella over him on the way back.

As he came up the steps with a Charlie Brown grin on his face, they asked, "Where *were* you?"

"I just went and bought a mask and fins and I'm ready to go." Someone poured him a paper cup of champagne. Mel looked at the others and blinked. "Now you make me want to cry."

As they pounded him on the back and kept congratulating him, his grin never changed. In his typically understated manner, he said, "Well, I guess today's the day," and he sipped his bubbly.

# Chapter 37

# The Marvelous Mother Lode

Confronted with the realization that this was the day he had been preparing himself to cope with for the last twelve years, perhaps more than any other member of Treasure Salvors, archaeologist R. Duncan Mathewson III felt the full burden of responsibility that fell on his shoulders, now that they had found the Mother Lode, the primary cultural deposits. The academic world of his peers would be watching to see how he handled it.

Most of the company divers were experienced treasure salvors. They knew how to bring up the finds. But the time-consuming work of doing the tagging, the measuring, the photography, and mapping—in short, all the necessary procedures of proper archaeology—was another thing. It was a prodigious job, far more than one person or even a few could handle. It called for trained experts and consultants in a variety of scientific specializations, ranging from shipwreck archaeologists, shipbuilders, and nautical historians, to artifact conservators and computer technicians capable of documenting the mountain of material it would generate.

Mathewson soon assembled his team of experts, but, before they arrived, he and his available helpers established a baseline down the middle of the site and began setting up their grids for mapping timbers and artifacts in place. Meanwhile, the crew of the *Dauntless* brought up loaf-sized silver ingots, weighing around 70 pounds apiece, from the pile.

The base line from which all artifacts would be measured was over 150 feet long through the middle of the deposit. From Mathewson's urging and Mel Fisher's ordering, the treasure divers bridled their enthusiasm for grabbing everything in sight and getting it topside as fast as possible for the media to film. Fisher well knew the need to work the deposit archaeologically at the pace required for documenting everything where it was found. The find would then provide future generations with as much historical knowledge as possible relative to these centuries-old maritime treasures. To snatch them away without learning everything possible about their past would be the same as obliterating a unique historical time capsule.

Not too surprisingly, once Treasure Salvors divers realized the importance and responsibilities that went with their discovery, they soon were working with the archaeologists rather than against them. Older divers taught the younger divers what was required. The frenzied salvage activity that marked the first few days of working the site slowed down and became an organized effort to combine good shipwreck archaeology with modern-day salvage methods. The operation proved to be one of the first major successful working arrangements ever attempted between underwater archaeologists and professional treasure hunters.

Diving down to the over three and a half centuries old gravesite of this virgin treasure galleon is possibly the closest thing to time travel modern man will ever experience. Don Kincaid expressed it best when he said, "It's a wonderful experience. You're going from the deck of a boat in twentieth century armor—all the diving gear—and you go down to the bottom and then you're in the seventeenth century. You're now walking on a deck that's three hundred and fifty years old. You can see the marks on the wood where the guy has hacked the wood into the shape it is to become a rib in the ship. You can see where the nails were driven in. You can see areas where something akin to putty, or material like that, you can see some guy's fingerprint in there. That fingerprint is three hundred and fifty years old. So you're shaking hands with history."

In many respects it was not unlike the intense excitement felt by Howard Carter upon opening and first viewing the marvels of King Tut's tomb. The first divers to view the *Atocha*'s tomb were amazed to see how close others had come to this fabulous pile of treasures—anchor ropes and fishing lines were entangled around the stack of silver ingots, the deteriorating chests of corroded coins, the bars of gold. Lobster antennas waved enticingly from the multimillion dollar cache. A short distance away, a skin diver's spear lay on the bottom. How close had someone swam to a huge stack of riches beyond one's wildest imagination? Perhaps he had been looking at a fish he hoped to spear for supper, rather than at the dusky, reef like pile of refuse in the shadowy depths 54 feet down in often murky Hawk Channel.

After several weeks of work, Mathewson and his assistants began learning facts about the deposit that furnished vital missing historical answers to what had happened to the *Atocha* during its final death throes. The Mother Lode measured 75 feet long, 30 feet wide, and 4 feet deep at its center, amazingly similar to the size deposit Mathewson calculated they would find. His prediction was made eight years earlier in a masters thesis on the *Atocha* work.

The material was strewn along a line going from the southeast to the northwest. Timbers and planking of the ship, identified as the stern portion, lay to the northwest, while the vessel's bow was pointed southeast. Experts believe that the already dismasted ship crashed into the outer reef, severely damaging its bow. The hurricane force winds then caught the high-pooped sterncastle, and weather cocked it like a weather vane, turning the vessel end for end and pushing it backward through the seas. As she tore out her keel and keelson in her journey over the reef, she quickly went down under the tremendous load of treasure and cargo in her hold.

There she remained with her mizzen mast above water, as

described by the first Spanish salvagers to reach the sunken vessel. But a second severe storm apparently tore away the entire stern of the ship, along with the towering bow and stern castles, pushing them northward toward the shallower waters of the sand shoals over 9 miles away. Treasure Salvors finds in that area called the Quicksands are believed to have come from the stern castle portion. An early historical report said that Keys Indians found part of the *Atocha*'s bow washed ashore on the Marquesas Key.

On extremely rare days the water visibility over the site is clear enough to provide up to 20- or 30-foot visibility. More often than not the site remains shrouded in an underwater fog. Then, one has the feeling of diving in pale green opaque warm pea soup, an illusion sometimes fostered by the presence of a late summer sea bloom, consisting of yellowish green marine algae in the water.

As one descends through this soupy void into the darkening green depths, the first sight of the Mother Lode is her dark brown planks and timbers, lying loglike beneath a jumble of ballast rock, scattered treasure, and assorted wreckage. Here are the much sought after rounded river rocks that Mathewson and his divers knew had to mark the final grave site. Scattered among the 40 tons of ballast are the rough-edged course clay pottery shards that carried the galleon's food supplies. Nearby lies a curved, rusty barrel hoop. But for their different shapes, all the rubble looks alike with a common color—the patina of age. A small, curved piece proves to be a rib bone. A blackened squared-edged, peg-shaped object proves to be a chunk of silver. A palm-sized cluster of blackened small disc-like pieces of metal fused together, as if by a coating of hard, brittle tar, are clusters of Spanish silver coins—pieces of eight with silver sulphide encrustations ½ inch thick, making them appear to be worthless, easy-to-overlook debris. Then there are the silver bars resembling kiln-scorched pig iron. In this area, nine hundred of them stacked in a 5-foot-thick reef of pure silver, each ingot 15 inches long, weighing 60 or 70 pounds apiece.

Even some of the shipping chests containing pillow-shaped clumps of fused silver coins still remain. Prolonged immersion of such encrusted conglomerates in chemical baths will be necessary to reduce this lump to its original pile of glittering silver coins. Other wooden crates are found to contain hundreds of gold bars, bits, and discs of gold.

Southward through the lukewarm pea soup brings divers to an area where the ship's pilot's chest and giant ceramic Ali Baba jars were found. Mathewson's team learned the pilot's centuries-old secret, when they began examining the contents of his chest.

Lifting its lid, they found the usual navigational instruments in view: an astrolabe, an ivory sun dial, the pilot's dividers, and compasses.

"And what do you suppose we found underneath all that?" asks Mathewson. "Contraband."

To avoid paying Philip IV, Spain's monarch, the usual royal fifth in taxes levied by the king on such treasure brought back to Spain from the New World, there, hidden by the tools of his trade was the pilot's personal hoard: a 41-foot gold chain, gold nuggets, eight gold two-escudo pieces, a pouch of gold dust, and enough silver coins to fill eleven bags. But the pilot was not the only smuggler aboard.

Apparently, smuggling contraband treasure back to Spain was widespread enough that it might amount to half again as much as was recorded in the ship's manifest.

"Gold was stashed all over the ship," Mathewson said.

The penalty for smuggling the precious metal in those days was two hundred lashes and ten years at a galley oar. Still, illegal goods accounted for as much as a quarter of galleon cargo. Considering the severity of the penalty and the widespread practice of smuggling treasure aboard these ships, it must have been an extremely lax law.

Timbers and planks of the wreck once buried beneath the Pile and the protective sand, now exposed by the dredging operations, look reasonably modern despite their centuries of age. A diver may slide his hand along a smooth deck plank that passengers and crew walked on 363 years ago.

When Mathewson's archaeological team, which soon grew to fifteen members, sampled and analyzed the wood, they learned another of the *Atocha*'s long kept secrets. The Havana shipwright who had built the *Atocha* substituted mahogany for oak for some of the beamwork. In shipbuilding terms this was a serious breach of contract. When under great stress, oak has a slight bend and give to it, while mahogany tends to break. Worse, the archaeologists found that the shipwright skimped on nails. When spiking together some of the more important beams, he was supposed to use five fasteners. He had instead used two. These discrepancies would not have been noticed until the ship was put under severe storm stress. Then, these points would have been the failure factors, causing the ship's more rapid destruction by cracking up and falling apart in these areas of weakness.

Of the thousands of pieces of eight found in the Pile at that time, historian Gene Lyon learned that 21,323 of the silver coins had been intended to pay a debt Spain owed to an heir of Christopher Columbus. Large sums came from papal indulgences; another portion was the proceeds from a head tax on the sale of 1,400 African slaves. Other cargo consisted of 525 bales of tobacco and large copper ingots, the size of manhole covers, that came from Cuba. These were being sent to a Spanish foundry, where tin would have been blended into the melted metal and it would have been forged into bronze cannon.

One of the highlights of the Memorial Day weekend find was a chestful of gold ingots and sixteen emeralds. The *Atocha*'s manifest listed 200 pounds of gold, twelve hundred silver ingots weighing from 63 to 100 pounds each, and more than two hundred fifty thousand silver coins. But no green emeralds were listed there. They were contraband. In this case they proved to be some of the world's most precious gemstones. Experts verified that emeralds of this quality, which had originated from emerald mines in northern Columbia, were so rare today, that they were more valuable per carat that diamonds. Eventually, some five hundred such rare quality emeralds were found. One 40-carat emerald is believed to be worth 1 million dollars. The total estimated appraisal from a qualified source felt that these stones would bring as much as $15 million.

The following Memorial Day, a year later, divers using airlifts found another cache of emeralds. Running in size from peas to jellybeans and grapes, the green gems were sucked into the 8-inch pipe, then showered back down on the divers. Suddenly, it was raining emeralds!

"We had them going down our collar," said diver Don Deeks. "We had them in our hair. There was a sea cucumber crawling through a field of emeralds, and he had one on his back. 'A-ha, stealing one of Mel's emeralds,' I said to myself."

Fisher, who was diving on the site at the time that the airlift struck emeralds, tried to get in on the fun by catching some of the green gems showering down.

"Everything I caught was a seashell or snail," he said, chuckling about it later. "I was diving for an hour and didn't find anything myself but a square nail."

This new cache of contraband emeralds amounted to almost three thousand of the uncut gems. Aboard the salvage vessel, Mel happily displayed them to everyone in a Planters peanut jar.

Examining the new find, emerald expert Manual Marcial, owner of Emeralds International in Key West, said, "Visually, they are not quite the quality of the earlier finds, but there could well be some valuable stones," he said. "The prior finds were of a darker vein and extremely expensive. One stone alone—about 57 carats— is worth seven hundred fifty thousand dollars."

All the artifacts from the site were brought to Key West, where the more interesting items were carefully cleaned, cataloged, and entered onto a computerized list of finds. In the archaeological laboratory cannon, coins and conglomerates were soaked in chemical baths to leech out centuries of saltwater, remove encrustations, and return the finds to some semblance of their original condition.

As soon as possible, many of these priceless recoveries were placed on view at Treasure Salvor's Key West Museum, so that the public could marvel at these recently recovered treasures of the deep. Heavy loaf-sized silver ingots purposely left encrusted with black silver sulphide sit stacked, row upon row, where visitors can see, photograph, and touch them. Displays of golden goblets, dishes, and dozens of gold bars fill glass cases. At one such display visitors slip their hand into a plastic display case to touch and heft a large gold bar, too large to withdraw through the hand hole. Other cases contain a handful of uncut emeralds, glowing in their own green aura, from cleverly hidden lights inside the case. An elaborate gem and pearl-studded priceless gold belt is an example of one of the more exotic finds. Other displays are draped with huge linked gold chains, representing some of the over 500 feet of gold chains recovered so far from the wreck sites. A solid gold cross, studded with large grape-sized cut emeralds, is displayed with an ornate gold ring, featuring a 16-carat emerald setting, along with the blackened silver box, in which the items were found. Large artist illustrations and a continuous video film details the history of the two treasure galleons and Treasure Salvors's efforts to find them.

For the first time the public got some idea of what comprised this long-sought Mother Lode, a goal that Mel Fisher had been trying to reach in one form or another for most of his life. And now, it was time for the financial reward. It was time for payday.

# Chapter 38

# Payday

All the artifacts, treasure, and shipwreck structure of the Mother Lode, had not yet been recovered, when it was decided that Treasure Salvors Company would have a division with its stockholders. The complexity of this action can better be understood when one has a small inkling of the intricacies of Mel Fisher's business arrangements.

During the leanest and most difficult years, Fisher's scramble for operating capital sometimes left a few of his business associates unhappy enough to sue. None, however, were successful in winning their suits. Unlike a public company—where investors buy stock on the open market and get a standard dividend—Fisher's investors dealt directly with him.

"I've had lots of deals," Fisher admits in a classic understatement. Among them were his "private placements," arrangements sometimes executed on the backs of napkins and envelopes, often with Key West locals. Large investors, such as Frank Perdue, the New Jersey poultry magnate, contributed a six figure sum. Delaware construction firm and speedway owner, Melvin Joseph, invested half a million dollars in Fisher's dream. Treasure Salvors's sharp attorney, David Paul Horan, received one thousand shares of the company, instead of money, because

Fisher owed him for legal services. That was how Fisher often paid off his creditors.

"To do it any other way," Horan said, "Fisher would never have made it." The firm has more than a million shares outstanding.

With operational expenses for the Treasure Salvors Company that could go up to one thousand dollars a day just to keep his salvage vessels working, times frequently got so rough, that Fisher was often long overdue with paying his people, unable to come up with the fifty dollars a week he paid divers in the early days. But then, bright, new young divers were always eager to go treasure hunting, even if they got nothing more than a place to sleep aboard his boats and decent meals, with maybe occasionally a silver Spanish coin or two thrown in to carry them over. To many of them, a real piece of eight, worn proudly on a chain around their neck was worth as much as a fistful of folding money in the pockets of their tattered jeans. After all, they were treasure divers working for the world's greatest treasure salvor, and *that* counted for something.

To find investors, Fisher worked all the angles he could, often selling stock through the classified ad section of the *Key West Citizen*. Gradually, however, as more significant finds were made, Fisher's operation attracted larger investors. One group of thirty wealthy businessmen, known as Treasure Company, provided a much needed financial helping hand when each member committed one hundred fifty thousand dollars to the search. From them, Fisher received $4.5 million to ease the Treasure Salvors financial crunch. This group was entitled to a 10 percent share of the treasure from both the *Atocha* and *Margarita* when found. Treasure Salvors's early recovery from the *Margarita* helped Fisher pay off this financial responsibility. The group recouped its investment with $4.5 million in treasure that was quickly bank vaulted for this purpose. Eventually, the rich investors expected to pick up another $20 million from the division of the Mother Lode.

Thanks to the tax laws then in effect, those investors already had written off their investment, according to their tax lawyer. One reason the Treasure Company investors planned to keep their treasure in a bank vault was to make more money from it. Under the law, 100 percent of the gain on treasure sales was taxable, if the sales were made within five years. Only 40 percent of the sales was taxed when investors waited out the five years before selling their loot.

In 1980, Fisher was persuaded to sell investors one thousand dollar year-long limited partnerships. These investors would only be paid a profit from treasure recovered during the time of the one year limited partnership with the firm. The idea caught a lot of limited investors. Fisher raised about $3 million this way.

The payoff came on Monday, October 13, 1986. For tax purposes, none of the treasure would be converted into cash. The treasure items themselves would be distributed to investors on a point system. It would be a partial treasure division; another would occur in 1987. The October amount included 130,000 silver coins; 956 silver ingots, with an average weight of 1,000 ounces or more; 315 emeralds; 115 small gold bars, ranging in size from 6 to 27 troy ounces; fifteen gold chains; 67 gold coins; and 22 other items of gold and jewels.

To make the division fair and equal, each treasure item was given a point value equal to its appraised worth. Total points would then be divided among investors and shareholders according to how much percentage they owned. Treasure Salvors Company Incorporated and its stockholders would get 30 percent of the total value. The remaining 70 percent would be divided among the investors, the computer randomly matching an investor's point value with treasure of equal number of points. Total point value of the treasure for this October division amounted to 3,280,286 points. A one thousand dollar investor would receive approximately 328 points of treasure.

As an example of some of the treasure values, Bleth McHaley explained that some of the emeralds were rated at anywhere from 2 points for a low to a high of 20,844 points. Gold bar bits started at 7.2 and ranged up to 3,741 points for an entire bar; gold coins ranged from 166 to 277 points; a copper ingot ranged from 2 to 37 points; silver bars ranged from 7 to 1,300 points; artifacts ranged from 3.33 to 4,500 points; and silver reals (coins) ranged from 3 to 30 points with a grade-1 coin valued at 24 points.

To start everything rolling, Mel Fisher pushed a key on Treasure Salvors's computer and the shareholder/investor division got underway.

The computer ran for two and a half days, assigning the six hundred investors and employees points for the twenty-seven hundred page artifact inventory. When it finally stopped on October 16th, at about 12:45 P.M., it flashed on its screen, "Division Complete, Congratulations Treasure Salvors."

Simultaneously, about three dozen champagne corks popped, people moved out of the computer room and, according to McHaley, "they just went bananas!"

Investors were asked to make appointments to pick up their treasure in Key West, or Treasure Salvors would ship it to them. Once the booty was signed for, the company was no longer responsible for it. Investors were requested to provide their own security, which Treasure Salvors agreed to arrange if needed.

Mel Fisher and his family received ten pages of computer printout for their share. Other company stockholders received varying amounts, according to their company status and other considerations. For the long-time faithful, it was the culmination of their long-awaited rewards—the first payment, with others yet to come. Reason enough for champagne and hilarity.

"What do you do with a 364-year-old 131-pound copper ingot?" asked investor Shirley Harrington, who had an appointment to go to Miami and collect the ingot and several coins that were appraised at a total value of more than seventeen thousand dollars. She had bought a one thousand dollar share in Mel Fisher's company, before the Mother Lode had been found in July, 1985.

"I might give it to my boss as a paperweight," quipped Ms. Harrington, "but then I would have to give him a ceiling hoist to lift it to get paper out from under it."

One person suggested she have a foundry melt it into 1-ounce copper ingots certified as having been part of the *Atocha* treasure. Then she could sell them mail-order to others wanting a piece of the *Atocha* treasure. Later, however, Harrington learned that, in addition to copper, the ingot contained platinum. So, at last report, she was still in a quandary about what to do with her manhole-cover-sized share of the treasure.

How has life changed for Mel Fisher?

"Well, I'm getting more and more famous all the time," he smiled distractedly, not really bragging, but just stating the facts. He looks hardly changed—a bit older, a bit heavier, a bit grayer. One news account said, "He has yet to upgrade his sartorial style. His shirts are old and unironed; the polyester snagged and puckered. But fame has its predictable botherations."

"Strangers spot me on the street of Key West and start shrieking, 'Mel Fisher! I want to shake your hand!' You get tired of all that yelling," said Fisher, "along with the crunching handshakes."

He is traveling more. He returned from Spain, where they wanted to borrow a few museum-quality pieces for an upcoming 1992 Columbus exhibit. In the fall of 1986 he was the subject of a network TV movie. The *National Geographic Magazine* featured his efforts three times, and the society is marketing a videotape of the treasure quests they featured earlier in their program series. Mel Fisher, at 65, was particularly proud to attend the August 11th Mel Fisher Day at his hometown, the Gary suburb of Hobart, Indiana.

Not only there, but throughout the world, Mel has become something of a folk hero in the manner of Don Quixote. For sixteen years, Mel jousted with the windmills of adversity, and won. People *like* that.

He says he will never retire, that he might liquidate Treasure Salvors Incorporated, but that he would never be entirely out of the salvage business.

"Oh, there's lots of neat treasure all over the world," Mel says. "I know this volcano crater in Peru . . ."

# Epilogue

Keeping up with the various adventures and enterprises of our six most successful treasure hunters is about as easy as keeping up with droplets of spilled mercury. Over the years, their courses often fly off in a myriad different directions. Here, however, are updates on our key players in this drama, along with the treasures they sought, found, and sometimes lost again. As we all know, treasure hunters come and go, but throughout the centuries, what continues to endure long after their passing are the treasures and the legends they leave behind.

One of the best liked and most respected of the treasure hunters, Art McKee, Jr., often called the "father of Florida treasure hunting," left a void among all who knew him when he died. His Pirate Treasure Fortress on Plantation Key closed. Art's second wife, Gay McKee, let the public have a last nostalgic look at McKee's treasure collection at Key Largo in March, 1983, during the "Treasures from the Sea" show sponsored by the Historical Preservation Society of the Upper Keys. After that, the collection was divided among the McKee children. Gay McKee has placed some of it on display in a museum on Grand Cayman, the island on which she grew up, and where she first met the lovable treasure-hunting leprechaun, Art McKee.

Though Kip Wagner and his now defunct treasure salvage company, Real Eight, are no longer with us, the scattered treasure of the 1715 Spanish fleet along Florida's east coast is still being found. After Mel Fisher's Treasure Salvors Company recovered over three thousand gold coins from the Gold Wreck site, south of Fort Pierce, recoveries quickly diminished. When Treasure Salvors moved to the Keys in 1970 to search for the *Atocha*, Fisher's Cobb Coin Company, which holds titles to most of the Florida east coast state salvage sites, subcontracted the work to other salvage firms. Slim pickings discouraged long-term efforts, until the advent of pulse-induction metal detectors in 1978, at which time the wreck sites and east coast beaches opposite the sites began producing increasing numbers of coins, jewelry, and artifacts for hunters. Over the next four years, the areas produced over $1 million worth of treasure for those persistent enough to keep pursuing it. In the *Plus Ultra* quarterly newsletter from Florida Treasure Brokers, part-time treasure salvors, Bob Weller and Ernie Richards, keep readers informed of returns from the wrecks and finds from the beaches. In early 1986, Weller wrote of a good couple of days salvaging treasure from the Gold Wreck south of Fort Pierce, where Treasure Salvors recovered over $5 million in gold and silver coins, from 1965 to 1969.

"Good underwater detectors were put to use and began paying off in gold and silver coins, as well as exquisite jewelry," wrote Weller. "During a two-day period, John and Judy Halas recovered twenty-seven pieces of worked gold jewelry, including a 10-carat emerald ring. . . .The state of Florida became the beneficiary of a gold Madonna with a trace of emeralds; rings, countless artifacts, and the only gold chain the group had recovered to date." Then, after twenty-six years of treasure diving along that coast, Weller made his most spectacular find— "three large gold medallions connected by a series of gold filigree links, with black ebony beads between each link, which all formed a cross about 6½ by 8 inches." Fellow diver Whitey Keevan soon turned up the necklace part—60 inches of filigree gold, alternating with small black ebony beads, each capped with a floral gold motif. It was an exquisite rosary.

Near another of the 1715 wreck sites, three young scuba divers were casing the reef for lobsters when one, Alex Kuze, found a 5 by 9-inch elaborately carved, solid gold footed tray designed like the flattened petals of a sunflower. Appraised at twenty-three thousand dollars the divers traded it to Florida for six rare eight-escudo gold coins valued together at twelve thousand five hundred dollars.

Nor were the treasure finds limited only to the ocean. Treasure hunters soon learned that, opposite certain of the wreck sites, coins and artifacts often turned up after a bad beach-scouring storm. Reporting on a particularly severe Thanksgiving Day tempest that uncovered a beach bonanza in 1985, Weller described the scene: "By Friday afternoon, over fifty treasure hunters waving metal detectors had converged on the beach, as high tide passed. Before that day and the following day had ended, a reported two thousand silver coins and at least thirty-five gold coins had been retrieved, most of them within a few feet of the cut-away bern line. An unexpected bonus turned up in the form of two 4-foot cannon and some ship's rigging . . ."

What few people realized was that the scatter patterns of treasure actually touched shore in some areas for over a mile and a half. This fact came to light with the computerized record of all the treasure returns made from the mid-sixties to the present time. Eventually, this information became available with the publication of a fact-filled shipwreck chart, showing the locations of all the 1715 treasure wrecks, those of the 1733 treasure fleet, and fifty other period shipwreck sites. Based on information provided by long-time treasure divers and shipwreck research from Florida's Department of Archives and History, the detailed *Snorkelers' and Divers' Guide to Old Shipwrecks of Florida's South-east Coast* ($15.95 from Spyglass Publications, 308-B West

Marion Street, Chattahoochee, Florida, 32324) for the first time gave the public some idea of the concentration of old shipwrecks in Florida's coastal waters, which included at least two major treasure fleets. The visual picture of the 1715 treasure scatter patterns now told beachcombers and amateur treasure hunters why Kip Wagner had been so successful locating concentrations of valuable silver and gold coins along the beach between Sebastian and Wabasso. For centuries the treasure was washing ashore! And better still, any treasure found on coastal property that did not belong to the state or federal governments, was finder's keepers. So scattered are these treasures, that beachcombers will undoubtedly continue finding coins and other shipwreck artifacts from 1715 and earlier along this coast for decades to come. But any such historical artifacts found from the high watermark out to Florida's 3-mile limit belong to the state of Florida. Finders may not be prosecuted for making an accidental find, but Florida's Archives and History Department would like to be informed. Said James J. Miller, Chief of the Bureau of Archaeological Research for the department that deals with these matters:

> "It is not the state policy, nor has it been the practice of the agency, to confiscate material accidentally found on state lands, or to prosecute the finder. Rather, we are interested in learning about historically important finds and would hope to discuss with the finders ways that the state may acquire or exhibit important artifacts such as ships' rigging or structure, tools, weapons, coins, and Oriental or Spanish pottery. This policy, however, is not intended in any way to encourage recovery of archaeological material from shipwrecks or other sites."

Divers who find artifacts they believe are significant should call the Bureau of Archaeological Research in Tallahassee at (904) 487–2333. Those wishing to know the complete story of the 1715 Spanish fleet and eventual treasure recovery will find it detailed in *Florida's Golden Galleons* ($13.95 from Spyglass Publications, 308-B West Marion Street, Chattahoochee, Florida 32324).

What happened to the treasure of the *Maravilla*, after Bob Marx left the site? For a few years others contracted with the Bahamian government to salvage the wreck. None, however, were too successful, until the bow section of the wreck was found again in the summer of 1986 by Marine Archaeological Research (MAR) Limited, a Grand Cayman-based firm headed by Captain Herbert Humphreys, Jr., a Memphis businessman. Owner of investment companies, hotels, and air-charter services, Humphreys had searched the Caribbean for years in pursuit of sunken treasure, when he and his company finally obtained a Bahamian government search and salvage lease for the *Maravilla* site.

By February, 1987, MAR's divers had recovered an estimated 1 million dollars worth of artifacts and treasure including a 51.76-carat Columbian emerald, said to be one of the largest ever found on a Spanish shipwreck. Long-time treasure salvor, Art Hartman, who in the past had made significant recoveries on Florida's 1715 wrecks, is MAR's salvage master. He said the ship is the best he's seen in nearly thirty years of diving. "There's an immense amount of treasure still down there waiting to be found."

Some believe the *Maravilla* carried between 30 and 40 tons of treasure valued today around $1.6 billion. According to Hartman and Humphreys, one of the *Maravilla*'s prize treasure items that they are searching for is a pure gold 1,800-pound life-size Madonna and Child statue. According to news reports, the salvors will use a gold-sensitive laser device that can pinpoint an ounce of the precious gold from a quarter-mile, Herbert Humphreys has allegedly said. If that is true, we should soon be reading an account of the recovery. Eighteen hundred pounds of gold should make that laser device light up like a magic wand. Humphreys is said to be building a treasure museum on Grand Cayman to house what will be left after Bahamian officials select what they want from their 25 percent share of the treasure.

Meanwhile, not one to waste time in getting on with other

adventuresome projects, Bob Marx went on a worldwide ship-wreck and sunken cities survey, working in conjunction with archaeological or historical institutions of the various countries involved. Here is a thumbnail resume of his adventures, which began in October, 1975:

> Off the north coast of Israel investigating ancient harbor works, a crusader shipwreck, and locating several Phoenician, Roman, and Hellenistic shipwrecks.
> Exploring both the Atlantic and Pacific coasts of Panama to locate forty-four old pre-1800 shipwrecks.
> Off Belize in Central America where seven virgin wrecks were found.
> Explored four seventeenth and eighteenth-century Dutch wrecks off the west coast of Australia.
> Surveyed several shipwrecks in the Dutch Antilles.
> Search and excavation of several 1733 shipwrecks in the Florida Keys.
> Located thirteen seventeenth-, eighteenth-, and nineteenth-century shipwrecks around Salvador.
> Found amphorae-bearing Greek and Roman galleys off Majorca in the Baleric Islands.
> Excavated two Dutch warships off Brazil.
> Found possible Roman amphorae-bearing vessel believed second century B.C. during underwater survey off Rio de Janeiro.

More recently, this underwater Indiana Jones is laying the foundation for his biggest and most spectacular project yet; the excavation of one or more of the fabled Manila Galleons, and then the construction of a replica that Marx and his companions will sail from the Philippines to North America. They will follow the same route as the legendary galleons, whose single longest navigation in the world sometimes resulted in a six-month-long sea voyage.

The story of the Manila Galleons is legend. Each year for almost two hundred fifty years, the Spanish sent a single galleon to Manila, where it purchased porcelains, silks, fine woods, spices, and elaborately worked gold and silver treasure items from the Orient. The returning galleon was such a prize, that nations sent their fleets half-way around the world to try to intercept it. In all those centuries, only a few of the richly laden ships ever fell to attackers, but when they did, their cargo was often valuable enough to pay off that country's national debt.

Storms claimed many of the Manila Galleons trying to reach the trade fair in Acapulco. Some perished on reefs before they even left the Philippines; others ended their existence in the bottleneck of treacherous reefs in today's mid-Pacific Marshall Islands; and still others met disaster along the coast of California. One, the *San Agustine*, was reportedly storm-driven onto a sandbar and destroyed in Drake's Bay near San Francisco. Marx proposes finding and excavating it.

While California authorities considered the pros and cons of this project, Marx went to the Philippines where he said he found a receptive Aquino government which authorized him to search 18,500 square miles of Philippine waters to try and find some of the missing galleons. The treasure hunter believes there may be thirty such ships carrying more than $13 billion worth of treasure to be recovered. His search will be backed by his Los Angeles-based Phoenician South Seas Treasure Limited, for which he is seeking wealthy investors willing to become General Partners by purchasing sixty-six units of the partnership at fifty thousand dollars per unit. Whatever bonanzas are found will be divided among investors and the host country.

Did Burt Webber, Jr. and his treasure salvage firm really find all the coral-covered treasure lost from the *Concepción*? A year or so after he called a halt to salvage operations, some of his associates returned to the site north of the Dominican Republic, and their efforts produced relatively few silver coins. Apparently, Webber and his divers had done a thorough job.

By the end of 1986, Webber and his company were completing negotiations with the Columbian government for an exclusive search and salvage lease for the Serranilla Bank. This treacherous ridge of reef and shoals, lying just west of the route of Havana-bound treasure fleets from Cartagena, was a natural trap for unwary or storm-driven ships. For 260 years, it took a heavy toll of Spain's treasure armadas. After accumulating extensive documentation during the last five years, Webber said, "I plan on doing a complete survey of the Serranilla Bank in quest of the lost galleons of the 1605 Tierra Firma Armada commanded by Luis Hernandez de Cordova.'' Included among the four galleons lost in that fleet were the Capitana *San Rogue* and the Almiranta *Santo Domingo*. According to Webber, "Both were carrying over a million pesos in gold, silver, and emeralds, whose realistic value of each of the two galleons would be something like $50 to 75 million.'' Webber and his Sub-Sea Ventures, Incorporated company should have their work cut out for them, since this site has been a target for generations of treasure salvors, including the venerable Art McKee in the 1960s. But using the same kind of high-tech tactics that cracked the centuries-old secrets of Silver Shoals may now do the same for the stony reefs of Serranilla. If so, the reward should be in the millions.

Barry Clifford looks forward to the day when all the bureaucratic problems over ownership of the *Whydah*'s treasure is a thing of the past and he can consummate plans for moving the artifacts into a pirate treasure museum. According to his current plans, the museum will be built with the help of Disney World technicians. Walt Disney Enterprises plans to make a movie of the pirate ship and Clifford's search for it. Barry said he will play himself in the movie role.

Also awaiting his salvage company's attention is the *H.M.S. Hussar,* a twenty-eight gun British frigate that sank in New York Harbor in 1780 with eighty American prisoners and a hefty British payroll aboard. Over the years, the stories of lost treasures in such ships have a way of expanding faster than gases in a rising hot air balloon. The *Hussar* is believed to have had aboard "fourteen cartloads of gold'' to pay British troops. Over the years, other salvors have tried, but have been largely unsuccessful in locating either the shipwreck or its treasure. Now, however, Barry Clifford and his company, using underwater sonar, believe they have pinpointed the wreck lying in 80 feet of water and New York Harbor mud, between 130th and 140th Streets, not far from the Bronx shore. Treacherous tides, inky water, soupy mud, and all the risks associated with deeper-water diving guard the hulk. A large amount of funding has already been brought together, but, before the *Hussar* project can begin, Clifford and his company must strike a deal with New York State to determine how the ship is to be salvaged, who will take possession of whatever artifacts are found, and what will happen to the treasure if, in fact, a treasure exists. Such are some of the less prosaic problems confronting today's treasure hunters.

For the time-being at least, such matters are all behind successful treasure salvor Mel Fisher. For the moment, Mel and his millions are bathing in the afterglow of finding the *Atocha*, the *Margarita*, and the fame and fortune associated with that achievement. Apparently, for tax purposes, the company has sold its rights to the treasure wreck, while still maintaining its Key West treasure museum. Company shareholders are gradually being paid off and *Atocha* treasure is much on the market for anyone interested in purchasing a piece of the historic action. Once it is gone, all that will be left is the memory.

In an effort to perpetuate some of that memory, archaeologist R. Duncan Mathewson III, has been instrumental in having some of the *Atocha*'s timbers and shipboard artifacts placed in holding tanks at Key West's Community College, where he will be teaching a course on marine archaeology.

Today, treasure diving and salvage is becoming big business. Pioneering equipment, such as water jets and shallow water blowers, are rapidly being displaced by sophisticated electronic sensing devices and radio-controlled robotics. In the vanguard will always be the adventurers, the dreamers, those who thrill to the challenges and the risks. But now, instead of being out on a financial limb all by themselves, big business will be right there keeping step with them. When such investment empires as E. F. Hutton begin backing big-time searches for sunken treasure, you can be sure that this is just the beginning of a new lucrative era of recovering some of man's most fabulous centuries-old lost treasures from the deep.

# Appendix

# How It Still Begins

"Since man's early stages of evolution, he has been drawn to the sea like steel to a magnet," said diver/salvage master Raymond J. Braun. "From the time I was a young boy I was always fascinated by the stories of sunken and buried treasure, Captain Kidd, Blackbeard the Pirate, the Spanish Armada filled with doubloons and pieces of eight. Many times I would fall asleep at night dreaming of all the Spanish gold and other various treasures never found and thinking just how exciting it would be if I could be one of the lucky ones to go exploring and find T-R-E-A-S-U-R-E! ! !

"I first started scuba training when I was 17 years old. At that time I had no idea of what I was looking for or where to find it. Although most of my time was occupied by college, the U.S. Army, a real estate business in Euclid, Ohio, and raising a family, I always managed to find a little extra time to steal away and read another book about treasure diving, sunken Spanish Galleons, or a new method or practice in underwater salvage. Before I knew it, researching the sunken Spanish Galleons became a full-time hobby, and I started to diligently practice and perfect my diving skills.

"Since 1966, while I was a student at the University of Miami, every chance I would get, I would go down to the Florida Keys for a month or so and get to know some of the treasure divers and dive with them on many of the known sunken Galleons and Admiralty Claims throughout the Keys.

This is where a large number of references indicated in the Legajo records of Madrid and Seville told of the catastrophes of the treasure galleons that had sunk in that area. Periodically, I would dive with my own group of friends looking for a virgin wreck. There were many specific references of treasure galleons that have not yet been found.[1] We searched with every piece of borrowed or rented equipment we could get our hands on.

"In the summer of 1986, we found indications of a wreckage trail that stopped suddenly and just as suddenly began again almost ¼ of a mile later. At the end of the trail we found a completely sand-covered ballast pile which indicated the remains of an untouched sunken ship below. We could only excavate a little over a foot down into the sand but the pottery shards and cannonballs clearly indicated that it was a Spanish ship from the period between the late 1600s through the mid-1700s. If our assumption is correct, we may have found a Spanish ship carrying over 30,000 pieces of eight in treasure that is valued today anywhere from $50 to $800 per coin depending on the condition of the coins, the date, mint mark and assayer's mark.

"Treasure diving and salvage work today has become a calculated and expensive scientific research project. Proper excavating of a wreck is time-consuming, difficult, and expensive. Under the rights of the United States Constitution, I have been able to file an Admiralty Claim No. 86-2187-CIV-SCOTT, in October, 1986, in order to protect my claim and interest in this sunken ship. I plan to start excavation before the summer of 1987."

[1] Between 1492 and 1830, approximately 1400 Spanish ships were sunk off the Florida coast in an area known as the Spanish Main. Less than 100 have been actually located and salvaged at this time. During this period, a total of $4,035, 156,000 pesos of gold and silver were extracted from the mines of the New World. It was the responsibility of the Spanish Treasure Galleons to transport this gold and silver along the hazardous Florida Straits of the Spanish Main.

# RAYMOND J. BRAUN, *Salvage Master*     Age 39

- 22 years open water diving experience
- 19 years general salvage experience
- 8 years treasure salvage experience
- 4 years research in the spanish archives of the ships sunk.

# WHAT IT COSTS TODAY

## Monthly Salvage Expenses

BOAT EXPENSES

| | |
|---|---:|
| Fuel—(averaging 10 hrs. per day at 10 gallons per hour for 25 diving days of a 30-day month) | $ 2,800.00 |
| Oil & lubricants | 75.00 |
| Hooka breathing rig, gas, oil & filters | 175.00 |
| Misc. dive gear (replaced periodically): masks, flippers, gloves, lift bags, tanks | 350.00 |
| B.C. expendable boat equipments, Buoys, floats, rope, anchors | 250.00 |
| Air tank fills (10 x 25 x $2.00) | 500.00 |
| Dockage | 300.00 |
| Contingency fund for maintenance of twin blowers, air lift compressor, suction dredge, boat engines, etc. | 500.00 |
| Food for divers and crew on a 12-hour day for 5 to 7 personnel | 750.00 |

SALARIES:     1 Salvage Master
2 Dive Masters

| | |
|---|---:|
| 3 Full-time Divers | 3,250.00 |
| 1 Support Diver & Auxillary contractors | 800.00 |
| Surface Personnel | 400.00 |
| Preservation and storage of artifacts and security | 1,200.00 |
| SUBTOTAL | $ 11,350.00 |
| Overall contingency of total boat allowances and expenses based on 10% (percent) of monthly expenses | 1,135.00 |
| SUBTOTAL | $ 12,485.00 |
| x 30-month project: | |
| TOTAL | $374,550.00 |

## Initial Expenses

| | |
|---|---:|
| Proton Magnetometer | $ 35,000.00 |
| Twin 18 in. Blower construction and mount | $ 4,500.00 |
| Transportation of dive & misc. equipment to Fla. | $ 450.00 |
| Transportation of 2 salvage boats to Fla. | $ 1,200.00 |
| Purchase of additional salvage vessel | $ 40,000.00 |
| Total | $ 81,150.00 |
| | |
| Combined totals | $455,700.00 |

Courtesy, Raymond J. Braun, SUB-SEAS TREASURE SALVORS INC.